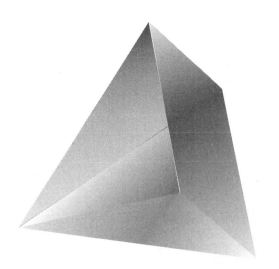

Server-Side JavaScript™

*Developing Integrated
Web Applications*

Robert Husted
JJ Kuslich

ADDISON-WESLEY

An imprint of Addison Wesley Longman, Inc.

Reading, Massachusetts • Harlow, England • Menlo Park, California
Berkeley, California • Don Mills, Ontario • Sydney
Bonn • Amsterdam • Tokyo • Mexico City

Many of the designations used by manufacturers and sellers to distinguish their products are claimed as trademarks. Where those designations appear in this book and Addison-Wesley was aware of a trademark claim, the designations have been printed in initial caps or all caps.

The authors and publishers have taken care in the preparation of this book, but make no expressed or implied warranty of any kind and assume no responsibility for errors or omissions. No liability is assumed for incidental or consequential damages in connection with or arising out of the use of the information or programs contained herein.

The publisher offers discounts on this book when ordered in quantity for special sales. For more information, please contact:

AWL Direct Sales
Addison Wesley Longman, Inc.
One Jacob Way
Reading, Massachusetts 01867

Visit AW on the Web: www.awl.com/cseng/

Library of Congress Cataloging-in-Publication Data
Husted, Robert, 1967–
    Server-side Javascript : developing integrated Web applications /
Robert Husted and J.J. Kuslich.
      p. cm.
    Includes bibliographical references.
    ISBN 0-201-43329-X. — ISBN 0-201-61624-6 (CD-ROM)
    1. Javascript (computer program language) 2. Web sites—Design.
I. Kuslich, J.J., 1972– . II. Title.
QA76.73.J39H877 1999   99-18619
005.2'762—dc21   CIP

Acquisitions Editor: Mary O'Brien
Production Coordinator: Jacquelyn Young
Compositor: Octal Publishing, Inc.
Cover Designer: Simone R. Payment

ISBN 0-201-43329-X

Text printed on recycled and acid-free paper.

 2 3 4 5 6 7 8 9 10-MA-0302010099

Second printing, July 1999

For my best friend, Wanda, and our three wonderful children:
Joseph, Rebekah, and Rachel.

—Robert

For the handful of amazing teachers who believed
in me and inspired me.

—JJ

Contents

Preface

Over the past few years both of us have spent a great deal of time educating people on how to use server-side JavaScript (SSJS) to build effective Web applications. As the technology evangelist for SSJS at Netscape, Robert gave presentations and wrote technical articles that expounded on the benefits of SSJS and showed developers new ways to use it. As a columnist for Netscape's *View Source* magazine and as a formal mentor in Netscape's SSJS newsgroup, JJ wrote articles on building well-designed Web applications with SSJS, and he helped SSJS developers overcome technical challenges they faced. So it made sense for the two of us to put our heads together and write a book on SSJS to introduce new developers to the platform and to educate experienced developers on some of the newer application programming interfaces.

However, we both knew from the beginning that we didn't want simply to perform a transfer of knowledge and write a simple SSJS reference manual. In fact, Netscape already has a great reference manual for SSJS on its Web site. Called *Writing Server-Side JavaScript Applications*, it gives the details of every keyword, operator, object, and method that an SSJS developer could ever want. We felt no need to rewrite such a tome (it is included on the accompanying CD-ROM), but rather we wanted to use much of the same information for a different purpose.

This book is intended to be a guide to writing better Web applications using SSJS. We set out with three goals in mind: to instruct, to cover, and to expand. First, we wanted to instruct developers new to SSJS on how it works and how to use it. Second, we wanted to cover as many of the capabilities of SSJS that we could in a single edition. Third, we wanted to expand on topics we covered: in addition to describing a feature, we wanted also to describe the proper way to employ the feature in your own SSJS applications through examples, real-world analogies, and discussions of common pitfalls. Throughout the book, you'll find a cohesive mixture of instruction, explanation, and advice that we hope will help you write better SSJS applications out there in the real world.

We both work as Web developers in the real world, just as you do. We hope that you find this book to be more than just a "how-to" manual. We hope it will serve as a guide to designing and implementing rock-solid Web applications.

What You Should Know

To use this book most effectively, you should be familiar with the way Web applications are built. If you have experience in writing applications with Common Gateway Interface (CGI), Microsoft Active Server Pages (ASP), or a similar platform, you have more than enough knowledge to understand all the material presented here. Knowledge of Java-Script, used either in a browser or on the server, would also be helpful. However, a working knowledge of Java, C, or VBScript would also suffice. Although this book discusses SSJS language specifics, it does not teach JavaScript language fundamentals, so you may want to have a JavaScript book as a companion to this one if you are unfamiliar with the JavaScript language.

About the Authors

Robert Husted is a technical lead at Qwest Communications Inc. in Denver. He recently worked for more than two years at Netscape Communications Corp. in Mountain View, California, promoting the adoption and use of SSJS. Robert started as a Web production engineer at Netscape, creating SSJS applications, in 1996. He worked on Netscape's App-Foundry initiative (free SSJS applications); the Virtual Intranet (a sample intranet site); and Netscape Insight, Netscape's first extranet. He created several sample applications for *View Source* magazine before becoming a technology evangelist in 1997.

Robert has written many sample applications, technotes, and *View Source* articles for Netscape's developer's site, DevEdge Online (http://developer.netscape.com/). He's given a variety of presentations on SSJS, Visual JavaScript, and other related technologies in the United States and Europe.

JJ Kuslich is a project manager and Web applications developer at the consulting firm Application Methods, Inc., a subsidiary of Rocky Mountain Internet, Inc. Since 1996, JJ has used SSJS, Microsoft ASP, and several other Web technologies—including JavaScript on the client, Java on both the client and server, and most recently Extensible Markup Language (XML)—to build fully functional intranets and e-commerce applications for corporate clients. He has also led development teams in the creation of reusable components for software industry clients, including Netscape and NetObjects, Inc. JJ also helped write the Video sample application that shipped with Netscape LiveWire 1.0 and the Compiler sample application that ships with Netscape Enterprise Server 3.5.1. Much of his work has included integrating applications or components with relational databases either natively or through Open Database Connectivity (ODBC).

For a year, JJ volunteered as the DevEdge champion for the SSJS newsgroup hosted by Netscape. As a champion, JJ used his experience with SSJS to mentor other SSJS developers in the group by answering technical questions and fostering peer-to-peer discussions on SSJS development issues. Since 1997, JJ has also written many articles on SSJS and Web development for Netscape's *View Source* magazine and for the Script-Builder.com Web site.

Acknowledgments

Although there are only two names listed on the cover, this book would not have been possible without the help of many talented people.

We'd like to thank the staff of Addison Wesley Longman for their professional guidance and understanding throughout the writing and editing process. This is the first book for both of us, and we'd also like to thank them for committing to two very excited first-time authors. Specifically, we'd like to thank Mary O'Brien, Elizabeth Spainhour and Maureen Hurley for their help in putting our drafts together into the refined, professional book you see before you.

Behind every book are special people who influenced the authors, the content, or both throughout the process. We'd like to express our gratitude for the guidance provided by Paul Dreyfus, the editor of Netscape's *View Source* magazine and the manager of technology evangelism at Netscape. Both of us have worked extensively with Paul, particularly in creating *View Source* articles for DevEdge Online. There is no doubt that this book would not have been the same without his support. We'd also like to thank Suzanne Anthony of Netscape for guiding us through the web of details required to start a book. Netscape's Basil Hashem offered encouragement and valuable assistance in the creation of this work—he was the catalyst who brought this book about. In this same vein, we'd like to thank Ray DePouli, John Fisher, Ron Stevenson, David Fail, Brendan Eich, Rob Weltman, Ken Smith, and Scott Johnston.

We also want to extend many thanks to the fine minds who helped improve this book by lending their time and expertise as technical reviewers: James Bender, Bill Binkley, Paul Dreyfus, Nate Kassenbaum, Willy Mena, Angelo Sirigos, and Mark Wilcox. Their help was instrumental in producing a text that is both accurate and interesting from the point of view of other real-world Web developers. Special thanks to Willy Mena, a Netscape employee and DevEdge champion for the SSJS newsgroup, for his many invaluable suggestions throughout the process. Nan Borenson and Suzanne Anthony also helped us in securing some of the great software found on the CD-ROM that accompanies this book.

We'd like to thank Netscape, Application Methods, Rocky Mountain Internet, and NetObjects for various contributions they made and for the support they offered to this project.

Finally, we'd like to thank some special people who helped influence this book through their relationships with us in our personal lives. We'd both like to thank all of our respective family and friends who gave us support and understanding (and occasional prodding, as needed) throughout the process.

JJ would like to thank four special teachers who, at various points in his life, inspired him, made him believe he could do anything he put his mind to, and helped prepare him with the tools he would need throughout his life and career: Lynn Stradley (science), Elaine Phelps (arts), Mindy Falnes (writing), and Marion Barchillon (technical writing).

Robert would like to extend special thanks to his parents (Dennis and Rita Husted and Kay Starr), who always encouraged him to continue learning, and to a few select individuals who inspired and helped him along the way: Mr. Rogerson (fifth grade); Mr. Harvey (English); Mr. Judd (English); Dr. Spainhour (English); Scott Knell; President Lloyd J. Cope (LDS mission president); Bill and Beth Flood; Connie Hatch-Frasier; Mary Covington; President Ray Martin (LDS stake president); Steve Smith; and Dr. Pat Logan. Last, but not least, he would like to thank his wife, Wanda, for her love and patience during the writing of this book.

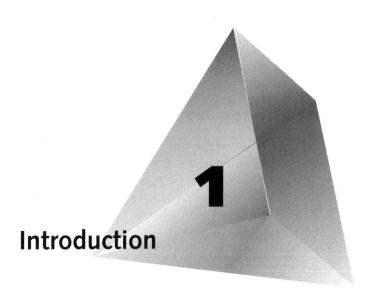

Introduction

In 1994, it seemed that everyone was hopping on the Web, from closet geeks to huge multinational corporations. It was the Internet Gold Rush, and everyone wanted in on the action. People could view information using any Web *client*, or *browser*, on any platform, and it was suddenly available anywhere on the planet at any time, day or night. Soon, businesses realized that the Web provided more than just access to static content. Indeed, it provided access to a whole new breed of application: the Web application.

Why create something in Visual Basic or PowerBuilder that can be run on only one platform, when you can create a Web application with server-side JavaScript (SSJS) that can be run on any existing platform (such as UNIX, Mac, and Windows) and even future platforms? The application might be hosted on a UNIX or Windows server and then accessed from a client browser on almost any platform imaginable.

To get a clear picture of how far we've come, let's step back to the late 1980s and early 1990s. Let's suppose that back then you wanted to provide a new service to your customers. You wanted to allow them to get an update on their orders: what was shipping and when, how many items they'd ordered, and so forth. You also wanted to let them add to or change their orders. However, you didn't want to hire an army of customer support people to work the phones. Instead, you wanted to let customers view and edit their own orders.

How would you have done it? Well, first you'd create an application using Visual Basic or PowerBuilder that would let your customers edit their own orders. Then you'd distribute this application via CD-ROMs or disks to all the customers who wanted to use it. But you had to ensure that the customer met certain minimum requirements:

- Operating system: They had to use the same operating system (OS) that you used for building the application (which was probably the same OS you ran at your company: Windows, MacOS, and so on).
- Computer hardware: They needed a minimum hardware configuration (modem speed, hard disk space, RAM, screen size, and so on).
- Network protocol: Everyone had to run the same network protocol (IPX/SPX, TCP/IP, NetBEUI, and so on).
- Connection: The customer needed a physical connection to your company (leased-line and the like) or dial-up capability via modem (and you had to provide a bank of modems to support the dial-up).

So you had a great application that would benefit your customers, but the barrier to entry was high. The customer had to do so much to run your application that it almost wasn't worth it. Moreover, if you wanted to change the application (fix bugs or add features), you had to worry about getting the update out to all your customers. You'd potentially have customers running several different versions of your application, and it became a logistical nightmare.

The Web has changed all that. It no longer matters what kind of hardware your customer runs, and the minimum configuration requirements have dropped significantly. Now, the customer must meet only two requirements:

- Web browser: Customers need only a browser, and they can use any one that they want (Netscape, Microsoft, and so on). The client browser allows all your customers to see exactly the same application regardless of the operating system installed on their computers. So now everyone can choose any desired OS (and version) and still be able to run your application.
- Internet connection: Customers need a connection to the Internet that they use to reach your company. The Internet is a giant network, a natural outgrowth of the local area networks (LANs) and wide area networks (WANs) of the 1980s. It allows people around the globe to communicate. If they have an Internet connection, they're running a common network protocol: Transmission Control Protocol/Internet Protocol (TCP/IP). Your customers probably already have a connection to the Internet, and they can use it for more than accessing your

application. They can use it to reach other companies and resources around the globe. So now anyone can access your application from anywhere on the planet.

Now the barrier to entry is greatly reduced, and it's easy for your customers to use your application and modify their orders. The Web has simplified everything. Even application updates are easier; because the application is hosted on your servers, when a change is made every customer around the world is instantly running the new version. You don't have to distribute your applications on CD-ROM or disk anymore. Everyone uses a common client browser, and everyone sees the same application. We've finally reached application development nirvana.

One additional advantage to Web development is that solutions such as SSJS take advantage of the so-called three-tier architecture. With two-tier client/server architecture, clients connects directly to the database. This means that every client must have a separate license to access the database. In addition, the database must maintain a connection for each client, something that can be expensive in database processing. With a three-tier Web architecture, multiple clients access a Web server, which maintains shared connections to the database. Clients don't need a database license or database client software. The Web server manages all communication with the database, and clients simply share a pool of common connections. The client need communicate directly only with the Web server and not the database. This means that you can more efficiently use a smaller number of database connections than you can in traditional two-tier client/server architectures.

The Three-Tier Client/Server Architecture

Figure 1.1 shows that in a two-tier client/server system every client is required to have a dedicated connection to the database (DB). So during latency periods when the user is reading or entering data, the database

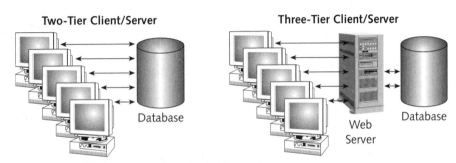

Figure 1.1 *Two-tier versus three-tier database architecture*

connection sits idle. The users must also connect to the database and disconnect from it at least once a day (for security reasons, you wouldn't leave a client connected to the DB all the time).

Three-tier client/server systems use database connections more efficiently. Notice that in the two-tier architecture, five database connections are required. In the three-tier architecture database connections are shared among all users so you can support more users with fewer connections. The connections are more efficiently used because there's a relatively continuous flow of traffic across the shared connections. In addition, the connections can be maintained for the life of the application because users log in to the application on the server and not to the database; as a result, you don't have to keep connecting with, and disconnecting from, the database. This is another reason that Web applications are generally superior to older, more proprietary two-tier solutions.

An Online Marketplace

Initially, businesses jumped on the Web to provide content. Although some companies still use the Web primarily as a distribution vehicle for content, others use it to create Web applications and to form relationships with their customers. For example, FedEx helps customers track their packages online; Wells Fargo gives customers access to their bank accounts over the Web; Amazon.com sells a variety of books over the Web. Slowly but surely, the Web is changing from a marketing vehicle to an online marketplace.

As the desire to offer services over the Internet increased, Web developers needed a way to write applications. They wanted to help their online customers download trial software, sign up for new accounts, order products, and so on. All these services required some kind of programming functionality, so most Web sites turned to the only thing that was available: the Common Gateway Interface (CGI). This technology enabled companies to make their sites interactive.

Unfortunately, CGIs had limitations: the server had to create a new process every time a CGI was executed, and that slowed down the Web server. When the CGI was finished sending values back to the Web server, the process would die, so all state or session information was immediately lost. This meant that you were limited in the types of Web applications you could create. Web developers wanted something more, something that would let them create complete database-driven Web applications.

In May 1996, Brendan Eich sent a copy of Mocha, his new scripting engine, to the team working on LiveWire, a product that would provide developers with an easier way to create database applications and do some Web site management. LiveWire was released in 1996 as a stand-alone product and was later rolled into Netscape Enterprise Server 3.0. It is now known as server-side JavaScript.

The purpose of this book is to teach you how to unleash the power of SSJS so that you can quickly script applications by adding JavaScript code to your Web pages. If you already know JavaScript, then learning SSJS simply requires learning to use a few additional JavaScript objects. If you don't know JavaScript, it's never too late to learn.

What is JavaScript?

Every Internet developer has heard of JavaScript—it's the standard general-purpose scripting language for the Web. Brendan Eich invented the language at Netscape in May 1995. He originally called it Mocha, and its syntax closely matched that of Java, a full-blown programming language for the Internet. (The Java syntax was, in turn, similar to C/C++.) When Eich created JavaScript he worked hard to develop a simple syntax that was similar to Java and C/C++ rather than yet another proprietary language syntax such as that employed by Visual Basic. In September 1995, Netscape changed the name of the programming language from Mocha to LiveScript and changed it again in December 1995 to JavaScript, following a deal with Sun Microsystems that let Netscape use the Java name.

In January 1996, JavaScript was included with Netscape Navigator 2.0 and became an instant success. Finally, there was a way for developers to do some work on the client. Developers had been clamoring for a way to create interactivity on the browser and to perform client-side processing. JavaScript made it easy for them to do this, and it was an easy scripting language to learn. The language was eventually embraced by Microsoft as JScript, and finally standardized in 1997 by the Internet Engineering Task Force (IETF) and the European Computer Manufacturers Association (ECMA). (Some browsers don't yet support the full ECMA standard. We won't mention which ones because we don't want to embarrass Microsoft.)

Founded in 1961, ECMA is an international standards body based in Europe. The group is dedicated to the standardization of information and communication systems. The ECMA-262 standard (ECMAScript) has been approved by the International Organization for Standardization (ISO) as ISO/IEC DIS 16262. ISO was established in 1947 as a worldwide federation of national standards bodies with representatives from more than 90 countries. Its mission is to promote the development of standardization to facilitate the exchange of goods and services.

JavaScript, arguably the most popular programming language in history, is used on more than 3.5 million Web pages (according to *Wired's* HotBot search April 9, 1998). Every Web developer knows about client-side JavaScript; it's the technology used on the Web client to validate form values, pop up new windows and alert messages, and enable dynamic HTML. Most people think of client-side JavaScript when they hear the term *JavaScript*, but JavaScript is composed of three parts, as shown in Figure 1.2.

The three parts of JavaScript are as follows.

1. Core JavaScript: the base JavaScript language. Functions written in core JavaScript can be run on the client *and* on the server.
2. Client-side JavaScript (CSJS): an extended version of JavaScript that enables the enhancement and manipulation of Web pages and client browsers. Functions that use CSJS objects can be run only on the *browser*.
3. Server-side JavaScript (SSJS): an extended version of JavaScript that enables back-end access to databases, file systems, and servers. Functions that use SSJS objects can be run only on the *server*.

Client-Side Javascript		Server-Side Javascript	
Objects		**Objects**	**Functions**
area	menubar	client	addClient()
applet	mimeType	Connection	AddResponseHeader()
anchor	navigator	Cursor	blob()
document	personalbar	Cursor Column	callC()
event	plugin	Database	debug()
history	screen	DbPool	deleteResponseHeader()
image	scrollbars	Lock	flush()
layer	statusbar	File	getOptionValue()
link	toolbar	StoredProc	getOptionValueCount()
location	window	ResultSet	redirect()
locationbar		server	registerCFunction()
		project	write()
		request	
		SendMail	

Core Javascript					
Objects			**Operators**		
Array	Number	function	== |= > >= < <=		delete
Date	String		+ - * / % ++ --		new
Math	RegExp		= += -= *= /+ %=		this
			<<= >>= >>>=		typeof
Control Statements			&= |= ^= && || |		void
if	do	label	& | ^ ~ << >> >>>		
else	while	continue			
?:	with	break	**Global Functions**		
for	switch		escape()	Number()	isNaN()
			unescape()	String()	parseFloat()
			Boolean()	eval()	parseInt()

Figure 1.2 *Core, client, and server JavaScript*

Core JavaScript

Core JavaScript is the basic JavaScript language and includes all the control statements, functions, objects, operators, and so on. It comprises all the core features of JavaScript, everything that can be used on both the client and the server. ECMA-262 (ECMAScript) version 1.0 is based entirely on core Java-Script. As one of the most popular programming languages in history, core JavaScript has been licensed by more than 175 companies for inclusion in their Web tools.

Core JavaScript contains objects that are applicable to both client and server (`Array`, `Date`, `String`, and so forth). If you know core JavaScript, you can easily write client-side and server-side JavaScript. Again, the only distinction is that client-side and server-side JavaScript have additional objects and functions that are specific to client-side or server-side functionality. Any JavaScript libraries (`.js` files) you create in core JavaScript can be used on both the client and the server.

Client-Side JavaScript

If you've ever created a Web site, particularly one with dynamic HTML, you probably already know client-side Javascript. CSJS is composed of core JavaScript and many additional objects (`document`, `form`, `window`, and so forth). The objects in CSJS enable you to manipulate HTML documents (checking form fields, submitting forms, creating dynamic pages, and so on) and the browser itself (directing the browser to load other HTML pages, display messages, and so on).

CSJS is better known than SSJS because it's used in the browser to pop up windows, move graphics and text on the screen, and even write out portions of an HTML page—things that users can see. It's also used to validate form values, check for required fields, and so forth. We delve a bit further into CSJS in Chapter 4 because you'll use it quite often in your SSJS applications.

Server-Side JavaScript

In 1995, Bill Turpin, Ken Smith, and Lloyd Tabb were hired by Netscape to create a product that would allow Web developers to easily script database-driven applications. Brendan Eich sent them his new Mocha engine to serve as the core language that would be used in the product. The LiveWire team added objects and functions to Mocha to make it easier for developers to create Web applications. The result of their efforts was server-side Java-Script. SSJS is implemented as an NSAPI (Netscape Server Application Programming Interface) plug-in that executes applications in-process with the server (see Figure 1.3). That means that the server isn't going through the time-consuming step of creating a new process for every request as it

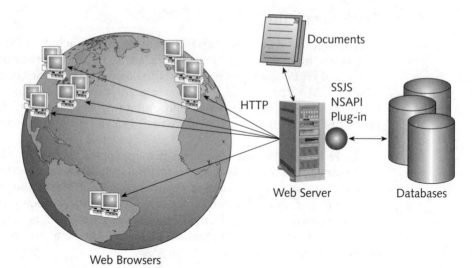

Figure 1.3 *SSJS request flow*

does with CGI. Instead, it just runs a portion of the Web application and returns the results to the requesting client.

Differences Between CSJS and SSJS

Table 1.1 compares CSJS with SSJS. Note that the only major syntactical difference between CSJS code and SSJS code is that for CSJS you use a <SCRIPT> tag rather than a <SERVER> tag in your HTML document. Remember, however, that SSJS provides a set of objects different from that of CSJS; if you try to use CSJS objects in your server-side application, errors will result. Note that CSJS can be served by any server but can be executed only by JavaScript-enabled browsers. SSJS must be executed by a JavaScript-enabled server but can be displayed by any browser. (At the time this chapter was written, only Netscape's Web servers supported SSJS.)

Table 1.1 *The difference between CSJS and SSJS*

Language Element	Client-Side JavaScript	Server-Side JavaScript
Tags	<SCRIPT></SCRIPT>	<SERVER></SERVER>
Execution	Runs on the browser only (interpreted at runtime)	Runs on the server only (compiled into JavaScript byte code)

Table 1.1 *The difference between CSJS and SSJS (Continued)*

Language Element	Client-Side JavaScript	Server-Side JavaScript
Compilation	Not compiled	Compiled into a Web application file
Required browser	A JavaScript-enabled browser	Any Web browser
Required server	Any Web server	A JavaScript-enabled server

What Is LiveWire?

You've probably heard the terms *LiveWire* and *server-side JavaScript* used interchangeably, but they're different technologies. When LiveWire was released as a product by Netscape in 1996, it contained Navigator Gold (for browsing and HTML editing), Site Manager (for Web site and application management), and SSJS (for application development). SSJS/LiveWire ran on Netscape Enterprise Server 2.0. In 1997, LiveWire was included with Enterprise Server 3.0, so it's no longer a separate product. Netscape began to refer to the database access engine as LiveWire to distinguish it from the language that the database applications are written in, which is SSJS.

Figure 1.4 shows that SSJS uses the LiveWire database engine to connect with a variety of databases (DB2, Informix, Oracle, Sybase, and ODBC-compliant databases). SSJS provides developers with a collection of objects (such as the `database`, `DbPool`, and `cursor` objects) that interact with the LiveWire database access engine to communicate with relational databases. Some of the objects that are part of SSJS (the `file`, `SendMail`, and `state management` objects) do not interact with databases via

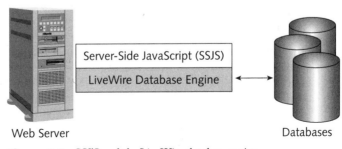

Web Server   Databases

Figure 1.4 *SSJS and the LiveWire database engine*

LiveWire. Remember that LiveWire involves database access only, whereas SSJS encompasses database access and additional scriptable server-side functionality.

CGI, SSJS, and NAS: What to Use

So what should you use to create your Web applications? CGI? SSJS? NAS (the Netscape Application Server)? It depends. Each approach has its own benefits and drawbacks, so you must decide the following:

- Functionality: what your application will do
- Scalability: how many users it will support
- Maintenance: how often it will be modified
- Usage: how often it will be used
- Reliability: how important it is that the application be available at all times

Using Common Gateway Interface

CGI is a basic, but flexible and powerful interface that enables developers to create programs on their Web sites to handle form data, perform file system tasks, and even interact with databases. However, CGI is generally slow, and it's not ideally suited to application development. The problem is that you must keep each CGI small because the server must load and run the CGI from scratch every time it's executed. If the CGI includes a library (Perl often uses libraries, and a large number of them are available free on the Web), then the library must also be loaded every time the CGI is run. Code libraries are useful because they facilitate code reuse.

SSJS also can use code libraries; SSSJ can access any JavaScript libraries (`.js` files) that are compiled into the Web application. In addition, SSJS supports LiveConnect, a kind of glue in JavaScript that lets you access Java classes. So you can also access Java libraries from SSJS. In Chapter 9 we talk more about LiveConnect and show you how to use Java in your JavaScript applications.

Basically, a CGI works this way: The customer clicks on a hyperlink or on a button on a form, and that action triggers a client request. The browser sends the request to the Web server listed in the uniform resource locator (URL). So a request such as `http://myServer.domain.com/cgi-bin/myprogram.cgi` is sent to the server `myServer` at `domain.com`. That server checks the designated `cgi-bin` directory on the server and runs `myprogram.cgi` if the file is found. The CGI `myProgram.cgi` runs through to completion and returns the results to the server. After the CGI ends, its process dies, and the Web server sends the results returned by the CGI back to the requesting client. Unfortunately, every time a new request comes in, the server must create a new process to run the CGI program, and that can be remarkably inefficient.

However, CGIs are great for specific tasks such as parsing logfiles, performing maintenance tasks, and so forth. You should standardize the language used to create CGIs in your company (usually Perl or C/C++) to make future maintenance somewhat easier. Generally speaking, use CGIs for one-time tasks—those that require heavy file-system access or functionality you can't get with SSJS or NAS—or use them if the application must be easily ported to other Web servers.

Using Server-Side JavaScript

Server-side JavaScript runs in-process with the Web server. As a result, it's generally faster than CGI and is ideally suited for the easy scripting of database-driven applications. Use SSJS for applications that need easy access to databases and need state or session capabilities (keeping track of application-specific and user data between HTTP requests). It's also great for application development because applications are easier to distribute (via a single .web file) and maintain when you use a standardized scripting language and a common application design. You can even place your application code inline with your HTML page. Everything stays together, making maintenance somewhat easier.

If you use SSJS to create your Web applications, you're using a common language syntax on both the client and the server. Any JavaScript libraries that are coded in core JavaScript can then be used on both the client and the server. Furthermore, it's generally easier to train Web developers to use SSJS than to train them to use Perl or C/C++ because they likely already know JavaScript (because it is the most popular programming language on the Web). Even if they don't already know JavaScript, it's an easy scripting language to learn, and the syntax is similar to that of Java and C/C++. For that reason, it's also generally easier for JavaScript developers to learn Java than it is for Perl developers.

Table 1.2 summarizes the benefits and drawbacks of SSJS and CGI.

Using Netscape Application Server

Netscape Application Server is a high-end solution intended for mission-critical applications that must be available 24 hours a day, seven days a week. (Other application servers also fall into this same category.) NAS applications are coded in Java or C/C++. You must pay extra money for a dedicated server that hosts applications, so you should get one only if you absolutely need one. You wouldn't use a backhoe to do your gardening; instead you'd

Table 1.2 *Advantages and disadvantages of SSJS and CGI*

Technology	Advantages	Disadvantages
SSJS	It provides built-in state management capabilities and easy database access.	It requires a JavaScript-enabled Web server, so it's not easily portable between Web servers.
	It is based on a standardized language (ECMAScript/ JavaScript), so client and server programs can be written in the same language, allowing code reuse between client and server applications.	It increases the size of your Web server process (because your applications run in-process with the Web server).
	It allows extended functionality using Java (via LiveConnect).	
	It caches database connections for faster performance.	
CGI	It is highly portable and can be run on any CGI-enabled Web server.	It is slow because a separate process is spawned every time the CGI is executed (which is taxing on the server).
	It can be programmed in a variety of languages (C, Java, Perl, and so on).	It makes state management difficult to implement; you must do it all yourself.
	Some languages (such as Perl) have a large number of code libraries available to simplify some programming tasks.	Database access is available only via separate libraries, so you must do more work to connect to a database.

use a shovel. By the same token, you should use a Web server and SSJS or CGI to create workgroup or departmental-size applications. Use an application server for enterprise-scale (thousands of simultaneous users), mission-critical applications.

Netscape Enterprise Server supports SSJS, CGI, servlets, and other methods of creating applications. Its primary mission, however, is to deliver content: HTML documents. In contrast, the mission of Netscape Application Server is to host applications. So NAS was created from the ground up to host applications in the most secure and robust manner possible and to allow maximum flexibility in tuning for optimal performance.

Remember that you're dealing with Web applications, so all the applications you write (CGI, SSJS, NAS, and so on) can communicate with one another. Potentially, you could have parts of a complex application written in CGI and other parts in SSJS. SSJS's strength is easy access to databases, easy state and session management, and ease of maintenance. Still, CGI is a valuable alternative. You should use whatever seems appropriate for the task at hand.

Writing SSJS Applications

In SSJS you simply add your application code to the Web page or to a Java-Script library that you access from a Web page (the preferred method). Table 1.3 shows two ways to code an SSJS application. Using JavaScript libraries is the preferred method because you can easily change the HTML page so that instead of calling a JavaScript function you call a Java servlet or some other server-side functionality. In this way, your applications will be easier to port to other programming models should you decide to do that in the future.

However, there are times when you'll want to use JavaScript interleaved with HTML. In the following example, portions of an HTML page are conditionally displayed. This technique can reduce the number of pages in your application because instead of redirecting to different pages based on input values, you can simply show different parts of a given Web page. This increases the flexibility and maintainability of your Web applications.

Table 1.3 *Interleaving versus using libraries in SSJS*

JavaScript Interleaved with HTML	Using JavaScript Libraries
`<HTML> . . .`	`<HTML> . . .`
`<BODY>`	`<BODY>`
`<H1>My SSJS Application</H1>`	`<H1>My SSJS Application</H1>`
`<SERVER>`	`<SERVER>`
`   // SSJS Code . . .`	`   // Call to JavaScript function`
`</SERVER>`	`</SERVER>`
`<P>Some text or other HTML code.`	`<P>Some text or other HTML code.`
`<SERVER>`	`<SERVER>`
`   // More SSJS Code . . .`	`   // Call to JavaScript function`
`</SERVER>`	`</SERVER>`
`. . .`	`. . .`

```
<HTML> . . .
<BODY>
<H1>My SSJS Application</H1>
<SERVER>
   if (condition1 == true) {
</SERVER>
<P>This text will be displayed if condition1 is true.
<SERVER>
   } else {
</SERVER>
<P>This text will be displayed if condition1 is false.
<SERVER>
   }
</SERVER>
<P>Some text or other HTML code that will always be displayed.
. . .
</HTML>
```

The Nuts and Bolts of SSJS

How is an SSJS application compiled and run by the Web server? First, you
create a series of HTML pages and embed your JavaScript statements in the
HTML page using <SERVER> tags (see Figure 1.5). (You can have client-side
JavaScript on the same pages. The JavaScript compiler ignores JavaScript
between <SCRIPT> tags and only compiles JavaScript between <SERVER>

jsac Compilation

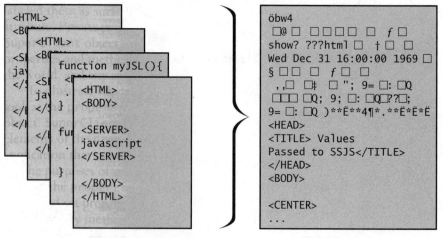

.html pages and .js Library Files   .web File

Figure 1.5 *Compiling an SSJS application*

tags.) Again, you should generally put most of your JavaScript code into JavaScript libraries (.js files) and simply call those JavaScript functions from within your HTML pages.

To increase the efficiency of an SSJS application on the server, it is compiled using the jsac compiler (or lwcomp for LiveWire 1.0 users). All HTML pages and JavaScript libraries in the application are concatenated into one large file (.web file), and all the server-side JavaScript is compiled into JavaScript byte code. (If your .web file becomes larger than 500K, try breaking the application into smaller pieces. Some Netscape customers have experienced performance problems with .web files that exceed 500K.) Every time you make a change to any HTML page that's included in your application (even documents that have no server-side JavaScript), you must recompile the application. If your documents do not change frequently, you may choose not to compile them with the application.

Note that only HTML and JavaScript libraries are compiled into a .web file. Java class files and images are not included in the compilation. When you add an SSJS application, an entry is made in the <server-root>/ https-myserver/config/jsa.conf file. You can manually edit this file to remove SSJS applications when necessary .

As shown in Figure 1.6, when the server receives a request for a document it first checks to see whether the document is part of an application. If the server recognizes the name **app** as the name of a valid SSJS application, the server checks the corresponding .web file to find **page3**. The server exe-

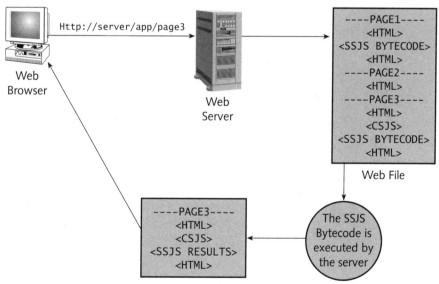

Figure 1.6 *The SSJS request flow*

cutes any SSJS byte code it finds on `page3` and returns the resulting HTML page to the client. If no JavaScript byte code is found on the page, the static page is returned to the client.

If the requested page is not found in the `.web` file, the server checks the directory where the `.web` file resides. If the document is found, it is returned to the client. (Any SSJS found on the page is rendered as text because the page was not compiled into the `.web` file.) If the page is still not found, the server checks the path from the server's doc-root to try to locate the page. If the page is still not found, an error message is returned. Preference is given first to SSJS applications, then to static documents in the directory where the `.web` file is located, and finally to static documents from the server's doc-root.

Note   Always give your applications a name that is different from that of the `.web` file. If a user enters the name of your `.web` file as the URL (`http://server.domain.com/myWebApp.web`), the entire contents of the `.web` file will be returned. If the user can decompile the JavaScript byte codes, he or she can potentially gain access to your database. Therefore, always give your `.web` files a cryptic name and always ensure that the Application Manager (`http://server.domain.com/appmgr`) is password-protected. (This problem with `.web` files has been corrected in the Netscape Enterprise server for versions later than, but not including, version 3.5.1. In addition, there is documentation on the Netscape Developer's Site, HTTP://Developer.Netscape.com/SSJS.)

Passing Values Between CSJS and SSJS

It's important to remember that SSJS and CSJS are entirely separate, even though both of them might appear on a single `.web` page. Think of a wall separating the two technologies: CSJS runs only on the client browser, and SSJS runs only on the server. They cannot share variables directly; they must be passed. CSJS passes values to SSJS via the URL:

```
http://server.domain.com/app/page.html?name1=value1&name2=value2&namex=valuex
```

or as part of a form submission. SSJS passes values to CSJS in one of two ways. It can write out CSJS code:

```
write"<SCRIPT>myVar=" + mySSJSvalue + ";</SCRIPT>";
```

or it can put the values in hidden form fields:

```
<INPUT TYPE=hidden NAME=myVar VALUE=`mySSJSvalue`>
```

You can reuse the same code on the client and the server if the functions are written in core JavaScript. However, variables can be passed between CSJS and SSJS only as shown in the preceding code examples.

Summary

Now you know a little about the history of SSJS; the differences between core, client, and server JavaScript; the advantages of Web applications; and the situations when it makes sense to use SSJS over CGIs. We've shown you the bare basics regarding SSJS applications: different basic ways of coding them, the request flow, and compilation into a .web file. In Chapter 2 we walk you through the creation of SSJS applications so that you can start creating your own database-driven Web applications.

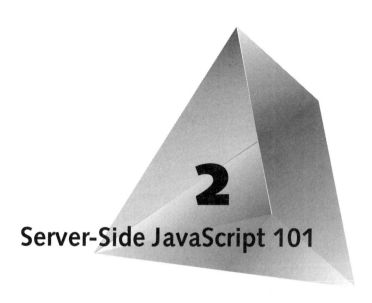

2

Server-Side JavaScript 101

In the next two chapters we talk about the mechanics of server-side JavaScript. In this chapter we show you how SSJS works, introduce you to some new language elements, show you some code, and finish with a brief discussion on recommended design techniques. Although we introduce the topic of session management here, Chapter 3 is devoted to an in-depth discussion of the Session Management Service and contains more-detailed information on handling HTTP requests, such as form submissions, and on managing user sessions.

This chapter introduces you to server-side JavaScript as a language and as a development platform. The official Netscape SSJS manual, *Writing Server-Side JavaScript Applications*, explains every object, property, method, and API in great detail, and it will serve you well as a reference manual companion to this book. For this reason, this section, much like the rest of this book, discusses some of the same material found in the manual but focuses more on helping you build good Web applications and less on explaining every minor detail of an already documented platform. In this chapter, we explain the mechanics of building an application for the SSJS platform, and we introduce the APIs that are part of it. Later chapters explain each API in greater detail, always with a focus on helping you build better Web applications.

Note   If you're an advanced user, already know SSJS, and purchased this book to find advanced information and techniques, you should skip to Chapter 3. The first half of Chapter 3 reviews the Session Management Service, which you may already be familiar with. The last half of the chapter shows you how to extend the `client` object into the `SuperClient` so that it can hold not only strings and numbers but also arrays, objects, or any legal JavaScript value. Don't miss it!

How SSJS Works

The SSJS engine is essentially a Netscape Server API (NSAPI) plug-in made by Netscape that ships with Netscape Enterprise Server and Netscape FastTrack Server. The SSJS engine executes code embedded in SSJS pages on the server and then generates HTML output, which is returned to the browser that requested the SSJS page. Whereas CGI pages are typically written in languages such as Perl or C, SSJS pages are written in server-side JavaScript, a variant of the widely used JavaScript language.

When a Web browser requests an SSJS page from Netscape Enterprise Server, the Web server checks to see whether the URL is pointing to a static HTML page, a CGI script, or an SSJS page. If the page is an SSJS page, the server invokes the SSJS engine to interpret the code on the page. The interpreter executes commands on the page from top to bottom in order. Usually, the SSJS developer generates some HTML output that is returned to the requesting browser or redirects the browser to another page. In other words, after the engine has processed the page, a response is returned to the browser. Figure 2.1 illustrates the interaction between the Web browser and the Web server when the browser requests SSJS pages, as discussed in Chapter 1.

A common example of an SSJS page that might be invoked on the Web server is a form handler that receives a form submission from a browser and then stores that data in a text file or relational database. After processing the form elements, the SSJS engine might return a response to the browser by generating HTML text stating that the form data was processed. After the text is processed and the SSJS engine reaches the end of the SSJS code, all SSJS output is returned to the browser in the HTTP response. To the requesting browser, the page looks like a static HTML page and the browser cannot tell that it was generated by an SSJS server.

Note   The Web server actually buffers generated HTML output before sending it back to the browser. If generated content is less than 64K, the output is not sent to the browser until the SSJS engine has finished processing the page or you call the `flush` function. Otherwise, SSJS sends content back to the browser whenever the 64K buffer fills up.

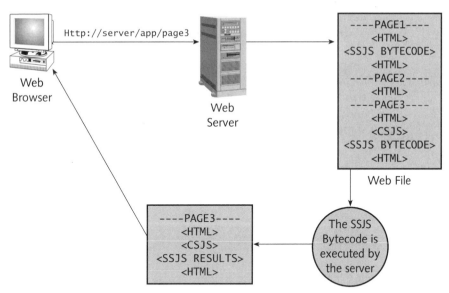

Figure 2.1 *Flow of requests from the Web browser through SSJS*

Elements of Server-Side JavaScript

Server-side JavaScript is an extension of the JavaScript core language. All the basic language elements that you find in JavaScript, such as loops, conditionals, and expressions, work the same in both client-side and server-side JavaScript. The primary difference between the languages rests in their different object models. With client-side JavaScript, you work with the browser's object model, which includes objects such as `document`, `window`, and `navigator`. With server-side JavaScript, you cannot access those client-side objects because there is no browser to provide such context. Instead, SSJS provides objects tailored to the Web server world and server processing tasks.

Writing SSJS Code

SSJS applications are built from HTML pages, which can have an `.htm` or `.html` extension; the HTML pages contain embedded server-side code and optionally SSJS library files, which must have a `.js` extension. We say that SSJS applications are built from these pages, as opposed to consisting of these pages, because SSJS applications are compiled. Source files with `.htm`, `.html`, and `.js` file extensions must be compiled into a single file with a `.web` extension before they can run on a Netscape Web server. This compiled model for Web applications contrasts with other popular server-side environments, such as Microsoft Active Server Pages (ASP) and CGI pages written in Perl, both of which are interpreted on-the-fly each time a server-side page is accessed. We discuss the compiler in more detail later in this chapter.

First, let's look at writing server-side code in HTML pages. There are two types of delimiters between which you can write SSJS code: server tags and back quotes. Use *server tags* for any code on the page that falls outside static HTML tags.

```
<HTML>
<BODY>
Static text<br>
<SERVER>
var txt = "Text";
write("Dynamic " + txt + "<br>");
</SERVER>
</BODY>
</HTML>
```

Use *back quotes* when you need to generate text inside HTML tags. Note that you do not need to wrap the value in quotes. The back quotes generate values wrapped in quotes automatically.

```
<HTML>
<BODY bgcolor=`(client.name == "JJ" ? "#FFFFFF" : "#DDDDDD")`>
This document will have a white background if the client.name property contains
the string "JJ" and will have a gray background otherwise.<br>
</BODY>
</HTML>
```

You should never use back quotes outside HTML tags, and by the same token never use server tags inside HTML tags. You can combine server tags and back quotes in the same page, and you can use them in multiple places within the same page. You're not limited to just a single block of server-side code.

From inside server tags, you can make any calls that are legal in core JavaScript or server-side JavaScript. You can call functions, reference objects, create arrays, define variables, and more. You can even define and call your own functions and objects, although, as you'll learn in the final section of this chapter, you should define functions and objects only inside SSJS function library files.

A file with a .js extension is an SSJS function library file. You may have used .js files with your client-side JavaScript code before, but be warned that .js files in SSJS have a bit less flexibility than their client-side counterparts. In client-side JavaScript, not only can you define functions and objects, but also you can execute any JavaScript statement from anywhere within the file. When the file is loaded, the browser simply inlines the code in the file and executes it as if it were part of the HTML file that referenced it.

SSJS treats library files a bit differently. Because all HTML and library files are compiled into a single application file, SSJS simply tosses all function and object definitions into a big global bucket and makes them available to every part of the application. It does not execute the code in library files but instead only adds any function and object definitions to the global bucket. Any statements executed outside of function definitions are ignored and are never executed. For this reason, library files in SSJS are nothing more than files that contain groups of function and object definitions. As we discuss in the final section of this chapter, function libraries are extremely useful, especially for larger applications.

Built-In Application Programming Interfaces

Server-side JavaScript comes with many APIs that are directly accessible from any page or library in an application. Each API focuses on helping you perform tasks common to a particular area of Web programming. We introduce these built-in APIs here and discuss each one in greater detail in later chapters.

Session Management Service

The Session Management Service provides four objects that help you build applications that interact with users, maintain information about the current state of user sessions, and store application-specific information. Each of the objects has a different scope and life span for maintaining different types of information, as described in Table 2.1.

Database Service

The Database Service, sometimes called the LiveWire Database Service, provides a basic API for interacting with relational databases. The service natively supports databases made by Oracle, Informix, Sybase, and IBM (DB2) and also supports many other databases through the ODBC standard. Truly one of the most attractive features of server-side JavaScript, the Database Service gives you the power to publish live data to corporate users or to Internet Web sites. You can combine the database API with HTML forms to create data entry applications so that your users can publish data to your corporate databases. You can even take advantage of stored procedures and triggers that might already exist in your databases so that you can reuse business logic and data validation rules the procedures may contain, thus

Table 2.1 *Objects of the Session Management Service*

Object	Life Span	Description
request	A single HTTP request	Relays data passed from forms and query string parameters and provides information about the client browser environment.
client	A single browser session, multiple HTTP requests	Holds application-specific information about a particular user. Use it to store numeric or string state information, such as items in a shopping basket.
project	Lifetime of a single application	Holds application-specific information for a single application installed on the server. Use it to store global application parameters such as database connections or for interuser communication.
server	Lifetime of the Web server process	Holds custom information related to a particular server and provides information about the server, such as its version. It can also be used for interapplication communication.

protecting the integrity of the data. In general, you send Structured Query Language (SQL) commands or stored procedure calls to retrieve or update data. If you're retrieving data, the Database Service holds the data in objects that make it easier for you to access.

The Database Service comprises several objects to help you interact with databases. Some of the most fundamental objects are described in Table 2.2.

Interacting with databases has become so important to building mission-critical applications, such as corporate extranets and e-commerce applications, that we've devoted two chapters in the book to building database applications with SSJS. Because there's a difference between writing an application that accesses a database and writing a good database application, in Chapter 5 and 6 we not only cover the database API, but also discuss the fundamentals of designing database applications for the SSJS platform.

Table 2.2 *Objects of the SSJS Database API*

Object	Description
DbPool	Establishes a pool of connections to your database that can be reused by many users.
connection	A single database connection pulled from a DbPool that you use to interact with the database. Methods of the object allow you to retrieve data, perform updates, invoke stored procedures, and execute other commands on the database server.
cursor	Represents a set of records retrieved from the database by invoking an SQL SELECT statement. You can create both read-only and updatable cursors. With an updatable cursor you can update records in the database without writing any SQL INSERT, UPDATE, or DELETE statements.
recordSet	Similar to a cursor object, it represents a set of records retrieved from the database by invoking a stored procedure. Data in a recordSet is always read-only.

File System Service

What Netscape somewhat overzealously calls the File System Service consists of a single object: the File object. With the File object you can read from, write to, and append to almost any text or binary file that your Web server has access to. You can even create files, although you must go through LiveConnect or an external library to delete files. In Chapter 7 we show you how to use the File object and delete files using LiveConnect.

Mail System Service

The single object that constitutes the ambitiously named Mail System Service provides an API for sending e-mail from SSJS applications through most SMTP servers. Using the SendMail object, you can define common parameters of e-mail messages, such as the to and from addresses, cc and blind cc fields, subject, body, and even MIME attachments. As of the 3.51 release of Netscape Enterprise Server, you cannot read e-mail messages with the Mail System Service, although you can use LiveConnect and custom or third-party Java classes to access POP3 and IMAP servers from your SSJS applications.

LiveConnect

LiveConnect is a window to a world of APIs. With LiveConnect, you can call external Java classes from inside your SSJS application code. Given that Netscape Enterprise Server and SSJS run on multiple versions of UNIX and Windows NT, the ability to call cross-platform Java code from SSJS makes LiveConnect an extremely valuable part of the SSJS platform. By using existing Java libraries you can save time. If you need capabilities that SSJS doesn't have, such as a way to connect to a Lightweight Directory Access Protocol (LDAP) server, you can extend the feature set of your SSJS platform by writing new code in Java that will work with any one of your SSJS applications. We discuss the LiveConnect API in depth in Chapter 9.

The Netscape Java Virtual Machine that ships with Enterprise 3.51 and earlier servers may not support all currently shipping Java APIs. Check the Enterprise Server release notes for information on supported Java APIs.

Top-Level Functions

As we just described, SSJS contains dozens of objects and methods that help you perform all kinds of useful tasks. However, there are also a number of functions that exist at the "top level" of SSJS; they are not methods of any visible object or part of any particular API. They are stand-alone functions that you can use anywhere in your SSJS applications. Table 2.3 outlines each of these top-level SSJS functions.

Table 2.3 *Top-Level SSJS functions*

Function	Description
addClient	Adds client object information to a URL (see Chapter 3).
addResponseHeader	Adds information to the HTTP response header sent back by the Web server.
callC	Calls a function from an external dynamic link library (DLL) or SO library.
debug	Writes debugging information to the debug window; visible only when you're running applications in Debug mode.
deleteResponseHeader	Deletes information from the HTTP response header sent back by the Web server.

Table 2.3 *Top-Level SSJS functions (Continued)*

Function	Description
`flush`	Flushes the 64K output buffer before the server has finished processing the page on which this function is called. The buffer is automatically flushed after the server generates 64K of content.
`getOptionValue`	Gets the selected option values from an HTML drop-down or scrolling list passed from an HTML form.
`getOptionValueCount`	Returns the number of selected option values in an HTML select list passed from an HTML form.
`redirect`	Redirects to a specified URL.
`registerCFunction`	Registers a function that is defined in an external DLL or SO library.
`ssjs_generateClientID`	Generates a unique identifier that can be used to uniquely identify a user session when used in combination with the `client` object (see Chapter 3).
`ssjs_getCGIVariables`	Retrieves values of server variables that are not already exposed in the `request` object.
`ssjs_getClientID`	Returns the current unique identifier for the current user session if you're using the `server-url` or `server-cookie` method for maintaining the `client` object (see Chapter 3).
`write`	Writes HTML text to the output buffer.

Building SSJS Applications

Now that you've seen an overview of what server-side JavaScript can do, let's look at how you go about building applications on the server-side JavaScript platform. We describe the process in reverse so that we can more clearly separate the application management process from the application coding process. Hence, first we describe installing the application into the server, then we describe coding the application, and finally we look at designing the application. Normally, these processes occur in the opposite order. There—you just learned your first fact about building server-side JavaScript applications. That wasn't so bad, was it?

Managing Applications

By this point, you have probably looked at the sample applications installed in the server, and you may even have modified some code and tried it out. If this is your first time using SSJS, your modifications probably didn't show up and you needlessly kicked your hapless server and said unspeakable things. By the time you're finished reading this section, you'll probably want to apologize to your server.

Unlike some other Web scripting platforms, such as Microsoft Active Server Pages, SSJS requires that you compile, configure, and install applications before they can be executed on the Web server. When you make modifications to pages that contain server-side code, you must recompile the application and let the server know that the application has been updated. In this section, we show you the process for making completed applications available for use on your Web server.

You must perform three steps before a Web server can run an SSJS application.

1. Compile the application with the SSJS compiler.
2. Install the application in the Web server.
3. Start the application in the Application Manager.

Compiling Applications

Let's face it—no one likes to compile applications. One of the reasons languages people like JavaScript and Perl so much is that they don't require that you sit around waiting for your compiler to churn out bits before you can try out your code. Of course, compilers have their benefits. Most compiled languages execute faster than interpreted languages. Additionally, compilers can catch errors before you waste time trying to run buggy code. So even though compilers might not be comfortable for those of us who are used to insta-scripting or who never write bugs into our code (ahem), as Mom said, "Eat your vegetables—they're good for you." And "Compile your SSJS applications." SSJS applications must be compiled before you can use them, so let us show you how it works and we promise we'll move to the fun stuff quickly.

First, let's take a look at where you can put server-side code. You can embed SSJS code in HTML pages with .htm or .html extensions. As with client-side JavaScript, you can also put libraries of functions in text files that have a .js extension. Any file that contains server-side code must be compiled before it can be executed by the server. When you compile an application, all the compiled code is output to a file with a `.web` extension, and the server reads from the `.web` file when pages with server-side code are requested by a browser.

Note   Any executable code that you write inside a `.js` file that falls outside your function definitions will be ignored by the SSJS engine.

Imagine that you have produced a small application made of four pages: `index.html`, `form.html`, `formhandler.html`, and `filelib.js`. Suppose that two of the pages—`formhandler.html` and `filelib.js`—contain SSJS code, and the other two pages contain only static HTML. To compile the files into a `.web` file, you must run the SSJS compiler, `jsac`, which you'll find in the `<server-root>/bin/https` directory. Although the compiler has several optional switches, the general syntax is as follows:

```
jsac -o <filename>.web <list of .htm, .html and .js files to compile>
```

The `-o` switch must be followed by the name of the `.web` file that the compiler will generate. The filenames are separated by spaces only. For our example application, the command to compile the files will produce a compiled `.web` file, `sampleapp.web`, that we can install and run on the server.

```
jsac -v -o sampleapp.web formhandler.html filelib.js
```

The first option, `-v`, tells the compiler to run in Verbose mode. In this mode, it will output all files it processes and any errors it encounters. By default, it notifies you only if an error occurs. The `-o` option is required and tells the compiler to write the compiled output to the filename that follows it. You can get more information on all the compiler options by running it with the `-?` option.

```
jsac -?
```

Notice that we're compiling only the two files that contain server-side code. You do not need to compile files that contain only static HTML, nor do you need to compile other resources such as graphics files. In fact, it would be a bad idea to compile static pages inside the `.web` file because a Web server can serve static pages faster than the SSJS engine can. There's no need to bog down the SSJS engine with the task of serving static pages, which the Web server process can serve more efficiently anyway.

Note   The compiler does not alter your source files in any way. It puts all compiled code into the `.web` file that you specify in the command line. The server uses only the `.web` files for execution and never touches the source files when handling requests.

Running the compiler command for our sample application produces the output shown in Listing 2.1.

Listing 2.1 *Sample compiler output*

```
JavaScript Application Compiler Version 21.11
Copyright (C) Netscape Communications Corporation 1996 1997
All rights reserved
Reading file formhandler.html
Compiling file formhandler.html
Reading file filelib.js
Compiling file filelib.js
Writing .web file
```

After we've generated the `.web` file, we must deploy the `.web` file and any static resources that belong to the application—including static HTML pages, graphics files, and so on—to the Netscape Enterprise Server that will execute the application. Deployment simply involves moving the files from the directory or server where you compiled them to their final destination. You can do this with any file transfer program, such as FTP, or with your operating system's file copying utilities. Just make sure that you keep the same directory structure you used to compile your applications. If you move files around, you'll likely wind up with a lot of broken links.

Note   For security reasons, do not deploy files that contain server-side code. You should deploy only the `.web` file and static resources. The `.web` file contains all the compiled code that the server needs to process requests for server-side pages. Keep files that contain your uncompiled source code in a protected area of your server. If you deploy your source code to a production server, you risk compromising it if someone breaks in or if you accidentally misconfigure the security settings on your server.

That's all there is to compiling an SSJS application! You'll find that the compiler is usually fast and efficient, so you don't have to wait around long to compile or recompile your applications. Unfortunately, you'll also find that the compilers that ship with Enterprise Server 3.51 and earlier don't catch all the errors that you'd expect a compiler to catch. Still, they're usually good enough to alert you to most common errors, such as syntax errors.

Note   Rather than compile your applications from the command line every time, we recommend that you build a script or batch file to execute your compiler commands. With a script you can rapidly run the compiler as many times as necessary when you make changes to your code without having to type the commands and filenames on the command line every time.

Installing Applications (Application Manager)

After you've compiled your application code into a .web file, you must install the application in the server. Installing the application not only lets the server know where to find the application but also configures the Web server to redirect requests for pages contained within the .web file to the SSJS engine. The SSJS engine must process pages and generate HTML before the Web server's HTTP process can return any pages to the user. Netscape Enterprise Server ships with an SSJS application called Application Manager that you will use to install and configure applications on the server.

As you can see in Figure 2.2, Application Manager is a browser-based application that allows you to install and configure applications from anywhere on the Internet, provided that you have the proper security access.

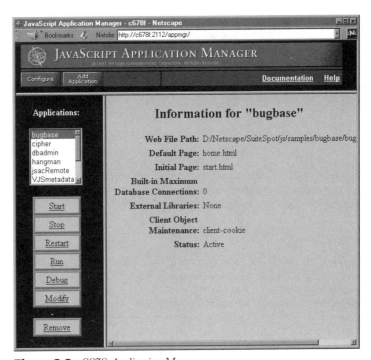

Figure 2.2 *SSJS Application Manager*

From Application Manager, you can add (install) and remove applications, start and stop installed applications, and change configuration settings of any application.

When you add an application to the server through Application Manager, you can specify several configuration parameters, as outlined in Table 2.4.

To install an application, click on the button labeled **Add Application** in the lower-left section of the top window frame. A form will appear in the main frame on the right; here you can fill in the necessary parameters.

Table 2.4 *Application Manager configuration parameters*

Parameter	Description	Sample Value
Application name	The reference that Web clients use to access the application on the server. An application named `HelloWorld` installed on the server `www.myserver.com` would be referenced as `http://www.myserver.com/HelloWorld/`.	`HelloWorld`
Web file path	The full path to the `.web` file.	`d:/projects/apps/app.web`
Default page	The page that will be fetched if the request does not specify a page name.	`index.html`
Initial page (optional)	A page that will be executed each time the application is started or restarted. Used to initialize application parameters such as global database connections.	`initial.html`
Built-in maximum database connections (optional)	The maximum number of database connections to allow the application to keep open at any one time. Use this to set limits based on the number of database licenses you own.	20
External libraries (optional)	A list of any external DLLs or SOs that your application uses.	`GetIMAPMail.DLL`
Client-object maintenance	The technique used to maintain properties of the client object throughout a user session.	`client-cookie`

When you click **OK**, Application Manager adds the application to its underlying `jsconf.config` file and attempts to start the application automatically. After an application is started, the Web server begins serving requests for its pages.

If you have applications that you do not want the server to run, you can stop the application from Application Manager. A stopped application is still installed and can be started at any time, but it is no longer accessible to the outside world. The server will return a "Not Found" error to any users requesting any SSJS pages in a stopped application.

Running Applications

Now that you know how to compile and install applications, you might wonder how you access your applications as a client. It's simple. When you install an application, you must give it an application name, such as `HelloWorld`. By appending this name to the end of the base URL for your server, you get the full URL of your application. If your server is named `www.myserver.com` and runs on port 8080, the URL to an application named `HelloWorld` would be `http://www.myserver.com:8080/HelloWorld`.

If users go to this URL without specifying a page name, the server will return the application's default page.

Your First SSJS Application: Hello World

As is the tradition in all books on programming, the first real example shown must be one that writes the string `"Hello World!"` to the primary user interface mechanism of the platform. In our case, the browser is the primary user interface device. This application is predictably simple, but who are we to defy the laws of computer publishing? Listing 2.2 shows the code, and Figure 2.3 shows the resulting output in the browser.

 Note   The top-level SSJS **write** function makes up most of the HTML generation "API" of the SSJS world, although we show you how to interlace HTML and SSJS output to reduce the number of **write** statements in your code.

Listing 2.2 *Hello World*

```
<HTML>
<BODY>
<H1><SERVER> write("Hello world!"); </SERVER></H1>
</BODY>
</HTML>
```

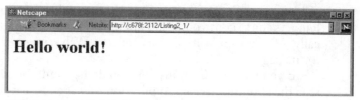

Figure 2.3 *Hello World in a browser*

Your Second SSJS Application: Son of Hello World

Let's look at a more interesting example and show you a few of the common elements you'll deal with in almost every SSJS application you build. Netscape's Enterprise and FastTrack servers ship with a number of sample applications that demonstrate how to use various features and APIs. One of those applications, called World, is an extended Hello World application that we dissect to point out interesting features of a typical SSJS application.

The World sample application is rather simple and consists of only a single page, but it illustrates three of the most fundamental features of SSJS (or any Web application platform, for that matter):

- Handling of HTML forms
- Session management
- HTML generation

Notice first that the application consists of generated text and an HTML form. The form submits to itself, and the page contains code to handle its own form submission. Essentially, it looks in the `request` object for the `request.newname` property because the only text input element on the page is named `newname`.

```
<P>This time you are <server>write(request.newname);</server>
```

Additionally, the page assigns this value to the client object property `client.oldname`. This essentially saves the current state of the page so that the next time a user submits the form, the page can write the previous state of the `newname` form element. The following code shows how the application dynamically generates the HTML using values from the `request` and `client` objects.

```
<server>write("<P>Last time you were " + client.oldname + ".");</server>
<P>This time you are <server>write(request.newname);</server>
<server>client.oldname = request.newname; // Remember name for next
```

The application also maintains two counters: one that tracks how many times a particular client has accessed the application, and a second one that tracks how many times the application has been accessed by any client. Because only one client can access the `client` object at a time, the application can simply increment the value each time the page is accessed.

```
// Initialize or increment number of accesses by this client
if (client.number == null) client.number = 0;
  else
client.number = 1 + parseInt(client.number,10);
```

However, because the application counter, stored in the `project` object, can be incremented by many different clients, it must protect the counter from simultaneous access, which might corrupt the value. Therefore, it must *lock* the `project` object before changing the value. You'll learn more about locks in Chapter 3.

```
project.lock();     // Initialize or increment total number of accesses.
  if(project.number == null)
    project.number = 0;
  else
    project.number = 1 + parseInt(project.number,10);
  project.unlock();
```

Listing 2.3 shows the complete listing for the world sample application. It is followed by Figure 2.4, which illustrates what the application looks like when executed.

Listing 2.3 *Complete listing of the World sample application*

```
<html>
<head>
<title> Hello World </title>

</head>
<body>
<h1> Hello World </h1>
<p>Your IP address is <server>write(request.ip);</server>

<server>write("<P>Last time you were " + client.oldname + ".");</server>
<P>This time you are <server>write(request.newname);</server>

<server>
//Remember name for next time.
client.oldname = request.newname;
</server>
```

Listing 2.3 *Complete listing of the World sample application (Continued)*

```
<h3> Enter your name... </h3>
<form method="post" action="hello.html">
<input type="text" name="newname" size="20">
<br>
<p><input type="submit" value="Enter">
    <input type="reset" value="Clear">
</form>
<server>
//Initialize or increment number of accesses by this client
  if (client.number == null)
    client.number = 0;
  else
    client.number = 1 + parseInt(client.number,10);

  project.lock();     // Initialize or increment total number of accesses.
  if(project.number == null)
    project.number = 0;
  else
    project.number = 1 + parseInt(project.number,10);
  project.unlock();
</server>
<p>You have been here <server>write(client.number);</server> times.
<br>This page has been accessed <server>write(project.number);</server> times.

</body>
</html>
```

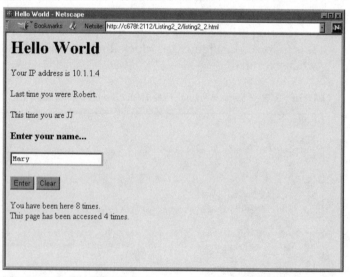

Figure 2.4 *The World sample application rendered in a Web browser*

The Sample Applications

You can find the sample applications on your server under the following directory:

```
<server-root>/js/samples
```

`<server-root>` is the root installation directory of your server. By default, the installer sets this directory to `Netscape/SuiteSpot`. Table 2.5 outlines each of the sample applications. Note that some applications are utilities you might find useful while building applications. These utility applications are noted in the table with an asterisk, and the description indicates their purpose.

Table 2.5 *SSJS sample applications*

Application	Description
Bank	Demonstrates how to communicate with remote applications through Internet Inter-ORB Protocol (IIOP). Not installed by default.
Bugbase	A bug-tracking application that demonstrates using LiveConnect to call Java classes.
Cipher	A simple game that asks you to decode a phrase.
Dbadmin*	A utility application that connects to any database supported by SSJS. Once connected, you can run any SQL statements and view results if your statement returns any results. Very useful for testing connectivity to a database and diagnosing connectivity problems.
Flexi	Another IIOP sample. Not installed by default.
Hangman	The traditional hangman game.
JsacRemote*	A utility application that allows you to remotely compile SSJS applications from any browser that has access to your Web server.
Sendmail	A simple application that demonstrates how to use the `SendMail` object to send mail through a Simple Mail Transfer Protocol (SMTP) server.

Table 2.5 *SSJS sample applications (Continued)*

Application	Description
Oldvideo	A simple video rental store application that demonstrates retrieving data from a database and updating data in a database. Works with DB2, Informix, Microsoft SQL Server, Oracle, and Sybase.
Videoapp	Essentially the same application as Oldvideo upgraded to demonstrate how to use Web cursors and Web transactions (see Chapter 6). Does not work with Informix.
Viewer*	A utility application that lets you view files on the server. Not installed by default. You must add this application to Application Manager yourself. This application poses a security risk because it allows anyone with access to read and write files on your server.
World	A "Hello World!" application that demonstrates HTML generation, session management, and form handling.

* indicate utility applications

Designing SSJS Applications

There's more to building applications than writing code, and that's one of the themes you'll find running throughout this book. Our goal is not only to show you how to use the features of SSJS but also to explain how to use them effectively. As you know, a good application design is the foundation on which all good applications are based. Therefore, let's explore some general design principles that we recommend for building good SSJS applications.

Client-Side JavaScript versus Server-Side JavaScript

The differences between client-side and server-side JavaScript often confuse novice Web developers. To help keep each environment straight, keep in mind the key point: server-side JavaScript cannot directly access client-side objects, and client-side JavaScript cannot directly access server-side objects. The object models on the client and the server platforms are very different. For example, you cannot directly call an alert box from server-side code. First, the `alert` method belongs to the `window` object, which exists only on the client-side platform. Second, on the server, there's no place to display an alert box. Similarly, in client-side JavaScript, you cannot directly access a database using the SSJS Database Service. The Database Service API exists only on the server.

When to Use What

Client-side JavaScript is popular because it's convenient to perform up-front processing tasks, such as data validation, without having to make a server request and wait for it to come back. Just because you can generate almost any HTML output with SSJS and validate form fields when a user submits a form doesn't mean that you should start using SSJS for everything. There are plenty of times when client-side JavaScript is a better choice. Following are some guidelines to help you decide when to use client-side JavaScript and when to use server-side JavaScript.

Use client-side JavaScript to perform these tasks:

- Access a client-side object or respond to a client-side event.
- Validate HTML form field values. Performing validation on the client can dramatically improve response times and reduce network traffic. Unfortunately, it sometimes requires that you put business rules in your client application.
- Prompt a user for confirmation.
- Reduce the processing load that the Web server must bear.

Use server-side JavaScript to perform these tasks:

- Access server-side objects or resources, such as databases, mail servers, and so on.
- Validate HTML form fields while keeping your validation logic in business objects on the server.
- Support several different browsers and browser versions on a limited budget. You can cut down on your testing costs by reducing or eliminating all client-side JavaScript and performing all processing on the server. Client-side JavaScript has notorious portability problems that mandate testing on every browser version that your application must support.

Communicating Between Client and Server

Communicating from client to server is relatively straightforward and doesn't require anything except simple HTML form elements and a basic understanding of HTTP requests. There are two ways to send data from the client to the server: URLs and HTML forms. To send values to the server by way of a URL, you can append data to the query string portion of the URL. That's the portion after the question mark, which you've probably seen at many sites on the World Wide Web.

```
http://www.netscape.com/mypage.html?id=ab+c&partition=left
```

By appending name-value pairs to the query string, you can send data to the server. The server will expose the name-value pairs in the SSJS `request` object so that they are accessible to your SSJS code. To add name-value pairs to a URL, you must make sure that all the values are URL-encoded. Characters such as spaces and question marks are illegal in URL-query strings. To pass an illegal character in a query string value, you must URL-encode it, which translates the character into a hexadecimal number that represents the ASCII equivalent of the character. Fortunately, both client-side and server-side JavaScript provide a function called `escape` that you can use to URL-encode all illegal characters in any string. Also, the SSJS `request` object automatically URL-decodes the values for you, so you don't need to worry about decoding them after they get back to the server. We talk more about handling HTTP requests in Chapter 3.

You can also return data to the server in form elements. Form element values are also exposed on the server side as properties of the `request` object.

There are two ways to return data from the server to the client so that client-side JavaScript code can take action on the data it receives: HTML form elements and dynamically generated client-side JavaScript. You can always generate HTML form elements from your server-side code that can be accessed by client-side JavaScript on the same page or in another frame. Additionally, you can generate client-side JavaScript code from SSJS and dynamically embed values into the client-side code. In Listing 2.4, the SSJS code generates client-side JavaScript code in `SCRIPT` tags and essentially passes a value to it by dynamically generating an assignment statement using the server-side value. After the server generates the page and returns it to the browser, the browser won't be able to tell that the client-side code was generated on-the-fly. It simply executes the code it's handed with the dynamically generated value. Listing 2.5 shows the generated code that the browser sees and executes, and Figure 2.5 illustrates the result as rendered in a Web browser.

Note   You cannot put **SERVER** tags between **SCRIPT** tags. Therefore, you must use an SSJS **write** statement to write the client-side **SCRIPT** tags if you're going to generate any client-side JavaScript code from the server inside **SERVER** tags.

Listing 2.4 *Dynamically generating client-side JavaScript from the server*

```
<HTML>
<HEAD>
<SERVER>
```

Listing 2.4 *Dynamically generating client-side JavaScript from the server (Continued)*

```
var userAge = 26;
write("<SCRIPT>");
write("var age = " + userAge);
write("</SCRIPT>");
</SERVER>
<BODY>
<h2>Static text here</h2>
<SERVER>
write("<SCRIPT>");
write("window.alert('User is ' + age + ' years old.')");
write("</SCRIPT>");
</SERVER>
</BODY>
</HTML>
```

Listing 2.5 *Code generated by the SSJS code from Listing 2.4*

```
<HTML>
<HEAD>
<SCRIPT>var age = 26</SCRIPT>
<BODY>
<h2>Static text here</h2>
<SCRIPT>window.alert('User is ' + age + ' years old.')</SCRIPT>
</BODY>
</HTML>
```

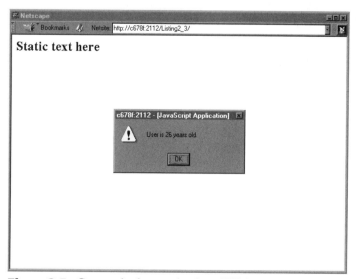

Figure 2.5 *Generated code as rendered in a Web browser*

Notice that we were able to generate a client-side alert command from the server. We said earlier that it's not possible to directly call an alert box from the server, and that's true. However, as we have done here, you can always generate client-side code that calls an alert box from the client. Don't be afraid to follow in our footsteps and find other ways to work around the apparent limitations of Web development.

Summary

In this chapter we introduce the basics of writing SSJS code and building SSJS applications. SSJS applications are compiled and not interpreted on-the-fly as are many competing Web application platforms. SSJS has several powerful APIs that you can use to interact with external servers and services, including database and mail servers, the file system, and external libraries. In this chapter you saw sample SSJS code to give you a feel for how to write SSJS applications. In the remaining chapters, we show you how to write a great deal more code, always keeping our examples in the context of building solid SSJS applications. After all, anyone can write code. We're here to help you build better applications.

Session Management

Session management is the act of passing and persisting information related to requests sent from a Web browser to a Web server. Session management is arguably one of the most fundamental and important concepts in Web application development. HTTP is a connectionless, stateless protocol, meaning that a new connection is created and broken on each request. Without a constant connection, such as with an FTP session, there is no way for the Web server to know whether the last request a user made is the final request or only one of many. As far as the Web server is concerned, each request from a browser is a request from an entirely new user.

A connectionless, stateless protocol presents a problem for developers who often need to store data that describes the current state of a client or of the application itself at any given moment. Suppose you're trying to display a customized view of an application for certain users. You could store all user preferences in a file or database on the server, but the overhead required to perform searches and updates for such small amounts of information across potentially thousands of users makes such schemes impractical. Alternatively, you can store such session information in the browser using mechanisms such as cookies, but cookies require that you write code to get, set, and manage the information they contain. What developers really need are built-in data structures on the Web server that allow them to manage session and state information.

The concept of session management applies to all Web applications and not just to SSJS applications, and it has its roots in the world of traditional client/server applications. In fact, Web applications are essentially a variant of client/server programming with a cookie-cutter client—the Web browser—and a cookie-cutter server—the Web server—to handle communication protocols for you. Yet, in the early days of Web programming, the generic client and server lacked a way to store information about a client's session between client requests to the server. In other words, Web browsers and servers had no way to remember what had just happened and how it affected the application user.

SSJS provides several mechanisms for maintaining client and application state so that you don't have to invent your own routines or write code that deals directly with browser cookies or databases. In this chapter, we explain the SSJS Session Management Service and show you how to extend it if you need additional functionality.

The Session Management Service

Server-side JavaScript provides an API called the Session Management Service for maintaining information about client and application sessions. The API consists of several objects that represent different levels of session scope from the Web server level to the individual HTTP request level. With these objects you can manage data passed at the request level or manage your own custom data at levels of scope that have longer life spans than a single HTTP request.

Overview of the Session Management Objects

The API consists of four objects, each of which relates to a different level of session scope: `request`, `client`, `project`, and `server`. Figure 3.1 shows the scope of each object. In this diagram, the smaller the scope, the shorter the life span of the object.

Starting from the inside out, you can see that the `request` object has the smallest scope and therefore the shortest lifetime. In fact, SSJS creates a `request` object for each HTTP request sent to a page contained in a `.web` file and destroys the object after the request is processed. Use the `request` object to access name-value pairs passed from HTML forms or URL query strings. SSJS interprets each HTTP request for a page within a `.web` file and creates one new property in the `request` object for each name-value pair sent in the request. Thus, many properties of the `request` object are context-dependent and highly dynamic. The `request` object also has some default properties, which are always part of the object, from which you can retrieve information such as the user's Internet Protocol (IP) address, the type of browser being used, and other information.

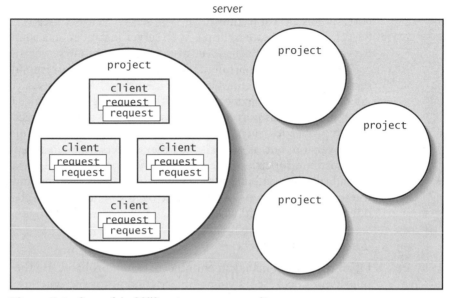

Figure 3.1 *Scope of the SSJS session management objects*

The object with the next longest life span is the `client` object. It corresponds to an entire user session, which can be made up of one or many HTTP requests. Each distinct user session has its own `client` object; a user session is defined uniquely by a combination of browser, IP address, and date-time. Primarily, the `client` object acts as a repository for user-specific settings, such as account numbers or parameters, that customize the look-and-feel of a site for each user. SSJS creates a `client` object as soon as you create its first property, and the object persists until the user closes the browser or a customizable timeout period expires. Each time the user makes a new request or reloads a page, SSJS resets the timer. Later in this chapter, we discuss how SSJS stores values held in the `client` object.

Continuing outward in the diagram, we find the `project` object. Recall from Chapter 2 that several SSJS applications can be registered under Application Manager for a single Web server. Just as HTTP requests and user sessions have their own objects, each active application on the server has its own `project` object. The `project` object has the same lifetime as the application; this means that whenever you start or restart the server or the application, SSJS re-creates the `project` object. You can store application-specific parameters in the `project` object, such as global database connections that you want all clients to use. If you want to make sure that certain parameters are reset whenever the application is started, just set them in the application's initial page, which is executed whenever an application is started or restarted.

Finally, we come to the `server` object, which holds information that corresponds almost to the entire Web server. With Netscape Enterprise Server, you can create multiple Web server instances on a single Enterprise Server installation. Each server instance has a unique server identifier and usually has a unique port number. A `server` object corresponds to a single server instance with a unique server identifier. In most cases, you can also say that a `server` object corresponds to a Web server instance installed on a given port (such as port 80, 81, and so on). The `server` object has some default properties, such as the Web server's IP address, port number, and server version, but, as with all the other objects, you can also define your own custom properties. The `server` object persists as long as the server is up and running, and it spans all applications, user sessions, and requests on the server. The `server` object is destroyed whenever the Web server is shut down and is re-created whenever the Web server is started up.

The `request` *Object*

Of all the session management objects, you'll probably use the `request` object most because it's your primary conduit for receiving user input. Let's look at it in more detail so that you can know exactly what you can do with it. Table 3.1 lists its default properties, and Table 3.2 lists its methods along with brief descriptions of each one.

Table 3.1   `request` *object properties*

Property	Description	Sample Value
`agent`	The client browser and version.	`Mozilla/4.0N (Windows; I; 32bit)`
`auth_type`	The type of authentication, if any, used to validate a user. Corresponds to the CGI `AUTH_TYPE`.	`basic`
`auth_user`	The user name entered if authentication was used. Corresponds to the CGI variable `AUTH_USER`.	`bobjones`
`imageX`	Set when the user clicks inside an image map. Contains the x coordinate value of the mouse position inside the image map.	15

Table 3.1 request *object properties (Continued)*

Property	Description	Sample Value
imageY	Set when the user clicks inside an image map. Contains the y coordinate value of the mouse position inside the image map.	27
ip	The IP address of the client.	198.3.230.76
method	The HTTP method used to submit the request.	POST
protocol	The protocol and version used for the request.	HTTP/1.0
query	The query string portion of the URL.	?name=bob&color=blue
uri	The portion of the URL after the protocol, machine name, and port number.	/sports/baseball/mac.html

Table 3.2 request *object methods*

Method	Description

httpHeader()	Returns an object that contains properties that correspond to each property of the HTTP request header. For example:
	
	`var hdr = request.httpHeader();`
	
	`// displays the value of the`
	`content-type of the request`
	`write(hdr.content-type);`

getPostData(numChars)	Used to get raw data sent in the body of an HTTP POST request. numChars instructs the method to return only numChars characters. Setting numChars to zero instructs the method to return all characters in the body of the request. For example:
	
	`// Assign entire body of the request to`
	`the variable "data"`
	
	`var data = request.getPostData(0);`

The request object wraps up most of the functionality needed to process incoming HTTP requests. When an application such as a browser makes an HTTP request, it generally submits one of two kinds of requests:

GET or POST. With the GET method, any data passed to the server, such as parameters in a URL query string, are put into the Web server's QUERY_STRING variable in URL-encoded format. With the POST method, data sent is put into the Web server's standard input buffer. If you were writing a CGI script to take an action on data passed in an HTTP request, you would have to parse out all the name-value pairs from the QUERY_STRING variable or standard input buffer, then decode them from URL-encoded format, and then parse each value from each name in every name-value pair found. Fortunately, the request object does all this decoding and parsing for you. Any values passed in an HTTP request, whether by GET or by POST, are placed in properties of the request object so that the name of the property corresponds to the name in the name-value pair and the property's value is that of the same name-value pair. For example, the following link sends a GET request and all the query string data to the Web server.

```
http://www.appmethods.com/thepage.html?var1=10&var2=20&var3=30
```

You could then access the name-value pairs in thepage.html as properties of the request object without writing any code to parse or decode the values.

```
write(request.var1);   // Will write out the value '10'
write(request.var2);   // Will write out the value '20'
write(request.var3);   // Will write out the value '30'
```

The client *Object*

When server-side JavaScript was introduced, Web developers were starting to build CGI applications that were sophisticated enough to require more than just routines to parse and decode form values and query string variables. However, there was no standard way in most cases for developers to manage client and application state information, and that functionality is critical to building complex applications. For example, retail e-commerce applications rely heavily on electronic shopping carts to make buying items online easy and convenient. But maintaining a shopping cart requires that you have a way to store information about the items that a user has purchased during the life of the session. You must have a way to identify an entire user session—and not just individual requests—and you must have the ability to store data about the entire user session. When Netscape released server-side JavaScript, it provided the client object as a standard way to maintain session state in any SSJS application.

Note   You can store only string and numeric values in the SSJS client object. You cannot store arrays, objects, or other values with other data types. Later in this chapter, we show you how to extend the `client` object so that you can store values of any data type, including arrays and objects, in a client-level object.

To maintain client properties across multiple requests, SSJS must store the data in a data store that lives longer than a single request. SSJS can store client data in various places, and it provides five ways to maintain data stored in the `client` object, as described in Table 3.3.

Note   Each SSJS application provides a separate `client` object to each client. So if a client jumps from one SSJS application to another, the `client` object properties assigned in the first application will not be available to the second application, and vice versa.

Table 3.3 `client` *object maintenance techniques*

Technique	Description
Client cookie	Stores all client object properties in browser cookies, one cookie per browser. Maximum of 20 properties allowed per application because of cookie limitation of 20 cookies per application.
Client URL	Stores all client object properties as URL-encoded values in the query string of all links in the application. Requires the use of the `addClient` function.
Server IP	Properties are stored in a server data structure and indexed by the client's IP address. Suitable only for networks in which every client has a fixed IP address.
Server cookie	Stores properties in a server data structure indexed by a unique identifier. The identifier is stored in a single cookie on the client's browser.
Server URL	Stores properties in a server data structure indexed by a unique identifier. The identifier is stored as a URL-encoded name-value pair in the query string of all links in the application. Requires the use of the `addClient` function.

Client Cookie As the table describes, SSJS stores each property of the `client` object in a cookie in the client's browser. You do not have to do anything special to work with the `client` object when using this method. To create a new property or assign a value to an existing one, use a simple assignment statement.

```
client.myProperty = "value";
```

The client cookie method has some limitations worth noting:

- There is a limit of 4K of data per property. If you attempt to assign any property values longer than 4K, the value will be truncated.
- There is a limit of 300 cookies per client. As mentioned in Table 3.3, you can have only 20 properties per application. In addition, you can have only 300 total properties per client for all SSJS applications. If you create more than 300 cookies, older values will be deleted.
- You must set properties before the buffer is flushed. Recall from Chapter 2 that the SSJS engine flushes the output buffer and returns data to the browser after generating 64K of data. When it returns the first 64K, it also returns the HTTP response header, which contains any cookie commands the SSJS code might have generated. Because property values for cookies are sent back to the browser with the first 64K of data, any cookie values set after the first 64K of data will never make it back to the browser. Therefore, if you're using client cookie maintenance, you must not set any client properties after the first 64K of generated data on the page. Any client properties that are set after SSJS returns the response header and the first block of data will disappear after the entire page has been processed. This limitation applies only when you're using the client cookie maintenance technique.

Client URL If you don't like relying on cookies but wish to use a client maintenance technique that doesn't require storage in server memory for property values, you can use the client URL technique to maintain client property values. With this technique, you must call the addClient function to generate all hyperlinks in your site. This function appends the client properties to a URL by adding them to the URL's query string and giving them a special prefix of NETSCAPE_LIVEWIRE. For example, if you want to prepare a link to Netscape's Web site in your application, you would make the following call to addClient:

```
addClient("http://www.netscape.com/index.html");
```

Suppose that you had previously assigned a value of 17 to the client object property client.myProperty. In this case, the function would generate the following URL, which users would see in their browser's location box if they click on it.

State

```
http://www.netscape.com/index.html?NETSCAPE_LIVEWIRE.myProperty=17
```

When a user clicks on the link, the server knows that any values prefixed with `NETSCAPE_LIVEWIRE` are special, and it generates a new `client` object on the server with all the property values that have the special prefix in the URL. With this maintenance technique, a `client` object is created and destroyed on the server with each request, and the values are maintained only in the URL.

This approach has some noteworthy limitations. Most important, all client properties are lost when an HTML form is submitted. This limitation isn't specific to SSJS but rather is the way HTTP requests work. When you submit an HTML form, you're no longer using URLs to navigate to the next page. Thus, whatever values you had in your URL query string will be lost when the form sends the browser to another page. Fortunately, you can implement a simple workaround to this limitation. Any HTML form has an `ACTION` attribute as part of its `FORM` tag that specifies the URL of a form handler that it must submit the form data to. You can insert any valid absolute or relative URL here, including URLs with query strings. If you generate your `ACTION` tags using the `addClient` function, your `client` property values will be appended to the query string of the `ACTION` tag and thus sent to the form handler along with all the other form values.

```
<FORM ACTION=`addClient("formhandler.html")`>
```

Again, when the SSJS form handler receives the form data and sees the specially prefixed values with a `NETSCAPE_LIVEWIRE` prefix, it will automatically pull them into a new `client` object.

This technique has one other important limitation for which there is no workaround. All `client` properties are lost when the user jumps to another site. If the site is not part of the same SSJS application, the URL will lose the query string that contains the `client` properties.

Note   Even though both client techniques store `client` object data in data structures on the browser, SSJS also creates a version of the `client` object on the server with each HTTP request, provided that the `client` object is not empty. SSJS pulls the `client` properties from the browser and creates the object. That object is what you actually reference in your SSJS code.

When SSJS processes the page and returns the response to the browser, it returns any new or changed `client` property values to the `client` data structures and destroys the version of the `client` object it created on the server. So even though the client techniques don't use server memory to store data across multiple requests, they still require server memory for every request made.

Server IP With the server IP technique, SSJS stores `client` object properties in an internal data structure on the server and uses the IP address of the client as part of a unique identifier that references the internal data structure. It cannot use the IP address alone because one client can access many applications, each of which has its own separate `client` object.

This maintenance method works in a limited number of situations and is highly dependent on how your network and the networks of your clients are configured. Generally, you should consider this maintenance method when you're running your applications over a fixed-IP address network and your clients are not connecting through a proxy server. In certain cases, this method may not work at all. For example, you may have problems in dynamic-IP-address networks because the IP addresses of the clients change and are reused and machines are rebooted. If your clients will be accessing the application through a proxy server, note that proxy servers present a single IP address for clients that must connect through them. Clearly, in such a situation this `client` object maintenance method will not work.

Server Cookie The server cookie technique stores `client` object properties in an internal data structure and references the structure using a generated unique identifier. SSJS then stores this identifier in a cookie on the client browser so that the client can be associated with the internal data structure on any HTTP request.

Server URL The server URL technique is similar to the client URL technique except that instead of storing the actual property values in the URL, you store the property values in an internal data structure on the server. The data structure is indexed by a unique identifier, and SSJS stores that identifier in the URL query string. Like the client URL technique, this maintenance technique is also vulnerable to form submissions, and the same workaround discussed for the client technique applies.

Note   You can view the unique identifier used by the server cookie and server URL techniques by calling the top-level SSJS function `ssjs_getClientID`.

The `project` Object

As mentioned earlier, the `project` object exists for the lifetime of an entire SSJS application, and every SSJS application has its own `project` object. You can use it to track the state of an application, such as the number of times it has been accessed. You can also use it to hold shared data that all clients accessing the application can access. For example, you could define parameters that your application uses to dynamically generate the look-and-feel of your application, including background colors, font styles, and so on. If you ever wanted to change the appearance of your site, you would only have to change the parameters held in the `project` object. Instantly, all clients would see the new look-and-feel.

The `server` *Object*

The `server` object contains predefined information about the server, as outlined in Table 3.4. In addition, you can store custom properties in the `server` object, much as you can with the `client` and `project` objects. However, you should store serverwide shared data in the `server` object. For example, you can create shared data structures and store them in the server if you need one or more applications running on the server to be able to communicate with each other.

State

Table 3.4 *Predefined properties of the* server *object*

Property	Description	Sample Values
jsVersion	The Web server version and platform	3.5.1 WindowsNT
host	The full address of the Web server, including port number	www.appmethods.com:80
hostname	The machine name of the Web server	www.appmethods.com
port	The port on which the Web server runs	80
protocol	The Web server protocol	http:

Locking

You have been introduced to two objects—`project` and `server`—that can hold shared data that more than one client can access. Not only can more than one client read the data simultaneously, but also more than one client can attempt to change the data simultaneously. Therefore, SSJS provides two ways to lock access to shared data structures so that only one client at a time can change data in a shared location.

First, both the `project` and the `server` objects have `lock` and `unlock` methods that, when called, provide exclusive access to the caller and release the exclusive access, respectively. Whenever you need to modify shared data in one of these objects, you should first attempt to get a lock on the object. However, because other applications attempting to access a locked `project` or `server` object must wait for the lock to be released, you shouldn't keep the objects locked for very long. Call `lock` just before you are about to modify your data. Then perform the modification and immediately call `unlock` to release the lock on the data so that other clients can obtain access.

Second, SSJS has a generic `Lock` object that you can use to lock any shared object. If you use the `Lock` object instead of the `lock` and `unlock` methods of the `project` or `server` object, you can protect only the shared data without locking access to the entire `project` or `server` object. In other words, you can build a finer level of control around shared data using a `Lock` object than you can with the `project` or `server` `lock` method. Table 3.5 describes the methods of the `Lock` object.

Table 3.5 *Methods of the* Lock *object*

Method	Description
`lock`	Attempts to lock the object for exclusive access
`isValid`	Returns true if a lock was successfully obtained, false otherwise
`unlock`	Unlocks the object

For example, suppose you are holding two shared data values in the `project` object. One, `project.counter`, is a counter in a custom property of the `project` object. The other property, `project.util`, holds an array of `Date` objects, one per client, that tell when the user last accessed the application. Both properties contain data that multiple clients will be changing throughout the life cycle of the application. If you use the `project.lock` method to lock access to the `project.counter` property when one client wants to access it, another client that wants to modify `project.util` will be locked out until the first client has released the lock. However, in this case, there is no reason to lock the second client out of a different shared data structure.

Instead of locking the entire object, you could create an instance of a `Lock` object and call its `lock` and `unlock` methods to obtain a finer level of control over concurrent access to each shared property. Look at the code in Listing 3.1. We first create an instance of a `Lock` object and store it in the `project` property `project.counterLock`. We'll use this lock to protect the `project.counter` property. Second, we create another `Lock` object and store it in the `project.utilLock` property. This lock will protect the `project.util` property. Typically, you should create these locks on the initial page of your application so that they are instantiated before any clients have had a chance to access the application.

Listing 3.1 *Creating locks to protect shared data*

```
project.counterLock = new Lock();
project.utilLock = new Lock();
```

Next, look at Listing 3.2. Here, we show what it would look like to use these locks to provide access to the shared `project.counter` property.

Listing 3.2 *Accessing a protected property*

```
project.counterLock.lock();
   project.counter++;
project.counterLock.unlock();
```

Note   If you decide to use locks, you must use them consistently throughout your entire application. If you locked every door in your house except one, you might as well have left all of them unlocked. A burglar will find your one unlocked door and rob you. The situation is no different for an SSJS application. Allowing even one line of code to change data in a shared data structure without first locking it can lead to corrupt data no matter how careful you are in the rest of the application.

You must be careful when using `Lock` objects to avoid creating deadlock situations. For example, suppose that our application contained the two routines shown in Listings 3.3 and 3.4. Imagine that a client calls the routine in Listing 3.3 at the same time that a different client calls the routine in Listing 3.4. The first client will get a lock on `utilLock` and proceed to wait to get a lock on `counterLock`, while simultaneously the second client obtains a lock on `counterLock` until it can get a lock on `utilLock`. Because each client is holding a lock that the other client is waiting for, we have a deadlock. Both objects are locked indefinitely, and no processes can access the locked resources.

Listing 3.3 *Routine that waits for* `counterLock` *while holding a lock on* `utilLock`

```
project.utilLock.lock();
   project.counterLock.lock();
      project.counter++;
   project.counterLock.lock();
   project.util[0] = new Date();
project.utilLock.lock();
```

Listing 3.4 *Routine that waits for* utilLock *while holding a lock on* counterLock

```
project.counterLock.lock();
    project.utilLock.lock();
        project.project.util[0] = new Date();
    project.utilLock.lock();
    project.counter--;
project.counterLock.lock();
```

Effective Session Management

As with almost any powerful resource, you can use the session management objects for good or for evil. Perhaps those words are a bit strong, but you can definitely misuse the session management objects and create maintenance and debugging nightmares. Following are some do's and don'ts that, in our experience, will help you build better applications.

First, do use the project and server objects to store shared data. As mentioned earlier, there are many kinds of data that you may wish to share between clients or between applications. Using the project and server objects provides quicker access to shared data than retrieving values from a text file or database. However, keep in mind that storing data in the project and server objects takes up server memory, so for large amounts of data you'll want to resort to a database or text file for storage.

Second, do not use the client, project, or server objects as global variable dumping grounds. Many books that discuss good programming techniques disparage global variables because they tend to create maintenance and debugging problems. This book is no different. Using global variables creates a maintenance problem, especially on projects with a large number of developers, because it's hard to keep track of exactly when and where different parts of the application are changing global data values. Global variables also create a debugging nightmare for the same reason. You can spend a significant amount of time trying to track down a misbehaving routine that is corrupting a global variable that the rest of the application depends on.

The client object appears to be a wonderful place to dump global variables, but you should resist the temptation! Only store data in the client object that's related to maintaining user state information, such as user preferences or the state of a shopping cart. If you start dumping global data in the client object simply because it's convenient, you may find yourself inconvenienced later when you are forced to track down the part of your application that keeps changing a client property at the wrong time.

Do not use the request object as a holder of temporary variables. JavaScript gives you a great deal of power for dealing with objects because you can create new properties on-the-fly almost any time you like. However, the `request` object represents, by definition, the data sent from a browser in an HTTP request. If you start using it as a convenient holder of temporary variables on your page or if you start changing the values that were passed in the original request, you could create a maintenance problem.

Suppose that you validate form variables on the server side and change the values of any invalid properties to null. You no longer know what data was originally passed in the form. What if a new developer comes along later to modify your form handler and doesn't catch the line where you set the request parameters to null. It could take him or her a while to figure out that you were changing the true representation of the HTTP request sent from the browser. Instead, keep this representation pure and use the Java-Script `var` statement to create temporary JavaScript variables that hold temporary values.

Extending the `client` Object

As you've learned, the `client` object can hold only string and numeric values. If you need to store an object beyond any one request, you can store it only in the `project` or `server` object. However, because these objects are shared by all users—and not just a single one as the `client` object is—you must write code to manage the data and partition it among multiple users. In this section, we show you how to use the `project` and `client` objects to build your own extension of the `client` object that will hold any value you need, including objects such as database connections and cursors.

This section discusses some basic object-oriented concepts and defines custom JavaScript objects. If you're unfamiliar with JavaScript's object-oriented features, please refer to Chapter 10 of *JavaScript Guide* and the paper titled "Object Hierarchy and Inheritance in JavaScript," both on the Netscape developer Web site at `http://developer.netscape.com`. For specific URLs for these manuals, See Resources.

SuperClient to the Rescue

Let's build an object called `SuperClient` that you can use in your own applications to store any values, including objects on a per-client basis. You can think of the `SuperClient` object as a superset of the `client` object, as its name suggests. It should still have the basic properties of the `client` object, such as the ability to store data related to a single user session across multiple user requests. Yet it should be able to store any kind of data, including other JavaScript objects. Additionally, it should be almost as easy to use in an application as the `client` object.

First, we show you how to use the `SuperClient` object and another object called `SuperClientCollection` that manages all `SuperClient` objects in an application. When you understand how to use the objects in your own applications, we take a peek under the hood and explain how the objects work by looking at how to build each object from the ground up.

Overview of the Objects

You can look at the SuperClient object as a custom version of the client object, and we use it in exactly the same way that you would use the client object. You can add properties, set property values, and get property values. Each connecting browser has one and only one SuperClient object, and it persists for the lifetime of the user session, just like the client object. Later, you'll find out that we're still using the client object under the hood, although not to store property values directly.

The SuperClientCollection object manages all instances of SuperClient objects for an application. Each application in which you wish to use SuperClient objects should have only one SuperClient Collection. To use SuperClientCollection, you create an instance of it in the initial page and store that instance in the project object so that it can be referenced from anywhere in the application by any user session. The object stores all SuperClient objects in an internal array and uses the ssjs_generateClientID function to index each SuperClient object with a unique identifier. It then associates each SuperClient with each user session by storing that unique identifier in the client object. Whenever an application needs user-specific information, it can call the getSuperClient method of the SuperClientCollection, which uses the unique identifier stored in the client object to find the associated SuperClient object in the collection.

We've already built these objects for you, and you'll find them on the CD-ROM included with this book. They are generic and reusable for almost any application, although you can modify them to suit your needs. We show you a sample application that uses the SuperClient shortly. First, let's briefly review the important methods of the two objects we've discussed. You must call these methods in order to use the objects in your applications:

- SuperClient.setProperty adds a new custom property to the object or sets the value of a property if it already exists.
- SuperClient.getProperty retrieves the value of a custom property.
- SuperClient.deleteProperty permanently removes a property from the object.
- SuperClientCollection.getSuperClient retrieves the SuperClient property that corresponds to the current user session from the SuperClientCollection stored in the application's project object. It must be called on every page where you wish to use SuperClient.

You now have everything you need to employ `SuperClient` in your own applications. You can use the object without modification or modify it to suit your custom application needs. Either way, you now have the ability to store any kind of data you want—from simple strings to custom objects—in a repository that will persist for an entire user session.

Note You can store any valid JavaScript identifier in the `SuperClient` object, including instances of Java objects that you create through the SSJS LiveConnect interface described in Chapter 9. You can even store instances of JavaBeans and make them available to any page within your application!

Using `SuperClient` and `SuperClientCollection` in an SSJS Application

Let's look at a simple example that shows how to use the `SuperClient` and `SuperClientCollection` objects in an application. As you'll discover, employing the objects requires very little overhead, and `SuperClient` is almost as easy to use as the built-in `client` object.

To use the `SuperClient` and `SuperClientCollection` objects in an application, you must compile `SuperClient.js` into your application's `.web` file. You must also instantiate one and only one instance of a `SuperClientCollection` object in the initial page of your application, as demonstrated in Listing 3.5.

Listing 3.5 *Instantiating* `SuperClientCollection` *in the initial page*

```
// In seconds, the timeout period for SuperClient objects
var timeout = 10*60;  // 10 minutes
// In seconds, how often SuperClientCollection cleans up old SuperClient
objects
var cleanup = 30*60;  // 30 minutes
project.SuperClientCollection = new SuperClientCollection(timeout, cleanup);
```

Let's put this initial page to use in a simple two-page example. On the first page, we store a string and a JavaScript `Date` object in the `SuperClient`. On the second page, we retrieve these elements and write them to the page to show that we were able to persist data across requests inside the `SuperClient`.

Listing 3.6 shows the first page, `setclient.html`. It contains a static link to the second page and SSJS code that sets two properties of the `Super-Client`: a string and the current date and time. To create the properties, we call the `setProperty` method and provide a property name and the value. Figure 3.2 shows what the page looks like in a browser.

Listing 3.6 *Setting* SuperClient *properties in* setclient.html

```
<HTML>
<HEAD>
<META NAME="GENERATOR" Content="NetObjects ScriptBuilder 3.0">
<TITLE>Set SuperClient Properties</TITLE>
</HEAD>

<BODY>
Setting properties...
<hr>
<SERVER>

var sc = project.SuperClientCollection.getSuperClient();
var timestamp = new Date();

// Set two custom SuperClient properties
sc.setProperty("name", "Mozilla");
sc.setProperty("timestamp", timestamp);

</SERVER>
<TABLE BORDER=1 CELLPADDING=3 CELLSPACING=2>
<CAPTION><b>SuperClient Properties Set:</b></CAPTION>
<tr><td>name:</td><td>"Mozilla"</td></tr>
<tr><td>timestamp:</td><td><SERVER> write(timestamp); </SERVER></td></tr>
</TABLE>
<hr>
End.  Go to <A HREF="writeclient.html">page 2 to view the stored
properties</A>.
</BODY>
</HTML>
```

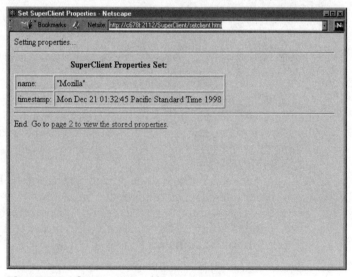

Figure 3.2 *Output generated by* setclient.html

When users click on the link in `setclient.html`, they are sent to `writeclient.html`, which displays the properties set on the preceding page. Listing 3.7 shows the SSJS code that reads the properties from `SuperClient`, and Figure 3.3 shows a sample of the output. The date and time displayed reflect the date stored in `SuperClient`, and the current date and time are displayed below that to show that they are different. To retrieve the values, we call `getProperty` and pass the name of the property as a parameter. Additionally, to prove that we're really getting a `Date` object back from `SuperClient` and not just a string value, we call the `getSeconds` method of the stored timestamp, which is a JavaScript `Date` object, and write it to the page.

Listing 3.7 *Getting* `SuperClient` *properties in* `writeclient.html`

```
<HTML>
<HEAD>
<META NAME="GENERATOR" Content="NetObjects ScriptBuilder 3.0">
<TITLE>Get SuperClient Properties</TITLE>
</HEAD>

<BODY>
Getting properties...
<hr>
<SERVER>

var sc = project.SuperClientCollection.getSuperClient();
var currenttime = new Date();

// Get stored SuperClient properties
var name = sc.getProperty("name");
var timestamp = sc.getProperty("timestamp");

</SERVER>

<TABLE BORDER=1 CELLPADDING=3 CELLSPACING=2>
<CAPTION><b>SuperClient Properties Set on the Previous Page:</b></CAPTION>
<tr><td>name:</td><td><SERVER> write(name); </SERVER></td></tr>
<tr><td>timestamp:</td><td><SERVER> write(timestamp); </SERVER></td></tr>
<tr><td>timestamp.getSeconds():</td><td><SERVER> write(timestamp.getSeconds());
</SERVER></td></tr>
<tr><td>currenttime.getSeconds():</td><td><SERVER>
write(currenttime.getSeconds()); </SERVER></td></tr>
</TABLE>
<hr>
End.
</BODY>
</HTML>
```

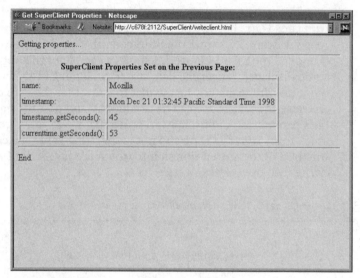

Figure 3.3 *Output generated by* writeclient.html

Building the SuperClient

First, let's build the SuperClient object. After that, we'll look at how to build the SuperClientCollection object that manages all SuperClient objects in an application. We'll design the SuperClient object as a user-defined server-side JavaScript object. As with client-side JavaScript, you can define your own objects in server-side JavaScript. In fact, that's one of its most appealing features. We need to be able to set and get property values from the SuperClient object and to delete property values. We also need for it to expire at some point so that it does not reside in server memory after a user session has expired. Table 3.6 lists the methods the object needs to accomplish these tasks.

The getProperty, setProperty, and deleteProperty methods do just what their names suggest. However, the touch and getLastTouched methods need a little explaining. Earlier in this chapter, we mentioned that by default native client objects expire after a certain amount of time elapses without their being accessed. The Web server must allocate memory for the data stored in a client object, and because there's no way to know when a user has accessed an application for the final time, the server must periodically clean up client objects that have not been used for a while. The server must assume that client objects that go unused for long periods must be abandoned and that the associated user has gone away. The SuperClient object must follow similar requirements to ensure that the memory required by its data members can be reclaimed by the server when

Table 3.6 *Methods of the* `SuperClient` *Object*

Method	Description
`getProperty`	Gets a property by name from the `SuperClient` object.
`setProperty`	Sets a property value or creates a property if it does not already exist.
`deleteProperty`	Deletes a property by name.
`touch`	Records that the `SuperClient` object has been accessed. `SuperClient` objects that have not been touched for a certain period of time must be deleted to free server resources.
`getLastTouched`	Gets the timestamp that tells when the `SuperClient` was last touched by the associated user.

its associated user session has closed. To manage the reclamation process, we need a timer that will tell us that `SuperClient` has expired. Because SSJS does not support the concept of timers, we'll invent one of our own using the `touch` method.

The `touch` method sets a property of the `SuperClient` object, `lastTouched`, to reflect when the object was last accessed. The `getLastTouched` method retrieves this property in the form of a JavaScript `Date` object. To determine whether a `SuperClient` has expired, we must know when it was last accessed and then compare that time with the current time to see whether the elapsed period is longer than the allowed period. If it is, we assume that the associated user has left and will not return and that therefore we must delete the object to reclaim server resources. Because any form of access means that the associated user is still using the application, we must call the `touch` method to record any type of access, including simple reads of a property. Therefore, in our object, we call the `touch` method whenever the host application accesses any property of `SuperClient` through the `getProperty`, `setProperty`, or `deleteProperty` method.

At this point, the `SuperClient` object we've described isn't capable of cleaning up after itself but instead only makes sure that its `lastTouch` property is maintained accurately. Therefore, some other method or process must clean up `SuperClient` objects that have expired. We discuss that cleanup process shortly. For now, let's look at the code behind the `SuperClient` and see how it works.

Listing 3.8 shows the constructor method for the `SuperClient` object. In the constructor method, the object's properties are defined and links to the functions that defined the object's methods are also established. In Java-

Script, you define a method by assigning a function to an identifier associated with the object:

```
this.getProperty = _sc_getProperty
```

Here, `getProperty` identifies the public name of the method that applications will call to invoke the method, and `_sc_getProperty` is the name of an SSJS function that defines the method's code.

Listing 3.8 `SuperClient` *constructor method*

```
function SuperClient() {
    // Private Properties
    this.lastTouched = new Date();
    this.properties = new Array();

    // Public Methods
    this.getProperty = _sc_getProperty;
    this.setProperty = _sc_setProperty;
    this.deleteProperty = _sc_deleteProperty;
    this.getLastTouched = _sc_getLastTouched;

    // Private Methods
    this.touch = _sc_touch;
} // END Constructor for SuperClient object
```

The object has two properties and five methods. Although SSJS does not enforce the concept of public or private properties and methods, we've labeled them as such as a reminder of the appropriate scope of each attribute. Private properties and methods should be accessed only within the `SuperClient` object, and never by any outside object or function. Public properties and methods, on the other hand, define the public interface to the world, and any application code can reference public attributes.

To illustrate why it's important to stay true to the intended scope, let's look at the `properties` array, which is a property of the `SuperClient` object. `SuperClient` stores each of its user-defined session properties as elements of the `properties` array. As with the native `client` object, an application that uses `SuperClient` can add new properties to it at any time for the purposes of maintaining new user session information. However, by making the `properties` array private, we say that we wish for applications to get and set property values only by the use of the `getProperty` and `setProperty` methods. If an application misbehaves and manipulates the `properties` array directly, the `touch` method will not be called automatically and the object will not know it has been accessed. Therefore, it might expire prematurely. Rather than place the burden of calling the `touch` method on applications that use `SuperClient`, we defined the public and private interfaces to the object so that well-behaved applications need not bother themselves with the internal working of the object. If applications employ the public interface properly, `SuperClient` will take care of its internal status automatically.

Listing 3.9 shows each of the `SuperClient` object's method definitions for both private and public methods. The combination of the constructor method and the method definitions makes up a complete `SuperClient` object definition.

Listing 3.9 `SuperClient` *method definitions*

```
function _sc_getProperty(name) {
    this.touch();
    return this.properties[name];
} // end _sc_getProperty

function _sc_setProperty(name, value) {
    this.touch();
    this.properties[name] = value;
} // end _sc_setProperty

function _sc_deleteProperty(name) {
    this.touch();
    if (this.properties[name])
        delete this.properties[name];
} // end _sc_deleteProperty

function _sc_touch() {
    this.lastTouched = new Date();
} // end _sc_touch

function _sc_getLastTouched() {
    return this.lastTouched;
} // end _sc_getLastTouched
```

To create a new instance of `SuperClient`, you must use the JavaScript new operator, as you would when creating an instance of any user-defined JavaScript object.

```
mySuperClient = new SuperClient();
```

This code invokes the constructor function, creates a new instance of the `SuperClient` prototype, and assigns it to the variable `mySuperClient`. However, as you'll see, you won't be creating instances of it in this fashion yourself.

Using `SuperClientCollection`

The `SuperClient` object is nothing more than an object that stores an arbitrary number of name-value pairs. By itself, it has no direct link to any one user session or the native `client` object. Furthermore, were you to instantiate a `SuperClient` object on an SSJS page, just as with any other object it would be destroyed at the end of a single user request. To make `SuperClient` useful, it must be associated with a user session and stored somewhere that has a lifetime at least as long as a user session. Recall that we must also deal with expired `SuperClient` objects. It would seem that we still have quite a bit more code to write before we have an object that serves our purpose. At this point, we could stop and simply show you how to implement the code needed to use `SuperClient` in your SSJS applications, but that might not lead to code that you could easily reuse in your own applications. Fortunately, we can organize this management code into yet another reusable, user-defined SSJS object.

Just as SSJS provides a single instance of a `client` object for each user session, we should provide only a single instance of `SuperClient` per user session. Thus, an entire application will have a collection of `SuperClient` objects, one for each connected user. Where better to store application-specific data, such as a collection of `SuperClient` objects, than the SSJS `project` object? We need to store an array of `SuperClient` objects in the `project` object and then come up with a way to associate each `SuperClient` object with a single user session.

To associate `SuperClient` with a user session, we use the built-in `client` object. Just because we're building a better session-level object doesn't mean that the `client` object has lost its utility. If we store a unique identifier as a property of the `client` object and then use that identifier as an index into the array of `SuperClient` objects, we can associate one `SuperClient` to one user session through the unique identifier. When an application needs to retrieve user-specific data, it can use the identifier stored in the `client` object to find the associated `SuperClient` in the array of `SuperClient` objects stored in the `project` object.

We could invent our own unique identifier to link `client` and `SuperClient`, but SSJS provides a top-level function, `ssjs_generate ClientID`, that returns a unique identifier for us. Every time the function is called, it returns a new, unique identifier, so we must make sure that we call it only one time for any one user session.

We can wrap all the management functions described so far into an object we'll call `SuperClientCollection`. Thus far, the object requires only one property and one method. We need a property, which we'll call `elements`, that holds an array of `SuperClient` objects. We also need a method, which we'll call `getSuperClient`, that does one of two things depending on whether a `SuperClient` exists yet for the user session that is requesting a `SuperClient` object:

1. The method checks the `client.__SuperClientID` property for an identifier. If one exists, it attempts to find the corresponding `SuperClient` object in the `elements` array by looking for an index in the array that matches the identifier. If it finds a corresponding object, it returns it to the calling routine.

2. If no `SuperClient` is found in the array, the method does the following:
   - Creates a new `SuperClient` object
   - Generates a unique identifier
   - Stores the `SuperClient` in the array indexed by the identifier
   - Stores the identifier in the `client.__SuperClientID` property

Now that we know what we need to do to create new `SuperClient` objects in the `SuperClientCollection` and to find existing objects in the collection, we need a way to clean up old `SuperClient` objects when a corresponding user leaves an application or the session times out. You didn't forget about that, did you? If we don't clean up old objects, the collection will continue to collect objects until the server eventually runs out of available memory.

In SSJS, there is no way to know exactly when a user ends a session or exactly when the session times out. No events are fired, nor are any notifications sent. The only way we can tell that a session has timed out is to set a timer of our own and define its expiration to mean that the user session has ended. This technique is tricky, so let's walk through it step by step.

First, we need a routine that checks a timer and determines when a `SuperClient` has expired. Second, we need a routine that uses the timer check routine of the `SuperClient` collection to check all the `SuperClient`s it holds and find any that have expired. Third, we need a method to delete expired clients to free server resources. Together, these three pieces of logic constitute a cleanup routine. Respectively, they translate into three methods of the `SuperClientCollection`: `isTimeout`, `removeOldSuperClients`, and `deleteSuperClient`.

Now we need to start this cleanup routine at some point and make sure that it gets called regularly. Any application that wants to use a `SuperClient` object must first call the `getSuperClient` method. Let's call our cleanup logic from this method because we know it will be called often enough to ensure that the collection will be cleaned up on a regular basis.

Note   Recall from earlier in the chapter that the `client` object has an expiration timer of
its own. By default, it expires after 10 minutes of inactivity unless overridden by a
call to the `client.expiration` method. This means that after 10 minutes of inactivity, the `client` object and any properties it contains will be destroyed.

In the proposed scheme, we store a reference to the `SuperClient` in the
`client` object, so, after 10 minutes, that reference will be destroyed and we will no
longer be able to reach the `SuperClient`. Therefore, no matter what life span we
give to the `SuperClient` in the `SuperClientCollection`, our reference to it is
ultimately controlled by the `client` object's life span. When the `client` object dies,
the `SuperClient` effectively also dies, even though it might continue to exist in
memory until our cleanup routine removes it.

At this point, let's review what we have designed so far and see whether
we have enough to make a complete `SuperClientCollection` object that
will properly manage all `SuperClient` objects for all user sessions accessing
an application.

Whenever any application wants to retrieve a `SuperClient` or create a
new one, it must call `getSuperClient`. This method attempts to find one in
the collection and return it or create a new one if no matching `SuperClient`
was found. Additionally, `getSuperClient` calls a cleanup routine,
`removeOldSuperClients`, that checks every `SuperClient` in the collection
to see whether it's expired. We can tell whether a `SuperClient` has expired
by comparing its `last touched` property, retrieved by calling its
`getLastTouched` method, to the current time. If the difference between
the times the `SuperClient` was last accessed is greater than the allowed
expiration period, we can say that the `SuperClient` has expired and delete
it from the collection with `deleteSuperClient`. These methods are summarized in Table 3.7.

Table 3.7 *Methods of the* `SuperClientCollection` *object*

`getSuperClient`	Gets a particular `SuperClient` object from the collection using the `client._SuperClientID` property or creates a new `SuperClient` if one cannot be found in the collection.
`isTimeout`	Determines whether a particular `SuperClient` object has expired.
`removeOldSuperClients`	Searches the entire collection of `SuperClient` objects and removes those that have expired according to the `isTimeout` method.
`deleteSuperClient`	Removes a `SuperClient` from the collection and frees the associated memory.

It seems that we have everything we need to manage SuperClients in our collection, but you may have noticed a potential problem with the current scheme. Because applications will call getSuperClient frequently, the cleanup routine also will be run quite frequently. If a large number of users are hitting the same application and thus using the same SuperClient Collection, the application will run the cleanup routine quite often. The more users, the more SuperClients in the collection and therefore the longer it will take to run the cleanup routine. Yikes! In trying to save server memory, we've created a performance problem. So before we can declare the object design complete, we must deal with this performance issue because it could significantly affect the scalability of the application. Fortunately, there's a simple way to tweak the performance of the application. Unfortunately, it requires a classic trade-off between server memory and application speed.

Instead of running the cleanup routine every time someone calls getSuperClient, we can configure the cleanup routine so that it runs only once in a while. The getSuperClient method will still call remove SuperClients each time it's invoked, but the removeSuperClients method will check a timer of its own to determine whether it's time to run the cleanup routine. In other words, the cleanup routine will run periodically according to a predetermined timer. To add this functionality, we add a property to the SuperClientCollection called cleanupPeriod, which represents the cleanup timer, and a method called isCleanup, which determines whether the cleanup timer has expired.

Note   The cleanup timer is entirely different from the SuperClient timer. Expiration of the cleanup timer tells SuperClientCollection to look for old SuperClients. After the cleanup timer has fired, the cleanup routine looks through the collection and uses the SuperClient timer to determine whether a particular object has expired.

This policy has two consequences. First, it should improve performance by reducing the amount of time the application spends running the cleanup routine. Second, the application will place greater demands on server memory because SuperClient objects will be left in memory until the cleanup routine is run. So depending on the value we assign to the cleanup timer, expired SuperClient objects may sit in memory for quite some time before the cleanup routine removes them and restores the memory they occupy. This is a necessary trade-off and requires some experimentation to see which cleanup timer length provides the optimal balance between server memory and application speed.

Note   In general, adding memory to a server is cheaper than adding faster hardware. Although your results may vary, you will probably find that high-traffic applications will benefit more from longer cleanup timers and greater server memory requirements. Of course, if you avoid storing large amounts of data in `SuperClient`, you can also reduce the memory requirements for your applications.

If spending time tweaking application performance isn't your idea of fun, reconsider whether you need the functionality of `SuperClient`. If you can get away with storing only strings and numbers in the built-in `client` object, you don't need `SuperClient` at all. However, assuming that some of your applications will require it, let's conclude our discussion of the `SuperClientCollection` object.

Listing 3.10 shows the complete listing for the `SuperClient` and `SuperClientCollection` objects. Both objects are defined in a single Java-Script library, `SuperClient.js`, which you'll find on the CD-ROM included with this book.

Listing 3.10   *Complete listing for* `SuperClient.js`

```
function SuperClient() {
      // Private Properties
      this.lastTouched = new Date();
      this.properties = new Array();

      // Public Methods
      this.getProperty = _sc_getProperty;
      this.setProperty = _sc_setProperty;
      this.deleteProperty = _sc_deleteProperty;
      this.getLastTouched = _sc_getLastTouched;

      // Private Methods
      this.touch = _sc_touch;
} // END Constructor for SuperClient object

/* ***** Begin SuperClient Method Definitions ***** */
function _sc_getProperty(name) {
      this.touch();
      return this.properties[name];
} // end _sc_getProperty

function _sc_setProperty(name, value) {
      this.touch();
      this.properties[name] = value;
} // end _sc_setProperty

function _sc_deleteProperty(name) {
      this.touch();
      if (this.properties[name])
            delete this.properties[name];
} // end _sc_deleteProperty
```

Listing 3.10 *Complete listing for* SuperClient.js *(Continued)*

```
function _sc_touch() {
     this.lastTouched = new Date();
} // end _sc_touch

function _sc_getLastTouched() {
     return this.lastTouched;
} // end _sc_getLastTouched
/* ***** End SuperClient Method Definitions ***** */

function SuperClientCollection(cleanupPeriod, clientTimeout) {
     // Public Properties
     this.lastCleanup = new Date();

     // Private Properties
     this.elements = new Array();
     this.cleanupPeriod = cleanupPeriod;
     this.timeout = clientTimeout;

     // Public Methods
     // uses client.__SuperClientID to pull from elements array
     this.getSuperClient = _scc_getSuperClient;
     this.deleteSuperClient = _scc_deleteSuperClient;  // deletes from array
(and blanks client.__SuperClientID?)
     this.getCleanupPeriod = _scc_getCleanupPeriod;
     this.setCleanupPeriod = _scc_setCleanupPeriod;
     this.getSuperClientTimeout = _scc_getSuperClientTimeout;
     this.setSuperClientTimeout = _scc_setSuperClientTimeout;

     // Private Method
     this.removeOldSuperClients = _scc_removeOldSuperClients;

     // Initialize a global application Lock object
     project.lock();
          if (typeof(project.SuperClientCollectionLock) == typeof(void(0)))
               project.SuperClientCollectionLock = new Lock();
     project.unlock();
} // END Constructor for SuperClientCollection object

/* ***** Begin Method Definitions ***** */
function _scc_getSuperClient() {
     var sc = null;
     var now = (new Date()).getTime();
     // If the cleanup period has expired, run the cleanup routine
     if (this.lastCleanup.getTime() + this.getCleanupPeriod()*1000 <= now)
          this.removeOldSuperClients(now);
     // If this is the first time the function has been called,
     // or the client object no longer references a valid SuperClient
     // object in the collection, create a new SuperClient object
     // and index it by client.__SuperClientID.
     if(!client.__SuperClientID) {
          project.SuperClientCollectionLock.lock();
               client.__SuperClientID = ssjs_generateClientID();
               this.elements[client.__SuperClientID] = new SuperClient();
               project.SuperClientCollectionLock.unlock();
     }
```

Listing 3.10   *Complete listing for* SuperClient.js *(Continued)*

```javascript
        return this.elements[client.__SuperClientID];
} // end = _scc_getSuperClient

function _scc_deleteSuperClient(id) {
    if (this.elements[id]) {
            // Lock the global lock object so that no other threads can
            // access the collection at the same time we're trying to
            // delete an element.
            project.SuperClientCollectionLock.lock();
                delete this.elements[id];
                // If we just deleted the current client's SuperClient,
                // then delete the pointer to it, client.__SuperClientID
                if (id == client.__SuperClientID)
                        delete client.__SuperClientID;
            project.SuperClientCollectionLock.unlock();
    }
} // end = _scc_deleteSuperClient

function _scc_getCleanupPeriod() {
    return this.cleanupPeriod;
} // end _scc_getCleanupPeriod

function _scc_setCleanupPeriod(seconds) {
    if (typeof(seconds) == typeof(0))
            this.cleanupPeriod = seconds;
} // end _scc_setCleanupPeriod

function _scc_getSuperClientTimeout() {
    return this.timeout;
} // end _scc_getSuperClientTimeout

function _scc_setSuperClientTimeout(seconds) {
    if (typeof(seconds) == typeof(0))
            this.timeout = seconds;
} // end _scc_setSuperClientTimeout

function _scc_removeOldSuperClients(now) {
    this.lastCleanup = new Date();
    for (var elm in this.elements) {
            if ((this.elements[elm].getLastTouched().getTime() +
                this.getSuperClientTimeout()*1000) <= now)
                    this.deleteSuperClient(elm);
    } // end for loop
} // end _scc_removeOldSuperClients
/* ***** End Method Definitions ***** */
```

Summary

The Session Management Service of the server-side JavaScript API has four built-in session management objects.

- `request` handles data sent from the browser to an SSJS application and has the lifetime of a single HTTP request.
- `client` holds custom, session-specific data and has the lifetime of an entire user session.
- `project` holds custom, application-specific data and has the lifetime and scope of an entire application.
- `server` holds server-specific data and has the lifetime of the entire Web server.

The `SuperClient` object extends the functionality of the `client` object to overcome some of its limitations. The `SuperClient` object presented here is generic and reusable, but we encourage you to modify and extend it for use in your own applications.

The `project` object is used to hold shared data, and `Lock` objects are used to protect shared data structures.

It is virtually impossible to write any meaningful SSJS applications without using some of the SSJS session management objects. The topics covered in this chapter are fundamental to understanding how to write effective SSJS applications.

State

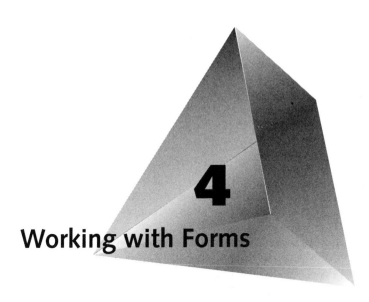

4

Working with Forms

How many times has this happened to you? You go into a meeting with your clients to tell them about all the cool things your new application will do. You tell them about the triggers, views, stored procedures, and other cool database functionality you'll use to process the data more efficiently. You tell them about Java and JavaScript and explain how you'll code the application in half the time and save them a bundle of money. You tell them that this application will make their work easier and change their lives into things of beauty. And what do they do? They look at you with serious faces and, without cracking a smile, say, "Do you have any screens to show us?"

They just don't get it. An application isn't about screens. Rather, you want to tell them, it's about cool functionality; efficient, succinct code; tons and tons of features; and a few well-placed bandages to hold the whole thing together. An application is a work of art, hundreds of hours of labor employed to craft an elegant solution to a problem. It's not a bunch of screens loosely tied together with code.

But you don't make that argument because you know you'll get no sympathy from your users. It's time to face reality. The user's only interaction with your application is through screens and, more specifically, forms. The sooner you come to grips with this fact, the better. You can have the coolest app in the world, but if the screens and forms are unattractive or poorly designed, the users will complain. After all, they may have to look at those screens every day of their corporate lives.

Forms are the lifeblood of server-side JavaScript—they allow you to gather information from users and submit that information to your SSJS application. Forms are the means by which users interact with a Web application. Some users judge the quality of an app based largely on its forms. (Reality check: the application must work correctly, but in this chapter we assume that you've created a working app with a minimum number of erroneous features, or bugs.) This chapter covers forms in detail, although we do not cover the entire HTML specification (plenty of good books already do that). Rather, we talk about the various input fields that can be placed on your form and how to manage them. In addition, we focus on the user interface (UI) as it relates to forms; we also don't cover general Web design because there are plenty of existing books on that topic.

We show code samples that demonstrate how to manipulate form values and form submission on the client using client-side JavaScript. We also show you how to access the field names and values from your submitted form in your back-end server-side JavaScript application—a process called form handling. We explain how to make forms visually appealing, validate form values, check for required values, and pass values from one document to another. We focus on creating forms that are pleasing to the eye, easy to use, and result in a positive experience for the user.

Note   This chapter is rather lengthy. You may wish to skim part of it.

The Importance of Forms

You should spend quality time designing the HTML pages and forms that make up your SSJS applications. Forms are the primary way that users interact with your applications, so it's extremely important to put a lot of effort into making them attractive and easy to use. Most users judge the quality of your application on the following four factors:

- Attractiveness: Are the HTML pages and forms visually appealing?
- Clarity: Is the application easy to understand, easy to navigate, and easy to use?
- Functionality: Does the application do what it is supposed to do? Can the data returned by the application be trusted?
- Performance: Do results come back in a reasonable amount of time? Is the site reliable?

HTML forms are the easiest way for users to communicate with an SSJS application, and that is why SSJS makes extensive use of them to gather transactional information and to allow users to modify that information. Generally, you should use forms only to gather data from the user and not to display data. In other words, use tables to display formatted data, and use forms to allow users to manipulate data.

Attention to the presentation and usability of your forms during design and development will result in increased user satisfaction with the finished product. You may do some clever things in SSJS to create a robust, reliable, and responsive application, but the user doesn't necessarily see these things. The user sees the user interface you create, which is composed of HTML pages. You should spend some time designing your pages to create a consistent look-and-feel and particularly spend time with your forms to ensure that they are easy to read and attractive.

Bad Form

The form in Figure 4.1 demonstrates how not to create a form. It shows plain HTML with little thought given to format, layout, and ease of use. Using forms of this nature is tedious and can be frustrating for the user.

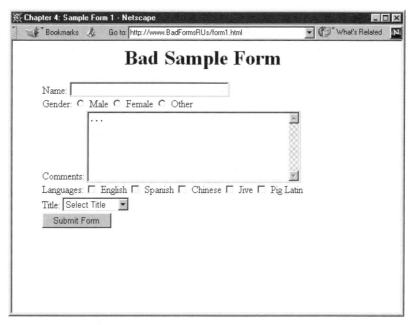

Figure 4.1 *An example of a poorly designed form.*

Here is the HTML code for the form in Figure 4.1. What mistakes can you spot?

```
<FORM METHOD="GET" ACTION="showValues.html">
Name: <INPUT TYPE="TEXT" NAME="name" SIZE=30<BR
Gender: <INPUT TYPE="RADIO" NAME="gender" VALUE="M" Male  <INPUT
TYPE="RADIO" NAME="gender" VALUE="F" Female><INPUT TYPE="RADIO"
NAME="gender" VALUE="O" Other><BR>
Comments: <TEXTAREA NAME="comments" COLS=40 ROWS=6...></TEXTAREA><BR>
Languages: <INPUT TYPE=checkbox NAME="english" VALUE="English">
English <INPUT TYPE=checkbox NAME="spanish" VALUE="Spanish" Spanish>
<INPUT TYPE=checkbox NAME="chinese" VALUE="Chinese" Chinese><INPUT
TYPE=checkbox NAME="jive" VALUE="Jive" Jive><INPUT TYPE=checkbox
NAME="piglatin" VALUE="Pig Latin" Pig Latin><BR>

Title: <SELECT NAME="title">
<OPTION VALUE="">Select Title
<OPTION VALUE="MR">Mr.
<OPTION VALUE="MS">Ms.
<OPTION VALUE="MRS">Mrs.
<OPTION VALUE="DR">Dr.
<OPTION VALUE="AGENT">Secret Agent
</SELECT><BR>

<INPUT TYPE="SUBMIT" NAME="submitButton" VALUE="Submit Form">
</FORM>
```

Here are a few things that are wrong with the preceding code.

- The form does not have a name, so it will be difficult to reference it from JavaScript. Always name your forms!
- The input fields do not have a MAXLENGTH property, so the user can input a value of any length. If your database accepts only 40 characters for this field, set MAXLENGTH=40. This prevents the user from entering more than 40 characters into this field.
- The textarea field does not contain a WRAP property. Without this property, textareas scroll to the right as users enter data, forcing them to press **Enter** to return to the left side of the entry area. If you set WRAP="VIRTUAL", the browser will show all the text entered in the field and users are not forced to press **Enter**.
- Avoid using words like "Jive" and "Pig Latin" that might be offensive to users.

There are additional problems with the form, but it's sufficient to note that it is not well designed. Try to avoid making the mistakes shown, and instead create concise, clearly worded, and attractive forms. You can use a variety of tools to create your HTML pages, including Netscape Composer, NetObjects Fusion, and so on. Layout tools are preferable because they help you better design and customize the appearance of your forms.

Making Forms Attractive

Now that you know what *not* to do, let's talk about what *to* do. Here are a few guidelines to follow when you create forms.

- To create attractive forms, use tables to format them. You may need to use multiple tables on a form to format each section properly.
- Use clear, concise wording in form labels so that users will know what information to enter in each field.
- Use colors when possible (within a table). This sets off your form from the rest of the page and can also be used to indicate related sections.
- If some fields require that values be entered, indicate it using italics, color, or boldface on the label. Before the form is submitted, you should check to ensure that the user has entered values in all the required fields.
- Always use drop-down lists (select lists), radio buttons, or checkboxes whenever you want to directly control input values, such as requiring that state and country be submitted in a particular format (for example, **CA, Calif.,** or **California**). Always use these elements when you know all the valid values for a field.
- When assigning values to the NAME property of a field, avoid space characters. Instead, use underscore ("_") characters to make the field easier to reference when using JavaScript.

Figure 4.2 shows a well-formatted form with clear labels and some shading to set it off from the rest of the HTML page. The labels are clearly defined, the layout is clean, and color has been used to separate the form from the surrounding document and to make it more attractive.

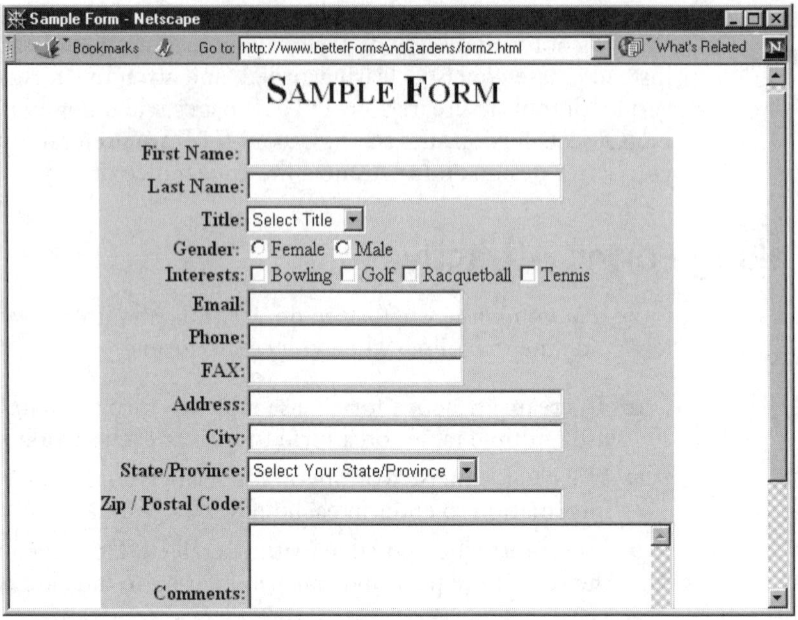

Figure 4.2 *An example of a well-designed form.*

Here is a portion of the code used in the form in Figure 4.2.

```
<CENTER>
<FORM NAME="myForm" METHOD="GET" ACTION="showValues.html">
<TABLE BGCOLOR=lightgreen CELLSPACING=0 CELLPADDING=0 BORDER=0>
<TR>
<TD ALIGN=right>
<INPUT TYPE=HIDDEN NAME="buttonPress" VALUE="">
<B>First Name:</B>
<TD><INPUT TYPE=text NAME="firstName" SIZE=30 MAXLENGTH=40>
<TD><FONT SIZE=-1 COLOR="#888888"></FONT></TD>
</TR>
. . .
<TR>
<TD COLSPAN=2><CENTER>
<INPUT TYPE=Reset NAME=Clear Value=Clear>
<INPUT TYPE=BUTTON NAME="add" VALUE="Add" onClick="submitForm(document.myForm, this)">
<INPUT TYPE=BUTTON NAME="update" VALUE="Update" onClick="submitForm(document.myForm,
this)">
<INPUT TYPE=BUTTON NAME="delete" VALUE="Delete" onClick="submitForm(document.myForm,
this)">
</CENTER>
<TD><FONT SIZE=-1 COLOR="#888888"></FONT></TD>
</TR>
</TABLE>
</FORM>
</CENTER>
```

Note the following regarding Figure 4.2 and the preceding code.

- The form has a name.
- A table is used to format the fields and labels.
- The labels are straightforward and easy to understand.
- Fields have a MAXLENGTH property to limit the number of characters that can be entered.
- Color is used to draw attention to the form.
- The most important fields appear first.
- The fields are logically grouped.

Remember that focusing attention on the visible aspects of your form will result in a positive user experience. If the forms in your application look good, many users will automatically assume that the application *works* well. We have written applications in our early programming days that weren't great, but the users loved them. They didn't know when an application was held together with rubber bands and prayers; they only knew that it was attractive and that it seemed to work. Perception, it seems, is often more important than reality.

Form Hierarchy

Before we talk about how to manipulate the elements that appear within forms, let's look at the JavaScript object hierarchy as it relates to forms. We start with an overview of the object model that governs forms so that you can better understand how JavaScript interacts with forms and form elements. As you can see in Figure 4.3, the top-level object is the window object, and it contains a document object. The document object contains a form object, and the form object contains a variety of form elements (text fields, select lists, buttons, and so on). The list of object properties in Figure 4.4 is not complete, but it gives you a basic listing of the properties available for each object and element in the form hierarchy. Please look closely now at Figure 4.3 to better understand the JavaScript object hierarchy as it relates to forms. (We apologize to those who get queasy looking at anything that resembles an org chart.)

Why is a book on server-side JavaScript spending so much time on client-side JavaScript? Remember that forms reside on the client, so you must use client-side JavaScript to manipulate them. Your server-side application can access the form's field names and their associated values only after the form has been submitted.

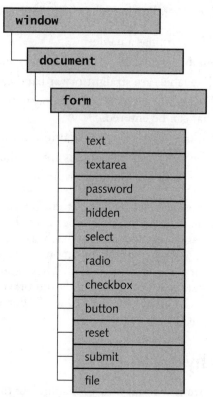

Figure 4.3   *Client-side JavaScript object
hierarchy for forms*

Figure 4.4 shows a nearly complete listing of the properties available for
each object shown in Figure 4.3. You can reference the properties using
standard object notation. For example, to reference the location for the document in the current window you'd write something like this:

```
var myLocation = window.document.location;
```

Note in Figure 4.4 that the window object contains an object called
document (shaded), the document object contains an array of form objects
(forms[]), and the form object contains an array of element objects
(elements[]). Figure 4.4 shows only the properties for each object we're
discussing. Keep in mind that there are also methods associated with the
objects.

Window			
top	document	innerHeight	screenX
frames[]	location	innerWidth	screenY
parent	history	outerHeight	status
self	length	outerWidth	secure
name	opener	pageXOffset	offscreenBuffering
	closed	pageYOffset	pkcs11
Document			
location	anchors[]	links[]	bgColor
URL	applets[]	height	alinkColor
domain	embeds[]	width	vlinkColor
referrer	forms[]	lastModified	linkColor
title	images[]	cookie	fgColor
Form			
name	action	elements[]	encoding
length	method		target
Element			

Hidden Field	Text/Password	Textarea	Select
type name value defaultValue length	type name value defaultValue length maxlength	type name value defaultValue length wrap	type name value defaultValue length options[] selectedIndex
Radio Button	**Checkbox**	**Button/Reset/Submit**	**File**
type name value length checked defaultChecked	type name value defaultValue checked defaultChecked	type name value	type name value defaultValue

Figure 4.4 *Form-related object properties*

Forms

Form Properties

Forms have specific properties that affect how a form is referenced and handled. Forms also have several types of input fields, each one used for specific kinds of data. It's a good practice to name the form so that you can reference it by name from JavaScript. You can reference forms by array value (`document.forms[0]`), but it's best to explicitly refer to them by name. It makes your code more readable and makes debugging and maintenance easier.

The name Property

When you process a form in your SSJS application, you will reference the fields and values on the form by their assigned names, so you should assign a name to every field. Get in the habit of placing quotation marks around the field name. (Quotes are required if you have a space character in the field name. However, as a general practice, you should avoid the use of spaces in field names and consider using capitalization (`myLastName`) or underscore characters (`my_last_name`) to separate the words.)

```
<FORM NAME="myForm" ...>
<INPUT NAME="lastName" ...>
```

Table 4.1 demonstrates how to refer to your fields using JavaScript. If you avoid using space characters in your field names, you can reference them more easily. In addition, after the form is submitted you can refer to the fields more easily in your SSJS code. We've found that by naming our forms and fields we can debug our code much more easily because we can immediately identify the exact field that is being manipulated.

Table 4.1 *Referencing form elements*

Field Name	Code Reference
"Last Name"	document.myForm.elements["Last Name"] document.myForm.elements[2]
lastName	document.myForm.lastName document.myForm.elements["lastName"] document.myForm.elements[2]
last_name	document.myForm.last_name document.myForm.elements["last_name"] document.myForm.elements[2]

As you can see in Table 4.1, it's easier and more straightforward to refer to elements in your form by name rather than by number. If you refer to form elements by number and later add elements to the form, you must adjust the reference numbers used in your client-side JavaScript code, a process that is extremely error-prone and remarkably tedious. Referring to elements on your HTML document directly makes your JavaScript code easier to read and maintain. Therefore, you should always assign names to the elements on your HTML documents (including forms, fields, images, and so on).

The `method` Property

You can submit forms using one of two common methods: GET and POST. (A third method, called HEAD, is rarely used.) Table 4.2 explains the difference between these two common methods. The GET method is easier to use and is more flexible, but the POST method is more secure. As a rule, you should use the POST method when submitting forms to an SSJS application.

Table 4.2 *The two methods of form submission*

Method	How Passed	Comments
GET	Name-value pairs are encoded and passed with the URL. The server stores the name-value pairs in the environment variable `query_string`.	This method is less secure than the POST method, but it is extremely flexible. The name-value pairs are submitted as part of the URL: `http://server.domain.com/myApp?name1=val1&name2=val2`. So the server actually saves some or all of the data in its logfiles. (Credit card numbers stored in server logfiles present an obvious security problem.)
POST	Name-value pairs are encoded and passed as part of the HTTP header. The server then stores the name-value pairs on the standard input (`STDIN`), and their length is defined by the environment variable `content-length`.	This method causes the browser to display a dialog box warning users if they are submitting data insecurely (HTTP port 80) rather than securely (SSL port 443). It is more secure than the GET method, and name-value pairs are not passed with the URL and are not stored in the server logfiles.

The form submission method is defined in your form:

```
<FORM ... METHOD="GET" . . .></FORM>
<FORM ... METHOD="POST" . . .></FORM>
```

Forms

The `action` Property

The `action` property defines what will happen when the form is submitted. Typically, you enter a URL here that tells the browser to pack up your form values and send them to the specified URL. In SSJS you generally send the form to another document in your app, where you process the form and enter the submitted values into a database or perform some other action. In the `action` property you can specify an SSJS URL, a static HTML page, a CGI program, or a `mailto` link. Table 4.3 shows the various ways to code the `ACTION` property of a form so that you can submit a form to an SSJS application, HTML document, CGI, or e-mail address.

Table 4.3   *How to submit forms to various targets*

Target	Code
SSJS application	`<FORM ...` `ACTION="http://server.domain.com/myApp/doc2.html">`
HTML document	`<FORM ...` `ACTION="http://server.domain.com/staticdoc.html">`
CGI	`<FORM ... ACTION="http://server.domain.com/cgi-bin/myapp.cgi">`
E-mail message	`<FORM ...` `ACTION="mailto:person@company.com?Subject=Sample Form Values">`

Each of the properties listed in Table 4.3 is a valid way to submit a form. If the application or document to which you are submitting the form is on the same machine as the form, you can use pathnames relative to your server's doc-root or relative to the form, rather than a complete URL (`"/myApp/doc2.html"` or `"../myDoc.html"` rather than `"http://server.domain.com/myApp/doc2.html"`). You can send forms to static HTML pages, SSJS application pages, and CGI programs, and you can even spawn mail windows to submit the form values. The form submission target you should use depends entirely on your application, as outlined in Table 4.4.

Table 4.4 *Determining the target of your form submission*

Target	Type of Application
SSJS application	Database applications, storing values in logfiles, sending HTML e-mail messages, and so on.
CGI	Heavy file-access or system maintenance tasks. SSJS, like any scripting language, has limitations. Rather than use it for everything, use an occasional CGI to perform tasks not ideally suited to SSJS.
HTML document	Interactive client-side JavaScript games or applications when you prefer not to use server-side processing.
Mailto	Sending e-mail messages. Formatting your mail message can be difficult, although it is possible. Mailto is seldom the ideal choice unless you want (or need) to avoid any server-side processing for sending form values via e-mail.

Giving Initial Focus to a Field

Sometimes I visit forms on the Web and want to begin entering values immediately. Unfortunately, I must move the pointer down, click inside the search field to give the field *focus*, and then shuffle my hands to the keyboard to start typing. (The most notorious offenders are search sites. The first thing you do is enter a query string in the form, so the least they could do is to give focus to the search field.) When an HTML document containing a form is loaded into the browser, you should give focus to the first field in the form. You can use the onLoad method in the BODY tag.

```
<BODY ... onLoad="document.myForm.myFirstField.focus()">
```

Giving focus to the search field makes it possible for users to begin entering values immediately without having to move the mouse pointer and click in the search field. This approach makes your users somewhat more efficient and helps them enjoy using your application more.

The idea is to make things as easy as possible, removing any unnecessary steps. In the preceding code example, focus is given to the first field on the form "myForm", which is "myFirstField".

Forms

Note   The onLoad method is executed after the HTML document is fully loaded in the browser.

Form Elements

Form elements enable the entry and submission of data by the user, and they also help you control how the data is entered. Each field element has a specific purpose to which it is ideally suited, and you should try to use the proper form element to get the precise data you need. Additionally, try to group like elements (keyboard-oriented entry fields, mouse-oriented entry fields, hidden fields, and buttons), as shown in Table 4.5.

Table 4.5 *Appropriate use of form elements*

Element Type	Element	Purpose
Keyboard oriented	Password, text, textarea	When the user must enter information from the keyboard. When the length of values varies (first name, city, and so on) or the value type varies (phone number, price, and so on).
Mouse-oriented	Checkboxes, radio buttons, select lists	When you know exactly what values will be entered (state, country, gender, and so on) and the total number of possible values that can be entered is limited. When you want to control the exact values allowed for a given field and precise formatting of those values.
Hidden	Hidden	When you don't want the user to see a given value but you want to send a specific value with the form (values passed from other forms; values you programmatically set; values that tell you what form or site the values came from, and so on).
Buttons	Button, reset, submit	When you want to submit a form, reset values on a form, execute JavaScript code, and so on.

By grouping like elements, you make it easier for the user to fill out a form. Try to group fields based on the type of data you are collecting (personal information, address and phone information, company or employment information, and so on) and try to group like fields where possible (radio buttons and checkboxes; text and textarea fields). If you create a form in which like fields are not grouped, the user is forced to shuffle between the keyboard and the mouse. It's almost guaranteed that users won't like that.

All the field types mentioned hereafter must appear within a form to be effective. Generally, if the input fields do not appear between <FORM> </FORM> tags, the browser will not display them. Perhaps you've put fields on forms and couldn't figure out why they didn't appear when you loaded the page in the browser. It's easy to forget to include <FORM> tags. Also remember to always enter a value for the TYPE and NAME properties of a field.

Hidden Fields

Following is the syntax for defining a hidden field.

```
<INPUT TYPE="HIDDEN" NAME="customerType" VALUE="OEM Customer">
```

Hidden fields are not displayed on the form; instead, they are hidden, so that the user does not see them. These types of fields are extremely useful for storing values the user does not need to enter or does not need to see when filling out a form. You may want to keep track of which form users submitted, the type of user, a value you may have prompted users for, and so on. If you have several forms in an application and you want users to fill in *all* the information on *all* the forms before you submit them, use hidden fields to store the values from previous forms. When you submit the final form in the series, you will have all the values together in one submission.

Remember that viewing hidden fields is *not* impossible. If users select **Page Source** from the View menu, they will see the HTML for your form, including the hidden fields and their associated values. Avoid using hidden fields for authentication or for storing any information that you do not want a user ever to see or potentially alter. Use hidden fields only for hiding information that the user does not need to see or does not need to enter. Hidden fields are useful, but you must always be aware that they are not a secure way of hiding values.

Text Fields

Following is the syntax for defining a text field.

```
<INPUT TYPE="TEXT" NAME="lastName" VALUE="" SIZE=30 MAXLENGTH=50>
```

Text fields, the most common fields that appear on a form, allow the user to enter a value from the keyboard. Unfortunately, with this type of field it is extremely difficult to control the value you will receive. You are therefore encouraged to do some field checking on these types of fields before the form is submitted, to check the fields in your application after the form has been submitted, or both. Eric Krock, of Netscape, has created a number of excellent field validation routines that you can use to check text fields on your forms. You can find it at the Netscape Developer's site. `http://developer.netscape.com/library/examples/javascript/ formval/overview.html`.

Specifying the SIZE of a text field determines the width of the input box that is displayed. The MAXLENGTH property strictly limits the maximum number of characters the user can enter. If you had a database column that held a 20-character value, you would set MAXLENGTH to 20, ensuring that you would not receive field values that could not be stored completely in the database. If a user tries to enter more than the number of characters specified by MAXLENGTH, the browser beeps every time a key is pressed, and no additional characters are displayed in the text field. The user is thereby forced to reduce the size of the entry. (This approach is far better than letting the user submit 40 characters and later discovering that only the first 20 characters were stored in the database. Users don't generally like such surprises.)

It's best to use the onChange event when you validate fields. Another event, called onBlur, can be used to validate field entries, but it's best not to use it. The reason is that onChange is activated only when a change has been made to the field since the last time the field had focus. onBlur is activated whenever the field loses focus. If you have two fields that are validated using the onBlur method, you can potentially put the user's browser into an endless loop.

The onChange event is activated immediately after the user has exited the field, provided that the field value has been changed. However, onChange is not activated if the field value was changed using JavaScript or if the field value was not changed since the field got focus. The user might enter an invalid field value, and your onChange event may validate that the field value is invalid and return focus to that field (after possibly displaying an error message). If the user does not alter the invalid value before leaving the field, the onChange event is not activated. Thus, an invalid value would remain in the field. For that reason, it's advisable to recheck all text field values for valid data before submitting the form. We discuss how to do this later in the chapter.

```
<INPUT TYPE="TEXT" ... onChange="validateField(this)">
```

Textareas

Following is the syntax for defining a textarea.

```
<TEXTAREA NAME="comments" WRAP="VIRTUAL" COLS=40 ROWS=6></TEXTAREA>
```

The TEXTAREA field lets users freely enter text of any length; you can't specify the maximum length as you can in text fields. For this reason, you may want to check the number of characters entered in the field using the onChange method:

```
<SCRIPT LANGUAGE="JavaScript">
<!--
    // CHECK FOR CHARACTER LIMIT ON TEXTAREA FIELD
    function checkSize(field, size)
    {
        var fieldValue = field.value;
        if (fieldValue.length>size) {
            alert ("Sorry, you have entered " + fieldValue.length +
                " characters\n in a " + size + " character field\n" +
                "Please revise your entry.");
            field.focus();
        }
    }
//-->
</SCRIPT>
...
<FORM ...>
<TEXTAREA NAME="comments" ... onChange="checkSize(this, 10)"></TEXTAREA>
...
</FORM>
```

Here the onChange method in the TEXTAREA field calls the JavaScript checkSize() function and passes the field object (this) and the maximum number of characters that should appear in the field. The field value is stored in the variable fieldValue. Next, the length is checked. If it exceeds size, an error message (Figure 4.5) is displayed and focus is returned to the TEXTAREA field. If users do not modify their entry, they can simply move to the next field. If you had used onBlur in this instance, users would see the error message every time they tried to leave the field, forcing them to enter less than the specified number of characters. It's up to you as to whether you use such heavy-handed enforcements in your form.

Figure 4.5 *Checking the size of*
TEXTAREA *fields*

If you want a value to appear in the TEXTAREA by default, place the text between the TEXTAREA tags:

```
<TEXTAREA NAME="comments" WRAP="VIRTUAL" COLS=40 ROWS=6>Your default
text here</TEXTAREA>
```

If you want to use JavaScript to set the value of a TEXTAREA field, use this code:

```
document.sampleForm.comments.value = "Your programmatically set text
here";
```

Textareas are useful for lengthy field values such as comments. Remember to specify WRAP="VIRTUAL"; otherwise, users must press **Enter** when they reach the end of each line. If they don't press **Enter,** the text they previously entered will scroll out of view as they pass the right side of the TEXTAREA. It becomes annoying to have to press **Enter** to move down to the next line to read what has been entered.

WRAP="VIRTUAL" automatically wraps the input line when the cursor reaches the right side of the TEXTAREA box. No return characters are sent with the field; rather, the text is sent in one long string. (This is generally best because return characters can cause errors in your SQL `insert` statements.)

Password Fields

Following is the syntax for defining a password field.

```
<INPUT TYPE="PASSWORD" NAME="login" SIZE=30 MAXLENGTH=50>
```

Password fields are similar to text fields. The major difference is that each character entered in a password is displayed as an asterisk ("*") character. This hides the value from anyone who might be watching the user enter values in the form.

Note

The value in a password field is no more secure than in any other field type except that the value is not displayed at the time it is entered. Suppose you used this code:

```
<INPUT TYPE="PASSWORD" NAME="login" SIZE=30 MAXLENGTH=50
onChange="alert(this.value)">
```

The value in the **PASSWORD** field would be displayed in an alert box as soon as the user exited the field. Also, when the form data is passed, the value in a password field is packed up and sent just as with a text field. Therefore, if you are using the **GET** method to submit your form, the user's password might end up stored in the server's logfiles with the other form data. Always use Secure Sockets Layer (SSL) to transmit forms whenever you are submitting sensitive information (credit card numbers, account numbers, and so on) to protect the data in transit. (Refer to your server documentation to learn how to set up a secure server.)

Select Fields

Following is the syntax for defining a select field.

```
<SELECT NAME="title">
<OPTION VALUE="">Select Title</OPTION>
<OPTION VALUE="MR">Mr.</OPTION>
<OPTION VALUE="MS">Ms.</OPTION>
<OPTION VALUE="MRS">Mrs.</OPTION>
<OPTION VALUE="DR">Dr.</OPTION>
<OPTION VALUE="AGENT">Secret Agent</OPTION>
</SELECT>
```

Select lists are one of the most useful fields on any form. They make it easier for users to specify values, and they strictly limit the values that can be submitted. (Basically, a select list is an implementation of the "domain" concept promoted by CJ Date, one of the pioneers of relational database theory.) The VALUE property in each OPTION of a SELECT field specifies the value that is sent with the form if that option is selected. If the VALUE property is absent and a given option has been selected by the user, the text appearing after the OPTION tag is sent as the value. (In the preceding sample code, if the user clicked on **Mrs.** and there was no VALUE="MRS" property, "Mrs." would be sent as the value for "title".)

Forms

The first option in a select list is generally displayed by default, but there is a way to specify which option is displayed by default. We often use this when we want to display things such as titles, states, and countries. Our users might use a form to enter a customer address, choosing from a list of states or countries in a select list. When we display the information so that they can update it, we display the state originally selected but also include all the other options so that they can select an alternative one. To make an option appear by default, you add SELECTED to the correct option. Here is an example:

```
<SELECT NAME="title">
<OPTION VALUE="">Select Title</OPTION>
<OPTION VALUE="MR">Mr.</OPTION>
<OPTION VALUE="MS">Ms.</OPTION>
<OPTION VALUE="MRS">Mrs.</OPTION>
<OPTION SELECTED VALUE="DR">Dr.</OPTION>
<OPTION VALUE="AGENT">Secret Agent</OPTION>
</SELECT>
```

In the preceding example, "Dr." would appear as the default option rather than "Select Title". By adding SELECTED inside the select tag, we tell the browser which option to display by default.

By default, a select list allows only one selection. To allow more than one selection, you add MULTIPLE inside the select tag:

```
<SELECT NAME="title" MULTIPLE SIZE=5>
```

If you add a SIZE property, the browser will display a select list with that number of items visible. If you include a select field in your form that allows multiple selections, always specify the SIZE property.

If you want to access the selected item from a select list (using CSJS), you would use code similar to this:

```
selectedValue = document.myForm.mySelect[document.myForm.mySelect.selectedIndex].value;
```

Note that the code for single-select lists is straightforward and simple. Two additional functions may come in handy when you're working with single-select lists. getListValue returns the value of the first selected item, and getListText returns the display text for the first selected item in a select list:

```
// RETURN THE VALUE FOR THE CURRENTLY SELECTED ITEM IN A SELECT LIST
function getListValue(list)
{
   var listValue = "";
   if (list.selectedIndex != -1) {
      listValue = list.options[list.selectedIndex].value;
   }
   return (listValue);
}
```

```
// RETURN THE DISPLAY TEXT FOR THE CURRENTLY SELECTED ITEM IN A SELECT LIST
function getListText(list)
{
   var listText = "";
   if (list.selectedIndex != -1) {
      listValue = list.options[list.selectedIndex].text;
   }
   return (listText);
}
```

For multiselect lists, the code used to collect all the selected values is more complex. You must loop through all the options and check to see whether they are selected because more than one can be selected. Here is an example:

```
var selectedValues = "";
var count          = 0;
var delimeter      = "|";
for (var i = 0; i < document.myForm.mySelect.options.length; i++) {
   if (document.myForm.mySelect.options[i].selected)
      // IF TWO OR MORE OPTIONS ARE SELECTED, THE VALUES WILL BE DELIMITED
      if (count) {
         selectedValues += delimeter + document.myForm.mySelect.options[i].value;
      }
      // IF THERE IS ONE SELECTED VALUE, OR THIS IS THE FIRST, DON'T INCLUDE A DELIMITER
      else {
         selectedValues += document.myForm.mySelect.options[i].value;
      }
      count++;
}
```

As you can see, the code for a multiselect list is more complex. When you try to access values from a multiselect list on the server side, you must do some special coding. Here's why. Suppose you post a form using the GET method with a select list:

```
<FORM NAME="testSelect" METHOD="GET" ACTION="showStooge.html">
<SELECT NAME="stooges" MULTIPLE SIZE=5>
<OPTION VALUE="joe">Joe</OPTION>
<OPTION VALUE="curly">Curly</OPTION>
...
<OPTION VALUE="shem">Shem</OPTION>
</SELECT>
...
</FORM>
```

If the user selects the original Three Stooges, the URL will look like this:

```
http://server.domain.com/ssjsApp/ssjsDoc.html?
stooge=curly&stooge=larry&stooge=moe
```

Note that the name portion of the name-value pair is `"stooge"` for all three values. Suppose you try to access the value in `stooge` on the server this way:

```
var stooges = request.stooge;
```

The variable `stooges` will contain only the value `"moe"`, which was the last selected option. As you can see, the values in the preceding URL share the name `"stooge"` because all of them are part of the same select list. The `request` object contains only the value of the last option selected (`"curly"` is assigned to the variable `stooges` but is subsequently overwritten by the value `"larry"`, which is then overwritten by `"moe"` in the SSJS `request` object). To get *all* the values in a select list of type `"select-multiple"`, you must do something like this in SSJS:

```
<SERVER>
var stooges = "";
var delimiter = ",";
for (i = 0; i < getOptionValueCount("stooge"); i++) {
    stooges += getOptionValue("stooge",i) + delimiter;
}
// Remove the trailing delimiter
stooges = stooges.substring(0,stooges.lastIndexOf(delimiter));
</SERVER>
```

In this way you can collect all the values selected in the select list into the variable `"stooges"` instead of only the last value.

Radio Buttons

Here is the syntax for defining radio buttons.

```
<INPUT TYPE="RADIO" NAME="gender" VALUE="M" Male>
<INPUT TYPE="RADIO" NAME="gender" VALUE="F" Female>
```

Radio buttons are used to strictly control input. Only one option can be checked, and the actual value associated with a given option is hidden from the user. Note in the preceding example that all related radio buttons share the same value in their NAME property. This is how the browser groups the radio fields so that only one of them can be checked.

We occasionally found the need for a routine to reset a group of radio buttons on a form. If a user clicks on a radio button and then later decides that he or she doesn't want any of the options to be selected, the user needs a way to deselect all the buttons (aside from resetting the form, which would force re-entry of all the values). If you want to reset a given group of radio buttons, you can execute the following JavaScript function:

```
function resetRadioField(form, name) {
    for (count = 0; count < form.length; count++) {
        // LOCATE CORRECT RADIO BUTTONS
        if (form.elements[count].name == name) {
            form.elements[count].checked = false;
        }
    }
}
```

So your link might look something like this:

```
<A HREF="JavaScript:resetRadioField(document.myForm, 'gender');" . . .>Reset</A>
```

Checkboxes

Following is the syntax for a typical checkbox.

```
<INPUT TYPE=checkbox NAME="english" VALUE="English" English>
<INPUT TYPE=checkbox NAME="spanish" VALUE="Spanish" Spanish>
<INPUT TYPE=checkbox NAME="chinese" VALUE="Chinese" Chinese>
```

Forms

Checkboxes are easy; each one is a separate field with its own name and value. If the box is checked, the name and value are sent with the submitted form. If the box is not checked, then neither the name nor the value is sent with the form. Each checkbox has a `checked` property. If the box is checked, the `checked` property is true; otherwise, it is false. The following example will generate an alert box that displays either "true" or "false," depending on whether the checkbox is checked.

```
alert(document.myForm.myCheckbox.checked);
```

Buttons

Here is the syntax for a typical set of buttons.

```
<INPUT TYPE="SUBMIT" NAME="add" VALUE="Add">
<INPUT TYPE="RESET" NAME="clear" VALUE="Clear Form">
<INPUT TYPE="BUTTON" NAME="add" VALUE="Add" onClick="addFunction()">
```

There are two types of buttons used to *submit* forms: `type=submit` and `type=button`. When creating your form, you must choose which type of button you will use to submit your form (see Table 4.6).

Table 4.6 *The two button types used to submit forms*

Type of Button	Description	Action
Submit	Automatically submits the form. The JavaScript specified in `onSubmit` is executed *if* users have JavaScript enabled in their browsers.	When a submit button is pressed, the value of that button is sent with the form. If you have two buttons—**Add** and **Delete**—and you press the **Add** button, that value is sent with the form data. The **Delete** value is not sent.
Button	Does *not* submit the form when clicked. It can call a JavaScript function, `form.submit()`, which then programmatically sends the form. If the user does not have JavaScript enabled in the browser, the form will not be submitted.	The button value is not sent with the form data. When a button is pressed, it executes or calls JavaScript code.

Buttons have three major properties: `type`, `name`, and `value`. The `type` property indicates which kind of button functionality you wish to use:

- `submit` submits the form.
- `reset` clears form values, resetting all form values back to their default state.
- `button` executes JavaScript code or calls a JavaScript function.

Let's discuss the merits and shortcomings of each type of button in detail.

Submit buttons are the most commonly used buttons on forms; they cause the form to be submitted. Submit buttons have the following syntax:

```
<INPUT TYPE="SUBMIT" NAME="add" VALUE="Add">
```

When the button is clicked, the name and value of the submit button (`add=Add` in the code example) are added to the form data, and the form is submitted. In your form you can specify an `onSubmit()` event handler; the code specified will be executed before the form is submitted. If the `onSubmit` event receives a `false` value from the JavaScript it executes, the form is not submitted. Any other value returned by JavaScript (including a JavaScript error) causes a form submission. If JavaScript is disabled in the browser, the `onSubmit` event is ignored and the form is submitted. Therefore, if you want to ensure that your JavaScript code is executed before form submission and that the form is not submitted unless certain conditions are met, use `type=button` rather than `type=submit`. If, however, you want to ensure that a user can submit the form using any browser and if the execution of your JavaScript code is not crucial (or you're not using any JavaScript code), use `type=submit`.

To summarize, the `onSubmit` method is not 100 percent reliable because of the following:

- If the user has JavaScript disabled, `onSubmit` is ignored.
- If the JavaScript executed via `onSubmit` returns anything other than `false`, the form will be submitted.
- If the JavaScript executed in the `onSubmit` routine aborts prematurely, the form *may* be submitted.

Reset buttons are used to reset all the fields on the form to their original (default) values. This button is helpful if the user wants to clear the form and start over. However, it can be a nuisance. Sometimes a user will fill out a form completely and inadvertently click on the **Reset** button, clearing all the data and forcing the user to fill in the form again. Use reset buttons judiciously.

```
<INPUT TYPE="RESET" NAME="clear" VALUE="Clear">
```

If you use buttons, you'll have greater control over your form submissions, but the user must have JavaScript enabled on the browser. A button forces the browser to check the form to ensure that the user has filled in all the required fields with proper values. If any error is found, the form is not submitted and you can prompt the user to fix erroneous values. If JavaScript is disabled on the browser and a button of `type=button` is used, the form will not be submitted. (The only exception is when the form has only one field and the user presses **Enter**. In this case, the browser submits the form automatically.)

Buttons of `type=button` look like this:

```
<INPUT TYPE="BUTTON" NAME="add" VALUE="Add" onClick="myJSFunction()">
```

Buttons require both an `onClick` event and JavaScript enabled in the browser. Otherwise, when the user clicks on the button nothing will happen. For this reason, buttons are not recommended for Internet forms (where your customer may be using a browser that does not support Java-Script or the customer may have disabled JavaScript). On an extranet or intranet, these types of buttons are useful to ensure that required fields are filled in with proper values.

When the user clicks on `type=button` elements, the name and value of the button are not sent with the form data. For this reason, you may wish to set the value of a hidden field before programmatically submitting your form to ensure that you capture information regarding which button was pressed. Consider a form that contains this field:

```
<INPUT TYPE=HIDDEN NAME="buttonPress" VALUE="">
```

the following buttons:

```
<INPUT TYPE=Reset NAME=Clear Value=Clear>
<INPUT TYPE=BUTTON NAME="add" VALUE="Add"
onClick="submitForm(document.myForm, this)">
<INPUT TYPE=BUTTON NAME="update" VALUE="Update"
onClick="submitForm(document.myForm, this)">
<INPUT TYPE=BUTTON NAME="delete" VALUE="Delete"
onClick="submitForm(document.myForm, this)">
```

and this JavaScript function:

```
function submitForm(form, field) {
    form.buttonPress.value = field.name;
    form.submit();
}
```

The form and the field (`button`) are passed to the function `submitForm`. The value of the hidden field `"buttonPress"` is set to the name of the button we clicked. Therefore, after the form has been submitted we know which button was actually pressed, so we know whether we should `"add"`, `"update"`, or `"delete"` the submitted data. Also note that the form is submitted using JavaScript. The button itself does not cause a form submission, so `form.submit()` is used to trigger the form submission. That's why JavaScript must be enabled on the browser for the form data to be sent.

Assuming you had three buttons (`"add"`, `"update"`, and `"delete"`), you could write the following SSJS code to see which button had been clicked on the submitted form:

```
<SERVER>
if (request.buttonPress == "add") {
...
}
else if (request.buttonPress == "update") {
...
}
else if (request.buttonPress == "delete") {
...
}
</SERVER>
```

Note   The text in the **VALUE** property of a button is the text that is actually displayed on the button.

Checking for JavaScript Usage on Forms

You may be wondering whether there is a way to check whether JavaScript is enabled in the browser. Absolutely. Simply create a hidden field as we did in the preceding example.

```
<INPUT TYPE="HIDDEN" NAME="JS_enabled" VALUE=false>
```

Unless this field is modified using JavaScript, we can be certain that the user does not have JavaScript enabled on the browser. We place JavaScript code in the onLoad method of the document, knowing that it will be executed after the entire page has loaded. In that way, we won't experience any JavaScript errors by trying to access a field that does not yet exist:

```
<BODY ... onLoad="document.myForm.JS_enabled.value = true">
```

On the server we use the request object to check the JS_enabled hidden field and see whether JavaScript is enabled on the client's browser. If JavaScript is enabled, request.JS_enabled will equal true; otherwise, request.JS_enabled will equal false.

Forcing JavaScript Usage on Forms

We mentioned earlier that it is possible to force JavaScript usage in your form. There are definite reasons to do this in an intranet or extranet environment, where you want to be sure that certain field checks have been accomplished before form submission. When doing this, you should put some indication on the form that the form is JavaScript-enabled so that the user knows to enable JavaScript in the browser before attempting to submit the form.

You can force JavaScript usage by avoiding the use of "type=submit" buttons and using only "type=button" buttons and then using JavaScript to submit the form. Here is another simple example of using JavaScript to submit a form rather than using a "type=submit" button:

```
<INPUT TYPE="BUTTON" NAME="submitForm" VALUE="Submit"
onClick="document.myForm.submit()">
```

 Note   There is no way to guarantee that your form will be submitted exactly as you constructed it. Users can alter the form they receive from your server and then submit it. It's unusual for anyone to do this (mostly because the benefit is vastly outweighed by the inconvenience), but it can be done, so take that into account when designing your applications and creating your forms. Remember that JavaScript checking of your forms on the client can still be circumvented. If it is critical that your application receive values in a strict format, consider formatting form values on the server rather than on the client. In nearly all cases, however, client-side formatting and validation are sufficient.

Field Validation

I always prefer to validate user-entered values before submitting the form to the server. It's best to notify the user of an invalid value right after it has been entered. To check an input value to ensure validity, you can use the following:

```
<INPUT TYPE="TEXT" NAME="masterCard" VALUE="" SIZE=30 MAXLENGTH=50
onChange="if(!isMasterCard(this.value)){alert('Sorry, you have
entered an invalid MasterCard number.\nPlease revise your
entry.');this.focus();}">
<SCRIPT LANGUAGE="JavaScript" SRC="formChek.js"></SCRIPT>
```

Checking for Required Fields

Have you ever used a form on the Web that contained some required fields? You submit the form and then wait and wait and wait. Finally, the server responds with an error message that you forgot to fill in a required field. The message doesn't always say which field was missing, and it generally tells you to press the **Back** button on your browser. When your form reappears, you must hunt all over it looking for the one field you missed. Sometimes it takes several tries before you finally get the form submitted—but only after your blood pressure has risen and some nearby object has paid a severe penalty.

Before allowing a form submission, ensure that any required fields on the form have been filled in. A form submission requesting student records is relatively useless if the student's name is not filled in. To eliminate unnecessary server processing and to give the user immediate feedback as to why the form cannot be submitted, do the required-fields checking on the client side whenever possible. In this way, you can immediately give focus to the problem field so that the user doesn't have to hunt for it. Users like this convenience.

The following code example demonstrates required-fields checking. The sample code checks the name of each field, looking for a required-fields indicator ("`req_`" in this example). If the indicator is found, the value of the field is checked. If a value does not exist in the required field, an error flag is set and the name of the field is added to the list of required fields that are missing values. If the error flag has been set, an error message is displayed that lists the field(s) users still need to fill in, and focus is given to the first field on the list.

Before the field names are displayed, they are cleaned up using the optional `alterFieldNames()` function to make them more readable (words are capitalized, underscore characters are removed, and so on), as shown in

Figure 4.6 *An example of the* checkRequiredFields() *function*

Figure 4.6. After all required fields have values entered in the form, the optional cleanNames() function is executed to remove the required-field indicators from all field names (so req_firstName is changed to firstName, req_gender to gender, and so on). Then JavaScript initiates a form submission.

The following submitForm function executes the checkRequired Fields() function and sends it a form object. If the check RequiredFields function returns a true value, it means that all the required fields on the form have been filled in, and the form is submitted using form.submit().

This example uses two optional functions: cleanNames() and alter Name(). The first function is used to remove required-field indicators before submitting the form. In this way, you don't have to worry about the required-field indicators (req_ in the example), making it easier for you to manipulate form values on the back end without having to worry about whether or not the field is a required value. The second function is used to make the field names look pretty before the user sees them. Seeing "req_firstName is missing a value" is confusing. As you know, it's painfully easy to confuse users, and it results in more work for you, so it's best to avoid that when possible. "First Name is missing a value" is less confusing.

```
// SUBMIT THE FORM (AFTER CHECKING FOR REQUIRED FIELDS)
function submitForm(form) {
    if (checkRequiredFields(form)) {
        cleanNames(form);
        form.submit();
    }
}
```

The getRequiredField() function sets the required-field indicator, which is used by several functions in this example (cleanNames(), alterName(), and checkRequiredFields()). This function lets you specify the required-field indicator in one place. Required fields start with "req_" in this example, so if you have a field on your form called "last-Name" and want to make it a required field, simply change its name to "req_lastName". That's all you need to do.

```
function getRequiredField() {
    var requiredField = "req_";
    return requiredField;
}
```

The getListValue(selectObject) function receives a select list object and returns the first (and only the first) selected value in the list. (We only need verify that at least one value has been selected in the list.)

```
// RETURN THE VALUE FOR THE CURRENTLY SELECTED ITEM
function getListValue(list) {
    var listValue = "";
    if (list.selectedIndex != -1) {
        listValue = list.options[list.selectedIndex].value;
    }
    return (listValue);
}
```

The optional cleanNames(formObject) function is used to remove all the required-field indicators from the field names before the form is submitted. (The field name req_lastName would become lastName before the form was submitted.) This means that you could make additional fields on your form required without having to modify any of your JavaScript code.

This function exists for the sake of convenience and is not needed for the
required-field checking to work properly.

```
// CLEAN FIELD NAMES PRIOR TO FORM SUBMISSION
function cleanNames(input)
{
    var requiredField = getRequiredField();
    for (count = 0; count < input.length; count++)
    {
        currentField = input.elements[count].name;
        if (currentField.indexOf(requiredField) != -1) {
            var tempString =
currentField.substring(0,currentField.indexOf(requiredField));
            tempString    +=
currentField.substring(currentField.indexOf(requiredField) +
            requiredField.length,currentField.length);
            input.elements[count].name = tempString;
        }
    }
}
```

The `alterName()` function takes a string argument that is then altered
so that it's more readable. In our sample form we used field names such as
`req_firstName` and `lastName`. We use `alterName()` to translate those
names into something more readable (and preferably something that
corresponds with the label for the field), such as `"First Name"` and `"Last
Name"`. All required-field indicators (`"req_"` in this example) are removed,
and all underscore characters (_) are replaced with a space. The characters
following an underscore are capitalized, as is the first character in the string.
If a character is uppercase, a space is added so that `"firstName"` becomes
`"First Name"` rather than `"FirstName"`. We adjust these strings so that
when we present the list of fields that are missing values, the user can more
easily find them.

```
// FORMAT FIELD NAME (FOR REQUIRED FIELDS DISPLAY)
function alterName(inString) {
    var newString = "";
    var ch        = "";
    var requiredField = getRequiredField();
    // REMOVE ANY REQUIRED FIELD INDICATORS FROM THE FIELD NAME
    if (inString.indexOf(requiredField) != -1) {
        var tempString =
        inString.substring(0,inString.indexOf(requiredField));
        tempString    +=
        inString.substring(inString.indexOf(requiredField) +
                        requiredField.length-1,inString.length);
        inString       = tempString;
```

```
    }
    // LOOP THROUGH THE FIELD REMOVING ALL UNDERSCORES,
    //  ADDING SPACES, AND CAPITALIZING WORDS
    for (i = 0; i < inString.length; i++) {
        ch = inString.substring(i,i+1);
        // REMOVE UNDERSCORES
        if (ch == "_") {
            i++;
            ch = inString.substring(i,i+1);
            newString += " " + ch.toUpperCase();
        }
        // ADD UPPERCASING TO FIRST WORD
        else if (i == 0) {
            ch = ch.toUpperCase()
        }
        // ADD SPACES FOR FIELD NAMES SUCH AS "firstName"
        else if (ch == ch.toUpperCase()) {
            newString += " " + ch;
        }
        else {
            newString += ch;
        }
    }
    return newString;
}
```

The `checkRequiredFields()` function takes a `form` object as its argument and looks for the required-field indicator in each field name in the form. If it finds the indicator, the field *type* is checked to determine how to access the field value. Next, the field *value* is checked. If the field has no value, the field name is added to a list of field names that are missing values. If some required fields are missing values, we display an error message showing the names of the required fields that are missing values. After the user clicks **OK**, focus is given to the first field on the list (provided it is not a radio button or checkbox). We return either a `false` value from the function, indicating that not all the required fields were filled in, or a `true` value, indicating that the form is complete and can be submitted.

```
// CHECK REQUIRED FIELDS - ENSURE THAT A VALUE HAS BEEN ENTERED FOR
// EVERY FIELD WITH A FIELD NAME STARTING WITH A REQUIRED FIELD CHARACTER
function checkRequiredFields(input)
{
    var fieldsNeeded  = "Sorry, you must enter a value\nin the following fields:\n\n";
    var fieldCheck    = true;
    var fieldName     = "";
    var fieldFocus    = "";
    var requiredField = getRequiredField();
    // LOOP THROUGH EVERY FIELD IN THE FORM
    for (count = 0; count < input.length; count++) {
        // GET CURRENT ELEMENT
        var element = input.elements[count];
```

```
    // CHECK TO ENSURE THAT FIELD IS REQUIRED
    if (element.name.substring(0,requiredField.length) == requiredField) {
        // IF FIELD IS A TEXT FIELD CHECK FOR A VALUE
        if ((element.type == "text") ||
            (element.type == "textarea") ||
            (element.type == "password")) {
            if ((element.value == "") ||
                (element.value.substring(0,1) == " ")) {
                if (fieldFocus == "") {
                    fieldFocus = element.name;
                }
                fieldsNeeded += alterName(element.name) + "\n";
                fieldCheck    = false;
            }
        }
        // IF FIELD IS A SELECT BOX, CHECK FOR A VALUE
        // SELECTED OPTIONS WITH A VALUE OF "" ARE NOT VALID VALUES
        else if ((element.type == "select-one") ||
            (element.type == "select-multiple")) {
            if (getListValue(element) == "") {
                if (fieldFocus == "") {
                    fieldFocus = element.name;
                }
                fieldsNeeded += alterName(element.name) + "\n";
                fieldCheck    = false;
            }
        }
        // IF FIELD IS A RADIO BUTTON, ENSURE THAT A VALUE IS CHECKED
        // LOOP THROUGH ALL RADIO OBJECTS
        else if (element.type == "radio") {
            var noneChecked = true;
            // RADIO BUTTONS MUST BE IN CONSECUTIVE ORDER ON THE FORM
            while (element.name == input.elements[count+1].name) {
                if (element.checked == true) {
                    noneChecked = false;
                }
                count++;
            }
            if (element.checked == true) {
                noneChecked = false;
            }
            if (noneChecked) {
                fieldsNeeded += alterName(element.name) + "\n";
                fieldCheck    = false;
            }
        }
        // IF FIELD IS A CHECKBOX, ENSURE THAT A VALUE IS CHECKED
        else if (element.type == "checkbox") {
            if (element.checked == false) {
                fieldsNeeded += alterName(element.name) + "\n";
                fieldCheck    = false;
            }
        }
    }
}
// IF ALL REQUIRED FIELDS HAVE A VALUE
if (fieldCheck) {
```

```
          return true;
    }
    else {
        alert(fieldsNeeded);
        // IF REQUIRED FIELD IS TEXTUAL OR A SELECT LIST, GIVE IT FOCUS
        if (fieldFocus != "") {
            input[fieldFocus].focus();
        }
        return false;
    }
}
```

Let's step through the checkRequiredFields() function to explain what is happening. Again, this code is used to ensure that the user has filled in all the required fields in your form before submitting it. This function is useful in SSJS applications and can also be used on any JavaScript-enabled form. (Sometimes people will click the **Submit** button on the form just to see what it does. This annoying habit can fill your database or logfiles with erroneous data or empty fields. Checking for required fields on your form discourages this practice and ensures that the data you receive and process is valid. It simply means less processing on the back end and a somewhat lighter load on your servers. It also means that the forms that *are* submitted generally contain good data.)

The checkRequiredFields function takes a form object as an argument. The function then parses the form, checking each element, and looking for required fields. First the field type is determined, and then the field value is checked to see whether the user entered one. We start by setting up some variables we'll need: the fieldsNeeded string, which will contain a list of required fields that are missing values; the requiredField indicator; and so on.

```
// CHECK REQUIRED FIELDS - ENSURE THAT A VALUE HAS BEEN ENTERED FOR
//   EVERY FIELD WITH A FIELD NAME STARTING WITH AN ASTERISK (*)
function checkRequiredFields(input)
{
    var fieldsNeeded  = "Sorry, you must enter a value\n" +
                        "in the following fields:\n\n";
    var fieldCheck    = true;
    var fieldName     = "";
    var fieldFocus    = "";
    var requiredField = getRequiredField();
```

The length of the form object (input.length) contains the number of elements in the form; this value includes all input fields, select lists, radio buttons, checkboxes, and buttons on the form. The function does not check button values or values in hidden fields because they are generally hard-coded by the designer of the form. However, the function checks every input element on the form and first determines the type of field and, when appropriate, checks for a value. We also assign each element in the form to a variable called `element` to make the code more readable.

```
// LOOP THROUGH EVERY FIELD IN THE FORM
for (count = 0; count < input.length; count++) {
    // GET CURRENT ELEMENT
    var element = input.elements[count];
```

We immediately check to see whether the field is required because there's no sense in checking the value if the field is not required.

```
// CHECK TO ENSURE THAT THE FIELD IS REQUIRED
if (element.name.substring(0,requiredField.length) == requiredField) {
```

We first check for text fields, the most common types of fields on a form. Text fields include text, textarea, and password fields. We then check text fields to see whether a value was entered and ensure that the first character is not a space. The reason is that sometimes users simply enter all spaces to avoid filling in required fields. Checking the first character to ensure that it's not a space will limit that practice. (It's almost impossible to idiot-proof an application because idiots are clever! However, we can try.)

```
// IF FIELD IS A TEXT FIELD CHECK FOR A VALUE
if ((element.type == "text") ||
    (element.type == "textarea") ||
    (element.type == "password")) {
    if ((element.value == "") ||
        (element.value.substring(0,1) == " ")) {
```

If a field is missing a value or has only a single space character, we add it to the list of required fields that have not been filled in. We also assign the first blank required field that we find to the `fieldFocus` variable. After displaying the list of required fields that still need values, we give focus to the first field. Notice that we clean up the field name by calling the `alterName()` function before adding the field name to the list.

```
if (fieldFocus == "") {
    fieldFocus = element.name;
}
```

```
                        fieldsNeeded += alterName(element.name) + "\n";
                        fieldCheck    = false;
                }
        }
```

If the field is a select list, a second routine is called (`getListValue()`) to return the first selected item in the list. If the item has no value, the name of the select list is added to the list of fields still needing values. Remember, a select list can be set up for the user to select a single value, or multiple values. However, `getListValue()` returns only the first selected value, which is all that is needed.

Forms

```
        // IF FIELD IS A SELECT BOX, CHECK FOR A VALUE

        // SELECTED OPTIONS WITH A VALUE OF "" ARE NOT VALID VALUES
        else if ((element.type == "select-one") ||
            (element.type == "select-multiple")) {
            if (getListValue(element) == "") {
                if (fieldFocus == "") {
                    fieldFocus = element.name;
                }
                fieldsNeeded += alterName(element.name) + "\n";
                fieldCheck    = false;
            }
        }
```

If the field is a radio button, we see whether it has been checked. Note that any *required* radio fields in your form must be in consecutive order (they usually are anyway) for this function to work properly. Even though all the radio buttons have the same name and are thus related (so that only one of them can be selected at a time), each one appears as a different element on the form and we must loop through subsequent elements to see whether they have the same name. If we find one that is checked, the entire group of related radio buttons is considered checked.

```
        // IF FIELD IS A RADIO BUTTON, ENSURE THAT A VALUE IS CHECKED
        // LOOP THROUGH ALL RADIO OBJECTS
        else if (element.type == "radio") {
            var noneChecked = true;
            // RADIO BUTTONS MUST BE IN CONSECUTIVE ORDER ON THE FORM
            while (element.name == input.elements[count+1].name)
                {
                if (element.checked == true) {
                    noneChecked = false;
                }
                count++;
            }
```

```
                    if (element.checked == true) {
                        noneChecked = false;
                    }
                    if (noneChecked) {
                        fieldsNeeded += alterName(element.name) + "\n";
                        fieldCheck    = false;
                    }
                }
```

If a field is a checkbox, we simply ensure that the box is checked. The only time this might be useful is if you want users to click on portions of an agreement or contract that they agree to be bound by. In this way, you make sure they've read a given section or agreed to a certain stipulation on the form because making a checkbox a required field means that you are requiring that it be checked, something you could just as easily set as the default.

```
            // IF FIELD IS A CHECKBOX, ENSURE THAT A VALUE IS CHECKED
            else if (element.type == "checkbox") {
                if (element.checked == false) {
                    fieldsNeeded += alterName(element.name) + "\n";
                    fieldCheck    = false;
                }
            }
        }
    }
```

If all the required fields have a value, return `true` to the calling function. In this case, the calling function is `formSubmit()`, which next calls an optional function to remove the required-field indicators and then submits the form.

```
    // IF ALL REQUIRED FIELDS HAVE A VALUE
    if (fieldCheck) {
        return true;
    }
```

If some required fields are missing a value, an error message is displayed (see Figure 4.7) that lists the name of all the fields that are missing values; then the first field on the list is given focus. Remember that the names of the required fields are altered before being placed on the list. Please see the description of the `alterName()` function for more details.

Figure 4.7 *List of required fields that are missing a value*

Notice in Figure 4.7 that the field names are easy to read (and should correspond to the actual field labels on your form). When the user clicks **OK,** focus is given to the `"First Name"` field (`req_firstName`).

```
    else {
        alert(fieldsNeeded);
        // IF REQUIRED FIELD IS TEXTUAL OR A SELECT LIST, GIVE IT FOCUS
        if (fieldFocus != "") {
            input[fieldFocus].focus();
        }
        return false;
    }
}
```

Note   You may wish to modify the preceding code to additionally check for field indicators such as `"mc_"` for a MasterCard number or `"digit_"` for a numeric character. Then you could call the appropriate function (`isMasterCard` or `isDigit`) to verify that the fields contain such values.

After you have verified that all required fields contain values (and optionally that all fields contain the proper type of data), you can perform any last-minute processing (such as assigning values to hidden fields to indicate which button the user pressed) and then submit the form. You can even set a hidden field that indicates whether the form was checked by JavaScript before being submitted. On the server side you can then skip the field checking if it was already done on the client, saving some server processing time.

Submitting Forms

When the form is submitted, the browser parses the information between the <FORM...></FORM> tags. The browser collects the name and value of all text fields on the form (even if a value was not entered), including text, textarea, password, and hidden fields. The browser also collects the name and value of all nontext fields, provided that a value has been selected (as is the case for select lists, checkboxes, and radio buttons). The names and values of TYPE=SUBMIT buttons are collected only if the button has been pressed to initiate form submission. All other buttons (reset and button) are ignored by the browser; their names and values are not collected. The field values that are collected may have been assigned by default, programmatically assigned using JavaScript, or entered or selected by the user.

URL Encoding

When the user submits a form that uses the GET method, the names of all input fields and the values associated with those fields are all encoded and packed together. The resulting URL-encoded string looks like this:

```
http://server.domain.com/path/file?name1=value1&name2=value2&namex=valuex
```

The string starts with a ? character to separate the name-value pairs from the actual URL; this is how the browser knows where the URL ends and the form data begins. Each field name appears first, followed by a = character and the actual value that appeared in the given field. Each name-value pair is separated by a & character. Table 4.7 lists and explains the values you might see in the URL if you submit a form using the GET method.

Table 4.7 *The characters used in URL encoding*

Character	Description
?	Starts the query string. It appears at the end of the URL and separates the URL from the form data.
=	Appears between each name and value in the form "name=value".
&	Appears between each name-value pair in the form "name1=value1&name2=value2".

Table 4.7 *The characters used in URL encoding (Continued)*

Character	Description
+	Replaces the space character. If you entered **Bjorn Free** in the form, it would appear in the query string as: `"Bjorn+Free"`.
%xx	Any special characters that appear in your form names or values are encoded before being sent with the URL request. The special character is replaced with a % character followed by two hexadecimal characters that represent the ASCII equivalent of the value you entered.
[a-z][A-Z][0-9]	All letters and numbers appear normally. Only special characters and whitespace characters are encoded.

You can imagine how confused a browser might get if you submitted a field name or field value that contained a ? or & character (because the ? character separates form values from the URL and & characters delimit the form values). This is why the name-value pairs on your form are encoded by replacing spaces with + characters and all other special characters with %xx characters. Numbers and letters appear normally.

In your HTML page or CGI you must decode the string of name-value pairs. However, in server-side JavaScript this is done for you by the `request` object. We include some code later to demonstrate how to approximate the `request` object using client-side JavaScript.

 Note If you submit your form using a `mailto:` link, the name-value pairs are not encoded before being added to your e-mail message. Your control over formatting is somewhat limited, but next we show a way to format your results.

Formatting `mailto` Form Submissions

The `mailer()` function takes a `form` object as an argument and launches an e-mail window with all form values formatted and packed into the body of the mail message. When the user clicks **Send** in the e-mail window, the message is sent. This method of form submission eliminates any server-side processing and allows you to format the mail message, but it requires that the client have JavaScript enabled on the client browser. So this function is useful if you don't have a server in which you can stage a CGI or SSJS application that accepts and processes form data. Your user can simply e-mail the data to you.

```
// FORM MAILER
function mailer(form) {
    var to      = "person@company.com";
    var subject = "Customer Enrollment Information";
    var current = new Date();
    var body    = current.getMonth() + "/" + current.getDay() +
                  "/19" + current.getYear() + "\n" +
                  "\nFORM VALUES:\n" +
                  getFormValues(form) + "\n";
    // BUILD MAIL MESSAGE COMPONENTS (YOU CAN ADD MORE PROPERTIES)
    doc = "mailto:" + to +
          "&subject=" + subject +
          "&body=" + body;
    // SEND MAIL MESSAGE
    document.location = doc;
}
```

The mailer() function calls the getFormValues() function to get
all the name-value pairs on the form. You can edit the getFormValues()
function to change the way the e-mail message is formatted. The
getFormValues() function takes a form object as input and then loops
through that form, collecting all name-value pairs. This list of name-value
pairs is then returned to the mailer() function for inclusion in the body
of the e-mail message.

```
// FORMAT FIELD NAMES & VALUES
function getFormValues(input) {
    var fieldList = "";
    var delimiter = ": ";
    // LOOP THROUGH EVERY FIELD IN THE FORM
    for (count = 0; count < input.length; count++) {
        // GET CURRENT ELEMENT
        var element = input.elements[count];
        // IF FIELD IS A TEXT FIELD, CHECK FOR A VALUE
        if ((element.type == "text") ||
            (element.type == "textarea") ||
            (element.type == "password")) {
            fieldList += "\n" + element.name + delimiter + element.value;
        }
        // IF FIELD IS A SELECT BOX, CHECK FOR A VALUE
        else if ((element.type == "select-one") ||
            (element.type == "select-multiple")) {
            fieldList += "\n" +  element.name + delimiter + getSelectValues(element);
        }
        // IF FIELD IS A RADIO BUTTON, ENSURE THAT A VALUE IS CHECKED
        else if (element.type == "radio") {
            if (element.checked == true) {
                fieldList += "\n" +  element.name + delimiter + element.value;
            }
        }
    }
```

```
        // IF FIELD IS A CHECKBOX, ENSURE THAT A VALUE IS CHECKED
        else if (element.type == "checkbox") {
            if (element.checked == true) {
                fieldList += "\n" + element.name + delimiter + element.value;
            }
        }
    }
    return fieldList;
}
```

The `getFormValues()` function calls `getSelectValues()` whenever one of the form elements is a select list. Select lists allow the selection of one or more values; the `getSelectValues()` function collects all the selected values in a select list and returns them in a delimited format. The delimiter is specified in the `delimiter` variable.

```
// GET ALL THE SELECTED VALUES FROM A SELECT LIST
function getSelectValues(list) {
    var selectedValues = "";
    var count          = 0;
    var delimiter      = "|";
    for (var i = 0; i < list.options.length; i++) {
        if (list.options[i].selected) {
            if (count) {
                selectedValues += delimiter +
                                    list.options[i].value;
            }
            else {
                selectedValues += list.options[i].value;
            }
            count++;
        }
    }
    return selectedValues;
}
```

Figure 4.8 shows a form that uses the mailer function (and related functions) to submit a formatted e-mail message containing all form values. Note that pressing the **Mail** button launches an e-mail window with the TO and SUBJECT fields filled in. In addition, the body of the message is filled in.

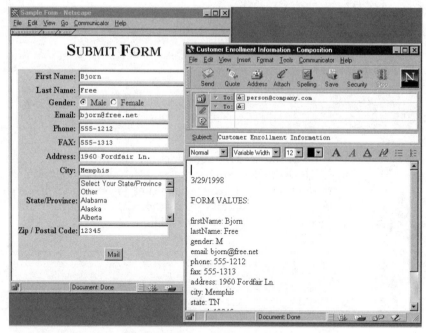

Figure 4.8 *A custom-formatted* `mailto:` *form submission*

The `onSubmit` Method

You can use the `onSubmit` method to do any processing before submitting the form. It's not our favorite, but it's still useful. If the JavaScript that the `onSubmit` method executes returns a `false` value, the form will not be submitted. Any other value returned to `onSubmit` (including JavaScript errors) will result in your form being submitted. `onSubmit` also requires the use of JavaScript. If the user has JavaScript turned off in browser preferences, or is using a browser that does not support JavaScript or if your JavaScript returns a nonfalse value, the form will be submitted when the user presses a submit button. This is why we prefer not to use the `onSubmit` method.

    `onSubmit` will call a JavaScript function or execute any JavaScript statements you indicate. You can include multiple JavaScript statements or functions in the `onSubmit` method; simply separate statements or function calls with a semicolon (;) character. `onSubmit` is often used for checking required fields, checking form values, or doing some last-minute processing (such as entering values in hidden fields) before the form is submitted. If you use `onSubmit`, you can rest assured that although your JavaScript code may not execute, the form will always be submitted. This arrangement is ideal if you are coding forms that will be used on the Internet or an extranet. If you are creating forms for use on an intranet and your company has standardized on a JavaScript-enabled browser, you can use other means to ensure that the JavaScript checking is always done before form submission.

The following example shows the syntax for the `onSubmit` method.

```
<FORM ... onSubmit="myJavaScriptFunction()">
<FORM ... onSubmit="if (!confirm('Submit form?')){return false};">
```

Figure 4.9 shows the message that is displayed if you use the second code example to ask users to confirm that they want to submit the form. If the user clicks **OK,** the form is submitted. If the user clicks **Cancel,** the form is not submitted because a `false` value is returned to the `onSubmit` method.

As you can see, you can either call a JavaScript function or execute your own JavaScript code. If you simply used the following JavaScript code, the form would be submitted regardless of the button you pressed because a `false` value wouldn't be returned.

```
<FORM ... onSubmit="confirm('Submit form?')">
```

You must explicitly return a `false` value or else the form will be submitted. Again, exercise caution when using `onSubmit` because the results are not always reliable. However, `onSubmit` is the best method of preprocessing form submissions if you must support browsers that are not JavaScript-enabled.

If your form contains a single input field, like many search engines you see on the Web, the form will be submitted if the user presses **Enter** (see Figure 4.10). Generally, when you're searching you want to start the search as quickly as possible, so you don't want to have to move from the keyboard to the mouse to submit a query. That's why a single-field form is always sub-

Figure 4.9 *Form submission confirmation message*

Forms

Figure 4.10 *An HTML page with a single-field search form*

mitted when you press **Enter.** Remember also to provide a search button so that the user can either press **Enter** or click on the button.

Submitting Forms Using Graphics

You can use images to make your forms more attractive, and those images can in turn submit your form. Simply include a JavaScript call instead of a URL in your anchor:

```
<A HREF="JavaScript:submitFormFunction()">
<IMG SRC="addButton.gif" HEIGHT=20 WIDTH=100 ALT="Add Form Values">
</A>
```

In this way, a user can click on a graphic image to submit the form, pop up a calendar to select a date, and so on. Graphics have one key disadvantage: they do not behave as a button when clicked. Buttons actually appear to depress when you click on them, but graphics do not.

Submitting Forms Using the **Enter** Key

If a form contains more than one input field, pressing **Enter** will not generally submit the form. Sometimes you may want to create a multifield form that allows the user to submit the form at any time by pressing **Enter.** To do this, you can use JavaScript 1.2 or later (Navigator 4.x and later). In the following example, the function `enableKeypress()` forces the browser to trap all keystrokes and pass them to the function `enterKey()`. The `enter-Key()` function checks the character to see whether it's an **Enter** key (ASCII value 13) and submits the form if it is.

```
<SCRIPT
// ENSURE USER IS USING NAV 4.x OR LATER
function enableKeypress() {
    if (parseInt(navigator.appVersion) 3) {
        document.captureEvents(Event.KEYPRESS);
        document.onkeypress = enterKey;
    }
}
// SUBMIT FORM ON KEYPRESS: ENTER
function enterKey(key) {
    // ASCII VALUE FOR ENTER KEY IS 13
    if (key.which == 13) {
        document.forms[0].submit();
    }
}
// ENABLE KEY TRAPPING AS DOCUMENT LOADS
enableKeypress();
</SCRIPT>
```

Form Handlers in Server-Side JavaScript

If you use CGIs to process your form values, you typically must separate the form's name-value pairs and unencode them for use in your application. However, in server-side JavaScript, the parsing of form name-value pairs is automatically done for you. The `request` object in SSJS contains information about a given request. Each field name on the form becomes a property of the `request` object on the target page. Let's look at the form in Figure 4.11.

For this form; the properties of the `request` object on the SSJS target page (ACTION="`http://server.domain.com/ssjsApp/ssjsTargetPage.html`") would be as follows:

```
request.firstName == "Bjorn"
request.lastName  == "Free"
request.address   == "1960 Fordfair Ln."
request.city      == "Memphis"
request.state     == "Tennessee"
request.zip       == "12345"
request.phone     == "(123) 456-7890"
request.fax       == "(123) 456-7891"
request.email     == "bjorn@free.net"
request.gender    == "M"
```

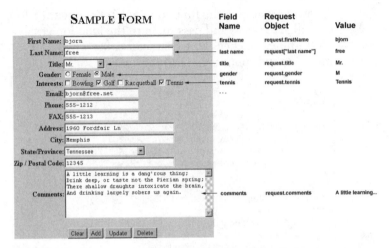

Figure 4.11 *How form fields map to the server-side JavaScript* request
object

The request object is freshly created for each HTTP request and contains properties and values specific to the current request, as described in Chapter 3. It also contains all your form values and makes it extremely easy for you to access them; they simply become properties of the request object You can reference values in the request object in any of the following ways:

```
request.fieldName
request[fieldName]
request[12]
```

You can also assign any of your form values to an SSJS variable so that you can manipulate them, use them in computations, and so on. Here is an example of how to assign request object properties to an SSJS variable:

```
var address = request.address;
var name    = request.firstName + " " + request.lastName;
...
```

Looping Through the SSJS request Object

You may want to create a generic routine that takes input from any form and loops through all the name-value pairs rather than having to reference each value by name (request.name). You might, for example, create a generic form handler. It would accept values from any form and then write them to a logfile, send them in an e-mail message, or insert them into a database. The following example demonstrates how to loop through all the name-value pairs in the `request` object. The `if` statement eliminates default properties in the `request` object so that you deal only with name-value pairs that came from your form or query string.

```
var message = "";
for (var propName in request) {
    // EXCLUDE DEFAULT REQUEST OBJECT PROPERTIES FROM MESSAGE
    if (propName == 'ip' ||
        propName == 'protocol' ||
        propName == 'method' ||
        propName == 'agent' ||
        propName == 'auth_user' ||
        propName == 'auth_type' ||
        propName == 'uri') {
    }
    else {
        ...
        // ADD THE NAME (propName) AND VALUE (request[propName]) TO THE MESSAGE
        message += "\n" + unescape(propName) + " = " + unescape(request[propName]);
        ...
    }
}
```

The preceding code packs all the name-value pairs into a variable called `message`, which you can display to see the values you received from the form submission. The variable `propName` contains the name of each field on the submitted form (with the exception of unselected select list options, unchecked checkboxes and radio buttons, and all buttons except any of TYPE=SUBMIT that were used to submit the form). You can use the name of the field with the `request` object to reference its value (`request[prop Name]`). Again, `propName` contains the name of each name-value pair, and `request[propName]` contains the associated value.

The preceding code example removes from the submitted form any default `request` object properties that are not part of the name-value pairs. There are additional properties (as explained in Chapter 3) that may need to be removed.

Creating a Client-Side `request` Object

Occasionally, you may want to test your forms on the client without having to create a special SSJS application for it. You can access the form values in client-side JavaScript, provided that you use the GET method of form submission and employ the following code. The `createRequestObject()`

function grabs all the name-value pairs from the URL and creates a
`request` object similar to that used with SSJS. Remember that
JavaScript 1.2 supports regular expressions, which we use in the following
example to split apart the name-value pairs from our form submission.

```
// createRequestObject():
// Author:   Duane K. Fields, Feb 1998
// Modified: Robert W. Husted, Mar 1998
//
// This function returns an object similar to server-side JavaScript's
// request object. Used to process forms on the client, in a method
// similar to SSJS.
//
// Usage: request=createRequestObject();
//        document.writeln("The Name was " + request.name);
//
function createRequestObject() {
    var request   = new Object();       // CREATE NEW REQUEST OBJECT
    var nameVal   = "";                 // HOLDS name-value ARRAY FOR A name-value PAIR
    var inString  = location.search;    // STRIPS QUERY STRING FROM URL
    var separator = ",";                // CHARACTER USED TO SEPARATE
                                        // MULTIPLE VALUES
    // IF URL CONTAINS A QUERY STRING, GRAB IT
    if (inString.charAt(0) == "?") {
        // REMOVE "?" CHARACTER FROM QUERY STRING
        inString = inString.substring(1, inString.length);
        // SEPARATE QUERY STRING INTO name=value PAIRS
        keypairs = inString.split("&");
        // LOOP THROUGH name=value PAIRS
        for (var i=0; i < keypairs.length; i++) {
            // SPLIT name=value INTO ARRAY (nameVal[0]=name, nameVal[1]=value)
            nameVal = keypairs[i].split("=");
            // REPLACE "+" CHARACTERS WITH SPACES AND THEN
            // UNESCAPE name-value PAIR
            for (a in nameVal) {
                nameVal[a] = nameVal[a].replace(/+/g, " ")
                nameVal[a] = unescape(nameVal[a]);
            }
            // CHECK TO SEE WHETHER NAME ALREADY EXISTS IN REQUEST OBJECT
            // (BECAUSE SELECT LISTS MAY CONTAIN MULTIPLE VALUES)
            if (request[nameVal[0]]) {
                request[nameVal[0]] += separator + nameVal[1];
            }
            else {
                request[nameVal[0]] = nameVal[1];
            }
        }
    }
    return request;
}
```

The `showFormValues()` function calls the `createRequestObject()`
function to generate a `request` object and then loops through all the values
in that object to display the name-value pairs in table format.

```
// USING THE CLIENT-SIDE REQUEST OBJECT, SHOW ALL FORM NAMES AND VALUES
// SUBMITTED TO THIS DOCUMENT (USEFUL FOR DEBUGGING FORMS)
function showFormValues()
{
    request = createRequestObject()
    doc  = "<CENTER>\n" +
           "<TABLE BGCOLOR=lightgreen CELLPADDING=0 CELLSPACING=0 BORDER=0>\n" +
           "<TR>\n" +
           "<TH ALIGN=LEFT> Name </TH>\n" +
           "<TH> </TH>\n" +
           "<TH ALIGN=LEFT> Value </TH>\n" +
           "</TR>\n";
    for (i in request) {
        doc += "<TR>\n" +
               "<TD> " + i + " </TD>\n" +
               "<TD> = </TD>\n" +
               "<TD> " + request[i] + " </TD>\n" +
               "</TR>\n";
    }
    doc += "</TABLE>\n" +
           "</CENTER>\n";
    document.write(doc);
}
```

Refer to Figure 4.12 to see the output from `showFormValues()`. The two functions are useful for debugging forms without using any server-side processing. When you are confident that the proper values are being submitted from the form, you can proceed to debug your CGI. These functions are also useful if you want to create an application that uses only client-side processing of form values.

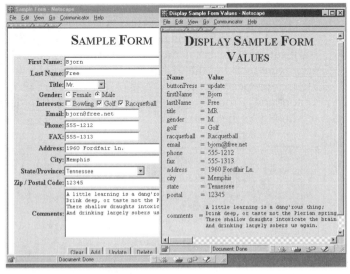

Figure 4.12 *Passing values between HTML pages using client-side JavaScript*

Forwarding Form Submission Values

There are times when you may want to redirect to another document in your application and include all the form values. You may also want to redirect to a CGI or even a static HTML page and pass your form values. You can do this by building an encoded URL that works in a way that's similar to the way the GET method of form submission passes form values. In SSJS, if you submitted your form using the GET method, you can use this code:

```
var url = "http://server.domain.com/ssjsApp/doc.html?" + request.query;
redirect(url);
```

In this case, we add the `query` property to the end of a URL and then redirect to that URL with all our name-value pairs intact. This option can be used only if your form was submitted using the GET method. You can also loop through the values in SSJS, build a URL, and then forward your form values. This approach is useful if the form was submitted using the POST method.

```
var query = "";
for (var propName in request) {
    query += propName + "=" + request[propName] + "&";
}
query = query.substring(0,query.LastIndexOf("&"));
var url = "http://server.domain.com/ssjsApp/doc.html?" + query;
redirect(url);
```

We loop through all the property names in our `request` object. (You can use the preceding code example for any object (client or server); just substitute the object's name for the `request` object.) You access each property name by using the variable `propName` and access each value by accessing that property in the `request` object's array of properties `request[propName]`. You can also manually create a URL that mimics the GET method of form submission:

```
var name1 = "name";
var name2 = "address";
var name3 = "phone";
var val1  = "Bjorn Free";
var val2  = "1960 Fordfair Ln.";
var val3  = "(123) 456-7890";
var url   = "http://server.domain.com/ssjsApp/doc.html?" +
            escape(name1) + "=" + escape(val1) + "&" +
            escape(name2) + "=" + escape(val2) + "&" +
            escape(name3) + "=" + escape(val3);
redirect(url);
```

Remember to always `escape()` your names and values before appending them to a URL. If you do not do this, your name-value pairs may not be
submitted correctly with the URL.

Passing Values from SSJS to SSJS, CSJS, and CGIs

Using a method similar to the one mentioned earlier for passing form values,
you can easily pass values between SSJS, CSJS, and CGIs by using the URL
(the same method of passing values used by the browser when you submit a
form using the `GET` method). The query string begins with a ? character and
is followed by name-value pairs. Each name-value pair is separated by the &
character. See Table 4.7 earlier in this chapter for more information on
URL encoding. The following example shows a query string:

```
?name1=val1&name2=val2&namen=valn
```

Next, you append the query string to a valid URL for any HTML document or CGI program. (It need not be part of an application. You can send
values to any URL on the Internet using this method.) In the following
example, the query string previously mentioned is appended to a URL:

```
http://server.domain.com/myProg.cgi?name1=val1&name2=val2&namen=valn
```

Now you simply redirect to the specified URL from SSJS. In the following example we also used the `escape()` function while creating our
query string. This is to ensure that any special characters from your variable
names and/or values are handled properly. Special characters (including
spaces) cause the URL to be misinterpreted by the browser. Therefore, you
should always escape your names and values unless you know for certain
that they are composed only of letters or numbers. The following example
builds a query string, appends it to a URL, and then uses the SSJS `redirect()`
function to redirect to the specified URL:

```
// PASSING VALUES FROM SERVER-SIDE JAVASCRIPT
var myVals = "?" + escape(myName1) + "=" + escape(myVal1) + "&" +
                  escape(myNamen) + "=" + escape(myValn);
var myURL = "http://server.domain.com/myDocument.html" + myVals;
redirect(myURL);
```

You can use the same process mentioned earlier to send values to and from standard HTML pages. (If you are using this method to communicate between HTML documents, you must use client-side JavaScript to extract the name-value pairs in the URL, as previously shown in the `createRequestObject()` function.)

```
// PASSING VALUES FROM CLIENT-SIDE JAVASCRIPT
var myVals = "?" + escape(myName1) + "=" + escape(myVal1) + "&" +
             escape(myNamen) + "=" + escape(myValn);
var myURL = "http://server.domain.com/myDocument.html" + myVals;
parent.document.location = myURL;
```

There is a security concern: the data you send using this method becomes part of the URL, and the URL is often stored in the server's logfiles. If the data you are sending is confidential, you should not use the preceding method. Instead, you may want to use cookies or other means to pass values. However, if you are simply passing values used within your application, the preceding method works well. If you are concerned about the URL looking cluttered, consider using frames in your application. Only the URL for the frameset document is displayed, so the URLs for the other pages in your application are hidden from the user.

Passing Server-Side JavaScript Variables or Values to Client-Side JavaScript

Often, you generate values on the server that you want to pass directly to your client-side page. There are two ways of doing this. The first technique is to use backquotes to put SSJS variables inside your client-side HTML tags. The second approach is to write JavaScript and assign the values to client-side variables as the page is loaded by the browser.

Back Quotes

You can use the back quote (`` ` ``) character to place SSJS values inside HTML tags. This allows you to use any state object (`request`, `client`, `project`, or `server`) properties in HTML tags or to use server-side variables. You can even use backquotes to display values in a form. Simply place a backquote character around the value you want to use, within an HTML tag. In this case, the document's name is `myDocument.html`.

```
<HTML>

...
<BODY BGCOLOR=`request.myColor` ...>
...
</HTML>
```

If you called the preceding document (`myDocument.html`) with the following URL, the resulting page would have a red background.

```
http://server.domain.com/myApp/myDocument.html?myColor=red
```

Again, the backquotes are used for placing server-side values inside HTML tags. You can include `request` object properties, JavaScript variables, and even database values (for example, `myCursor.salary`). Backquotes cannot be used outside tags, so save yourself some aggravation and use them only inside HTML tags. Trust us.

Writing Script Tags

The other method used to pass values from SSJS to CSJS is to write <SCRIPT tags and place your variables inside them:

```
<SERVER>
myFunction = "<SCRIPT>\n" +
                "var firstVar = \"firstVal\";\n" +
                "var secondVar = \"" + request.myVal + "\";\n" +
                "var thirdVar = " + client.id + ";\n" +
                "var nVar = 25;\n" +
                "</SCRIPT>\n";
write(myFunction);
</SERVER>
```

Your server-side values are assigned to client-side variables as the HTML document is loaded and rendered by the client browser. As the browser loads a document, it executes all JavaScript that doesn't appear within a function or an event. So these values get assigned immediately to client-side variables and can then be manipulated as you see fit.

A Tip on Displaying Data in Tables

You can use tables to display your data in any format you like. But be careful—if you use borders in your tables, some browsers will require a value in each cell or else the frame border for that cell will not be displayed.

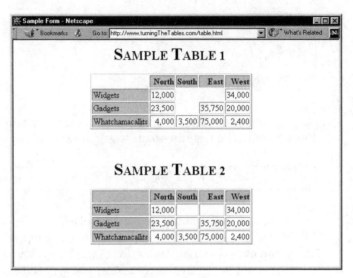

Figure 4.13   *Displaying data in tables*

Figure 4.13 demonstrates what we're talking about: values are missing in both the sample tables shown. Note that when no data exists in a cell in sample table 1, the frame border does not appear, making the presentation of data somewhat unattractive. To get around this problem, simply add a blank space in each empty cell:

```
<TD> </TD>
```

It's a simple trick, but it works. It forces the browser to display the border for the given cell even though the cell contains no actual data. Refer to sample table 2 for an example of a table that displays a border for several blank cells. This makes the table look a little better, and every little bit counts.

Summary

Sometimes it's hard to come to grips with the reality that users really understand only screens. As much as we'd like to believe that they understand the beauty of proper data modeling, the time-saving benefits of good application design, and the elegance of well-written code, they simply don't understand those things. They understand only what they see, and that's usually the pages and forms of your application. Therefore, because they're impressed only with color; clear, concise writing; clearly labeled, easy-to-understand forms; and a smattering of graphics, give them what they want. If your application actually *works*, that's an added benefit. Try to use client-side JavaScript to validate field values before the form is submitted. Remember that users don't see what you've done behind the scenes. Their interaction with applications is solely through forms and any output you display to them. For this reason, take time designing your forms to ensure that the user has a good experience.

5

Working with Databases

By this point, you've learned the basics of server-side JavaScript and are ready to move on to advanced topics. We've illustrated the differences between client-side and server-side JavaScript, we've shown you how to create simple applications, and we've discussed important state maintenance features that are built into the language. With the knowledge you have, you can create applications that generate dynamic content, maintain user state, and work with user input. But where will your dynamic content come from? Where will you store your user input?

Although it's true that many Web applications never require interaction with a database, chances are that if you're a Web developer, eventually you'll be faced with the task of writing a database-aware application. Have no fear—we're here to guide you through the process of writing applications that manage data in and pull data from databases. As you'll learn, working with databases isn't always simple—after all, people get paid good money to write this kind of software. But SSJS provides several mechanisms to make your life easier (although we make no guarantees about how it can improve your salary).

Note   This chapter assumes that you have a basic familiarity with relational databases and SQL.

In This Chapter

This chapter introduces the objects and methods that make up the SSJS database API. After reading this chapter, you should have a good understanding of how to work with databases from an SSJS application:

- Connecting to a database
- Retrieving data
- Generating HTML dynamically using cursors
- Inserting, updating, and deleting records
- Working with stored procedures
- Creating tables on the fly

Whereas this chapter shows you the basics of the SSJS database API, Chapter 6 builds on the fundamentals discussed here and talks about more-advanced topics related to creating complete database applications for the real world.

SSJS Data Basics

Organizations want database-aware Web applications for any number of reasons. Perhaps they want to provide their users with live data that is always up-to-date. They may want to collect data from users and send the information directly into a database. They may be building a sophisticated intranet application that requires live data display, live data updates, and data navigation. Whatever the reason, database-aware Web applications are extremely popular and are being built in increasing numbers as customers demand extranet access to supplier data and as more e-commerce applications are built. SSJS gives you the ability to create everything from simple, dynamically generated lists of data to full-scale e-commerce applications.

SSJS comes with a fully integrated database API, formerly called the LiveWire API, that allows you to connect to most major relational database servers on the market. The database API consists of several JavaScript objects that you can use to retrieve result sets and perform inserts, updates, and deletes in a uniform way across all supported database servers. This means that regardless of the database server you're using, you have only a single API to use. That's great news for those of us who write applications that must work with multiple database servers or who simply write a lot of applications and along the way must write to different databases. For this chapter, we make a simplifying, although not entirely true, assumption that the API works identically with all supported database servers. In practice, the API works *nearly* identically in most cases, but every database server has different features and sometimes you must account for those differences in your applications. Let's dive in to the SSJS database API and see what it can do. Along the way, we note any differences among the various database servers that may require you to code differently for different servers.

Supported Database Servers

The SSJS database API natively supports database servers made by Oracle, IBM, Informix, and Sybase. This means that under the hood, SSJS uses native drivers to talk to each supported database server. If you are working with a database that isn't supported natively or if you experience problems with the native support, you can also connect to some ODBC databases if you have a suitable ODBC driver for that database server. If you're writing on a UNIX operating system, ODBC may still be an option for you because it has been ported to a number of flavors of UNIX. Refer to the Enterprise Server documentation for the specific databases supported by your version of SSJS.

The SSJS Database API Objects

The SSJS API contains five primary objects that you'll find yourself working with frequently:

- `DbPool`: Use this object to establish a connection to a database. It maintains a pool of `connection` objects that provide a connection to the database.

- `connection`: After a connection is established, you use methods of this object to perform operations on the database.

- `cursor`: Spawned from a `connection` object, a `cursor` represents a record set returned by an SQL `SELECT` statement.

- `storedProc`: This object represents a call to a stored procedure on a database server.

- `resultSet`: Spawned from a particular `storedProc` object, a `resultSet` object represents the record set returned by the associated stored procedure. It behaves like a `cursor` object, but it can be used only to retrieve record sets from a stored procedure.

Connecting to a Database

Before you can do any work with a database in server-side JavaScript, you must first establish a connection to it. Establishing a connection involves telling SSJS what database driver to use, where to find the database you want to work with, and what user account you wish to use to log on. After you have a connection to a database server, you can perform any operation that your user account on the database server has permissions to execute.

The API has two objects for connecting to databases: `DbPool` and `database`. Both objects handle creation and release of database connections, and it is good practice to choose to use one or the other, and not both, when you write an application. The `DbPool` object creates a pool of connections to a database, and you can create as many such pools as your application needs. You can even create multiple pools of connections to entirely different database servers made by different database vendors and use all of them within the same application. The `DbPool` object inherently takes advantage of the built-in connection pooling features of SSJS. Using connection pooling, you can establish a pool, or group, of database connections that can be used and released several times throughout the life of an application without having to reconnect or reinitialize each time you use them. Establishing an initial connection to a database is an expensive operation and should be minimized. Taking advantage of connection pooling should help improve the performance of your database applications. You do not have to do anything special to turn on connection pooling.

Before Enterprise Server 3.0, SSJS used the `database` object for connecting to databases. This object was deprecated in version 3.0, meaning that it's still available for use but will no longer be advanced or improved in future releases. It also means that some future version of SSJS may eliminate the object entirely, so it's generally a good idea not to use the `database` object except perhaps for prototypes or smaller applications that can be easily upgraded to `DbPool`. The `database` object is also less flexible than `DbPool` because you can have only one connection to one database open at a time. Because the `database` object has been deprecated, this chapter discusses writing database applications with the more powerful `DbPool` object. For more information on using the `database` object, visit Netscape's developer Web site at `http://developer.netscape.com`.

Creating a pool of connections to a database is a simple process that can be performed in one or two lines of code. It involves two steps:

1. Create a new instance of a `DbPool` object.
2. Connect the pool to the database.

To use multiple `DbPool` objects in an application, you create multiple *instances* of the `DbPool` object using the JavaScript new operator.

```
// Create a pool of connections for users from Accounting
acctPool = new DbPool();
```

This step does not actually create any connections to a database. It merely creates a new `DbPool` object that you can use to manage your connections. Next, you explicitly call its `connect` method to create actual connections to the database.

```
connect(databaseType, serverName, username, password, databaseName, maxConn,
commit)
```

Let's look at the parameters in detail.

- `databaseType` indicates the database driver type. Valid values are `INFORMIX`, `ORACLE`, `DB2`, `SYBASE`, or `ODBC`.
- `serverName` is the name of the database server. Note that for ODBC databases, you must use the ODBC Data Source Name (DSN).
- `username` is a username stored on the database server. All connections in the pool have access permissions for the user account specified by this parameter.
- `password` is the associated account password.
- `databaseName` is the name of the database on the server. For DB2, ODBC, and Oracle, pass only an empty string because these servers do not use this parameter.
- `maxConnections` (optional) is the maximum number of connections that can be active in the pool at one time. If this parameter is left blank, the value defaults to the value set by the `Max Connections` property in Application Manager.
- `commit` (optional) is a Boolean flag that indicates whether to commit or roll back transactions when a connection is closed and finalized. Set the parameter to `true` to automatically commit open transactions when the connection is closed, or `false` to automatically roll back transactions. For the `DbPool` object, this parameter defaults to `false`, meaning that transactions that have been explicitly opened will be automatically rolled back when the connection is closed unless you have explicitly issued a `commit`.

Note   If you decide to use the `database` object instead of `DbPool`, you should note that it also has a `connect` method that takes the same parameters. However, the `commit` parameter of the `database` object defaults to `true` instead of `false`.

The following sample code creates a pool of 20 connections to an Informix database called `"OrdersDB"` on a server named `"IfxServ"` and sets the `commit` flag to `true` so that open transactions will be committed if not

Databases 1

otherwise rolled back before the connection is closed. Furthermore, each of the 20 connections has permissions only to perform operations that the database administrator has allowed for the account on the database server, acctg, that is specified in the connect method:

```
acctPool = new DbPool();
acctPool.connect("INFORMIX", "IfxServ", "acctg", "r18658", "OrdersDB", 20,
true);
```

Instead of performing each step of pool creation separately, you can create the same pool of connections with a single line of code. The DbPool constructor method, called when you use the new operator, accepts all the same parameters that the connect method accepts. So it's possible to create and connect the same pool of connections for the Accounting department in one line instead of two.

```
acctPool = new DbPool("INFORMIX", "IfxServ", "acctg", "r18658", "OrdersDB", 20,
true);
```

When you require a database connection from the pool, you can refer to the acctPool object, because it's an instance of DbPool and therefore shares all its properties and methods. The methods of the DbPool object are summarized in Table 5.1.

Table 5.1 DbPool *object methods*

connect	Creates a specified number of connections to a database and stores them in the DbPool.
connected	Tests to see whether the connections in DbPool are connected to the database.
connection	Retrieves one connection from the pool.
majorErrorCode	The major error code returned by the database server when an error occurs. The code returned is specific to the database vendor.
majorErrorMessage	The major error code returned by the database server when an error occurs. Gives textual information about the error.

Table 5.1 DbPool *object methods (Continued)*

`minorErrorCode`	The minor error code returned by the database server when an error occurs. This code is specific to the database vendor.
`minorErrorMessage`	The minor error message returned by the database server when an error occurs. Contains additional textual information about the error.

Using a Connection

You're now empowered with the knowledge you need to create a pool of connections. However, you need one more piece of knowledge before you can start performing operations on a database. When you have a bunch of connections bobbing around in your pool, you must entice one to hop out and do some work. The `DbPool` object provides a method for summoning a connection from the pool without any complaints.

```
acctConn = acctPool.connection("Betty", 20);
```

The `connection` method returns the next available `connection` object from the associated pool if one is available. The first argument to the method is an arbitrary name you can give to the connection. This parameter can be useful for debugging but is not required. The second parameter, also optional, specifies the amount of time in seconds that SSJS should wait for a connection to become available. If it is unspecified, SSJS will wait indefinitely. It's a good idea to specify a reasonable timeout period here so that connection requests don't hang your application indefinitely as it waits for a connection to be freed. Generally, you shouldn't keep users waiting for more than a few seconds. They don't know what they're waiting for and may wander off to one of your competitors' Web sites in the meantime. If you must make users wait longer than a few seconds, be sure to warn them and give them an approximate amount of time to wait. If successful, the variable `acctConn` will refer to a `connection` object, which has several properties and methods that allow you to perform most of the operations you'll need for manipulating a relational database. If unsuccessful, the method returns `null`. When you're finished with a connection, you can return it to the database connection pool for reuse by calling its `release` method. Table 5.2 lists the methods of the `connection` object.

Table 5.2 Connection *object methods*

connected	Returns true if the connection is still connected to the database, and returns false otherwise.
release	Returns a connection to its connection pool for reuse.
cursor	Creates a cursor object from an SQL SELECT statement.
execute	Executes a command on the database server. No results are returned, but you can call majorErrorCode and other functions to detect errors.
SQLTable	Generates an HTML table that displays all records returned by an SQL SELECT statement.
storedProc	Creates a stored procedure object and executes the specified procedure on the database server.
beginTransaction	Instructs the database server to start a database transaction.
commitTransaction	Instructs the database server to commit all database updates between this call and the call to beginTransaction.
rollbackTransaction	Instructs the database server to roll back all database updates between this call and the call to beginTransaction.

Connecting to a database sounds simple and straightforward, and often it is. However, when you're planning large applications you must consider many connection issues, such as security and performance, that can affect the design of the entire application. In Chapter 6 we revisit database connections, and you'll learn about several design strategies that will help you plan how and where to implement database connections. For now, you know all you need to know to move on to lessons that will show you how to work with data in a database after you have retrieved a connection.

Retrieving Data

In the world of relational databases, SQL (Structured Query Language) is king. Although some desktop databases, such as Microsoft Access, also have visual query interfaces, almost all major relational databases support SQL. It is the industry-standard language for interacting with relational databases, but it's not only a de facto standard. SQL has also been standardized in an effort to ensure that SQL statements work the same way on all databases that support it. In reality, not all databases support SQL to the same degree. In large part, however, SQL works the same way on any compliant database, with differences causing problems not so much in syntax as with data types and the level of support for complex statements. In Chapter 6 we talk about noteworthy pitfalls of writing cross-database SSJS (and SQL) applications.

You can query SQL databases and search for results using the SQL SELECT statement. The SELECT statement looks for matching records in one or more tables that you specify in the query and returns them to the caller. In the case of SSJS, the `cursor` object sends the SELECT statement to the database and handles the data returned. The concept, and even the terminology of a database cursor, is not unique to SSJS. Database cursors are a familiar concept to most database programmers. Think of a database cursor as a virtual table containing records returned by the SQL statement, a table that also has a pointer that points to the currently referenced record. When the records are returned, you can advance the pointer and retrieve the data in each record one at a time.

Note SSJS cursors execute SQL statements on the database server using pass-through SQL, which is simple to implement but has a performance disadvantage. Cursors simply pass the **SELECT** statement as plain text to the database server, where the **SELECT** statement is interpreted and executed. Every time the SQL is passed to the database server, the database must reinterpret and reexecute the query even if it hasn't changed from the last time it was executed. In some application platforms, you can execute precompiled queries that simply accept parameters to allow different criteria values to be used in the same SQL statement. A precompiled query is compiled by the database server only the first time it is executed; from that point on, it will execute much faster. It is similar to the way that compiled programs written in languages such as C run faster than programs written in interpreted languages such as BASIC. Currently, it is not possible to execute precompiled, parameterized queries from SSJS. If you require better performance than cursors and pass-through SQL offer, you should use stored procedures, which are also precompiled on the database server and should provide superior performance.

Database Cursors

Using a cursor to retrieve data is a five-step process:

1. Create the cursor.
2. Advance the cursor one position.

3. Pull data from the fields of the current row.

4. Repeat steps 2 and 3 until you reach the end of the cursor.

5. Close the cursor.

To perform step 1 and execute an SQL statement through a cursor object, you need a valid connection object. Then you call the cursor method of the connection object, passing your SQL SELECT statement as a parameter, and the method returns a cursor object.

```
myCursor = myConn.cursor("SELECT Name, Phone, DepartmentNum  FROM tblEmployee
WHERE CITY='Seattle'");
```

Assuming that myConn is a valid connection object, myCursor will contain all employee records from the table tblEmployee of employees who are located in Seattle.

Before you can access the data in the cursor, you must first perform step 2 and advance the cursor one position. Initially, cursors point not to the first record of data but rather to one position before the first record. Therefore, before you can access the data in myCursor to find the first employee in the list, you must call the next method once and "prime the pump," so to speak.

```
myCursor.next();
```

The next method returns true if the cursor was able to advance its pointer and returns false if it has reached the end of the record set. If it returns false the very first time you call it, you can assume either that your query returned no records or that a database error occurred. To find out whether a database error occurred, you call the majorErrorCode method of the associated connection object. If it returns a nonzero value, it means that an error occurred. If it returns zero, indicating that no error occurred, and if the next method returns false, then the record set is simply empty. For example, perhaps your company doesn't have an office in Seattle, and therefore there are no entries in tblEmployee where the CITY field contains the string "Seattle".

Now that the cursor is pointing at the first record, you can perform step 3 and pull data from every field in the query. Fields from the query, such as Name, Phone, and DepartmentNum, can be referenced in one of two ways. You can reference them by name or by their ordinal position in the query. When referenced by name, each field of the query becomes a property of the cursor object. So myCursor.Name refers to the Name field of the record that myCursor points to. When referenced by ordinal position, each field appears in a zero-based array indexed by the ordinal position of the field in the SQL statement. For example, `cursor[0]` refers to the `Name` property because `Name` appears first in the `SELECT` statement. You can use the two methods of access interchangeably. For example, both `myCursor[0]` and `myCursor.Name` return the data contained in the `Name` field for the record that `myCursor` references at any given time.

Step 4 calls for repeating steps 2 and 3 until there are no more records in the cursor. We can use a looping statement to repeat the steps, but to do so we must know when we've reached the end so that we can stop the loop. Recall that the `cursor` object's `next` method returns `true` if it was able to advance successfully, and returns `false` if it has reached the end. So calling the `next` method in the conditional statement of a `while` loop automatically advances the cursor with each loop iteration and stops the loop when the cursor has reached the end.

```
while (myCursor.next()) {
  // work with the cursor
}
```

Note that when you call `myCursor.next()` in a loop such as this, you need not call the `next` method initially to prime it. Remember that the first thing that happens in a `while` or `for` loop is that the expression between the parentheses is evaluated. In this case, the initial call to the `next` method is made at the start of the loop, and therefore the cursor points to the first record in the set for the very first iteration of the loop.

The final step, step 5, requires that we close the cursor when we're finished. This step is important because the version of SSJS in Enterprise Server 3.0 and later allows database connections and cursors to remain open even across multiple pages. If you don't explicitly close a cursor, it may remain open until its connection is released, and this can cause odd behavior. Additionally, keeping cursors open unnecessarily consumes server memory and is generally bad programming practice if your cursor is to be used on only a single page. Unless you need to keep the cursor open across multiple pages, you should always close your cursors and release connections when you're finished with them.

```
myCursor.close();
```

There are times when you might legitimately need to keep a cursor and connection open across more than one page. In Chapter 6 we discuss these situations when we discuss Web transactions and Web cursors.

Now let's put all the steps together in one cohesive code snippet that retrieves and displays data from a database. Listing 5.1 shows a code segment that creates a DbPool of connections to the database and runs all the way through retrieving records from it to releasing the connection. The code writes the name and phone number of every employee in the table tblEmployee.

Listing 5.1 *Displaying data with a cursor*

```
acctPool = new DbPool("INFORMIX", "AcctServer", "bob", "123", "Payroll");
acctConn = acctPool.connection();
acctCursor = acctConn.cursor("SELECT Name, Phone, DepartmentNum  FROM tblEmployee WHERE
CITY='Seattle'");
while (acctCursor.next())
   write("Name: " + acctCursor.Name + "<BR>");
   write("Phone: " + acctCursor.Phone + "<BR>");
}
acctCursor.close();
acctConn.release();
```

The BLOb

Stop giggling—BLObs (binary large objects) are serious business in some applications. No, we're not talking about the big green slimy stars of old B-movies. BLOb fields are special database fields that store almost any chunk of binary data you wish. They can store images, sound files, PDF files, Macromedia Shockwave presentations, or any other *blob* of binary data. SSJS supports images specifically—because they are commonly stored in BLOb fields—as well as any generic binary file (including images).

Suppose that you're building an online listing service for a real estate company that displays complete information about homes for sale. Everyone looking for a home wants to see a picture of it, so you need a way to display the picture dynamically based on the home a user selects. To display such a picture stored in a database, you call the blobImage or blobLink method of the cursor object to dynamically display the image.

Note For performance reasons, you shouldn't pull your images from BLOb fields in a database if you can avoid it. Instead, you should simply store the filenames of your images in the database and use them to dynamically construct the HTML image tag that points to the proper image that resides in a directory on your Web server. The Web server can serve up a plain image file much faster than it can pull binary data from a database, save it to a temporary file, generate a link, and then delete the temporary file.

Actually, the blobImage and blobLink methods are really methods of a cursorColumn object and, not of the cursor object. A cursorColumn object is the object returned when you reference a column either by name, such as `myCursor.Phone`, or by index, such as `myCursor[2]`. Both statements return a `cursorColumn` object and not just a value as you were led to believe earlier. Normally, you don't need to worry about the fact that the returned values are objects. SSJS takes care of converting the actual value for normal database fields such as strings, numbers, and dates. However, in the case of BLOb data, SSJS does not know the format of the binary data, so you must call either `blobImage` or `blobLink` to tell SSJS to extract the data for you and provide a way to display it.

In the case of images, `blobImage` instructs SSJS to extract the image to a temporary file, create an HTML image tag that points to the image, and then destroy the temporary file after it has been sent to the browser. The method has the following syntax:

```
cursorName.colName.blobImage (format, altText, align, widthPixels,
heightPixels, borderPixels, ismap)
```

The following line of SSJS code would produce the line of HTML that follows it.

```
myCursor.homeImage.blobImage("gif", "House");
<IMG SRC="LIVEWIRE_IMAGE37" ALT="HOUSE">
```

For more-generic BLOb data, you can call the `blobLink` method, which dynamically generates a temporary file containing the data and generates an HTML link pointing to that data. To give SSJS the kind of data it should tell the browser to expect, you enter the MIME type as the first argument to the method. The method has the following syntax:

```
cursorName.colName.blobLink (mimeType, linkText)
```

The following line of code would produce a link to a file containing a .WAV file stored in the database field `rockSong` in the record at the current position of `myCursor`:

```
myCursor.rockSong.blobLink("audio/x-wav", "Click here to listen to a song.");
```

Databases 1

The generated link would look like this:

```
<A HREF="LIVEWIRE_TEMP82">Click here to listen to a song.</A>
```

Note SSJS destroys the temporary file as soon as the user clicks the link and the file is uploaded to the browser, or after 60 seconds, whichever comes first. This applies only to `blobLink`.

Table 5.3 lists all the methods of the `cursor` object, not including `blobImage` and `blobLink`.

Table 5.3 *Methods of the* `cursor` *object*

`close`	Closes the cursor. The cursor becomes unusable after calling this method.
`columnName`	Given an integer for an argument, this method returns the name of the column at that position in the cursor. This corresponds directly to the order of the fields in the SELECT clause of an SQL SELECT statement. Note that if a wild card (*) is used in your SQL statement, there is no way of knowing in advance the order of the fields that are returned by the method.
`columns`	Returns the number of columns in the cursor.
`deleteRow`	Deletes the current row. Works only with updateable cursors. Returns 0 if the delete was successful, or returns an error code otherwise.
`insertRow`	Inserts a row into a table. Works only with updateable cursors. Returns 0 if the insert was successful, or returns an error code otherwise.
`next`	Advances the cursor to the next row. Returns `true` if the cursor was advanced, or returns `false` if the cursor is already at the end of the record set.
`updateRow`	Updates the current row. Works only with updateable cursors. Returns 0 if the update was successful, or returns an error code otherwise.

Aggregate Functions in SQL

In addition to returning data contained in table rows, you might want to call aggregate functions, such as MAX, COUNT, AVG, MIN, and MAX, in your SQL SELECT statements. When you call an aggregate function in an SSJS cursor method, you can retrieve the value only by using its ordinal position in the cursor array. For example, you could retrieve the highest salary in the Employee table using the following calls:

```
myCursor = myConn.cursor("SELECT MAX(Salary) from Employee");
myCursor.next();
```

However, because the returned aggregate value is not given a name by the SQL statement, you must use the following code to retrieve the value using the cursor array:

```
write("The maximum salary is " + myCursor[0]);
```

You can work around this limitation by assigning the count an alias in your SQL query, as illustrated next, and then referencing the column in the cursor by the alias name:

```
myCursor = myConn.cursor("SELECT MAX(Salary) AS MaxSalary FROM Employee");
myCursor.next();
write("The maximum salary is " + myCursor.MaxSalary);
```

Sometimes you might want to know how many records are returned by a SELECT query. You could display this number to let users know how many records they must sort through, as most Internet search engines provide. This information helps users decide whether they want to refine their search if too many records are returned. SSJS does not have a built-in property or method to return the record count, but you can return it nonetheless by using some slightly inefficient SQL code. The following query selects the names and phone numbers of all managers stored in the Employee table. It also returns the number of manager records returned by the query in an alias called EmpCount.

```
myCursor = myConn.cursor("SELECT COUNT(EmpID) AS EmpCount, Name, Phone " +
" FROM Employee WHERE Title="Manager" GROUP BY Name, Phone");
```

Databases 1

Note   SQL requires the use of a **GROUP BY** clause that contains all nonaggregated fields
listed in the **SELECT** clause when you aggregate other fields in a **SELECT** statement. In the example shown, the **Name** and **Phone** fields must be included in the
GROUP BY clause.

Nested Cursors

Some database servers, such as Informix Online Workgroup Server, allow
you to nest cursors or, in other words, to have more than one cursor open at
a time. Nested cursors can be useful for creating reports when disparate data
sets must be operated on at the same time using multiple SQL queries.
However, some database servers handle cursors differently than others and
either do not allow cursors to be nested at all or require a special kind of
cursor to take advantage of nesting. Before you try to use nested cursors in
your application, check your database vendor's documentation to see
whether your server supports them.

Note   ODBC specifies different kinds of cursors that database vendors can support. Type
A cursors are read-only cursors and cannot be nested. Type B cursors can be
updateable and can allow nesting. By default, SSJS creates type A cursors, so
even if your ODBC database supports nested cursors you will not be able to nest
them in your SSJS code. However, you can force SSJS to create a type B ODBC
cursor by creating an updateable cursor in SSJS. You can do this by passing **true**
as the second argument of the **cursor** method:

```
myCursor = myConn.cursor("SELECT * from Employee", true);
```

This trick does not work for some ODBC data sources, however, because not all
ODBC databases support updateable cursors in the first place. For example, SSJS
does not support updateable cursors when you're using Microsoft Access. Refer to
the Enterprise Server documentation for the most current list of supported databases and drivers.

Rendering a Record Set in Record Time

Listing 5.1 illustrates how to use loops to write data rows to the browser.
Using similar code, you can exercise a great deal of control over how your
data is formatted and rendered in the browser. You can set colors, font
styles, font sizes, and so on and can even render data rows in an HTML
table formatted in any way you like. However, if you're not concerned about
the format of your data, SSJS provides a simple method of the `connection`
object called `SQLTable`, which automatically displays any data returned by a
SELECT statement in an HTML table. The problem with `SQLTable` is that it
gives you no control over the format of the output. However, if you're

writing a prototype or simply need to display some down-and-dirty data quickly, calling `SQLTable` is the fastest way to dynamically render a record set in HTML. The following single line of code displays the results of the query shown in an HTML table. It is simple but inflexible.

```
connection.SQLTable("select * from customers");
```

If you're interested in this method for use in a rapid prototype, when style may not matter as much as getting something working, here's a useful tip. If the prototype application will be used as the basis for your production application rather than as a throw-away prototype, don't call `SQLTable` directly from any of your SSJS pages. A direct call would tie you to this method and would make it harder to replace later when you move to production code that renders pretty HTML. Instead, call a function or method such as `RenderCustomerList` and pass it the `connection` object. For your prototype, you can implement this function simply using the preceding line of code. For the production application, you can substitute a more robust implementation that gives you greater control over the HTML output without having to change the call to `SQLTable` on every page where a customer list is rendered. This technique can save you time when you build your prototype. It lets you use `SQLTable` for quick user interfaces initially without locking yourself into an inflexible table implementation for the final production application.

Updating Data

As mentioned earlier in this chapter, displaying live data isn't the only way you can interact with databases using SSJS. In this section, we look at how you can make your database applications more interactive using HTML forms to perform database inserts, updates, and deletes.

SSJS provides two ways to modify data: updateable cursors and pass-through SQL. Updateable cursors are extremely handy constructs because they allow you to add, modify, and delete records without having to write any SQL `INSERT`, `MODIFY` or `DELETE` statements. However, there are currently some limitations and bugs in SSJS that limit the practical use of cursors depending on your database server and your database schema. To obtain the latest information on limitations and bugs, review the known bugs list for Enterprise Server at `http://help.netscape.com`. The limitations are unfortunate because updateable cursors are designed to help eliminate differences in the way databases perform updates. Hopefully, future versions of SSJS will improve this important subsection of the database API. Despite our gloomy tone, however, updateable cursors are far from useless.

For many databases and schemas, they can be used intuitively to update your data. Without further ado, let's look at what they are and how you can use them.

Updateable Cursors

An updateable cursor is similar to the cursor that you've already learned about; in fact, it's really a `cursor` object that's configured a bit differently within SSJS. So far, you've seen one argument passed into the `cursor` method of the `connection` object: the SQL `SELECT` string. However, the `cursor` method has an optional second argument, which is a Boolean flag. When this argument is set to `true`, an updateable cursor is returned. When it is set to `false` or left undefined, a nonupdateable cursor is returned and it cannot be used to perform updates.

You can't create updateable cursors using just any SQL `SELECT` statement. Chapter 9 of the official Netscape SSJS manual, *Writing Server-Side JavaScript Applications*, states

> For a cursor to be updateable, the `SELECT` statement must be an update-able query (one that allows updating). For example, the statement cannot retrieve rows from more than one table or contain a `GROUP BY` clause, and generally it must retrieve key values from a table. For more information on constructing updateable queries, consult your database vendor's documentation.

You might also have problems with `ORDER BY` clauses and updateable cursors, and there are other limitations. Again, the manual states

> When you use cursors to make changes to your database, you should always work inside an explicit transaction. You do so using the `beginTransaction`, `commitTransaction`, and `rollbackTransaction` methods [of a `connection` object], as described in "Managing Transactions". If you do not use explicit transactions in these situations, you may get errors from your database. For example, Informix and Oracle both return error messages if you use a cursor without an explicit transaction. Oracle returns `Error ORA-01002: fetch out of sequence`; Informix returns `Error -206: There is no current row for UPDATE/DELETE` cursor.

Taking a cue from the Netscape manual, let's talk about transactions before we dive deeper into updateable cursors.

Database Transactions

A *database transaction* is a set of database commands that either execute all together, if committed, or not at all, if rolled back. Transactions are extremely important for maintaining data integrity and ensuring that proper values are stored when updates are performed to a database. The SSJS data-base API generally handles the configuration of a database server's auto-commit feature under the covers for individual statements. However, when you're using updateable cursors or executing multiple statements that must either succeed or fail as a single unit, such as a money transfer from one bank to another, you should always use explicit transactions to ensure data integrity.

Employing explicit transactions is simple and straightforward. To begin a transaction, call `beginTransaction`; to commit a transaction, call `commitTransaction`; and to roll back a transaction, call `rollback Transaction`. All of them are methods of the `connection` object, and none of them takes any arguments. Listing 5.2 shows an example of how to con-duct a transfer from one bank account to another. Such an operation should be performed in a transaction because two updates occur—a debit of the "from" account and a credit of the "to" account—and either both must suc-ceed or both must fail; otherwise, bank balances could be left in an incorrect state. Banks do not generally like their programmers to leave accounts with incorrect balances. Notice that both the debit from account A and the sub-sequent deposit into account B take place between a `beginTransaction` statement and an `if/else` block that calls either `commitTransaction` or `rollbackTransaction` depending on the success or failure of each update.

Listing 5.2   *Using transactions to transfer money between two accounts*

```
var result = 0;
// Assume bankConn is a valid connection object
bankConn.beginTransaction();
   accountA = bankConn.cursor("SELECT * from Accounts where AccountID='12345'", true);
   result = bankConn.majorErrorCode();
   accountA.next();
   accountA.balance -= 100;  // Debit the account $100
   result += accountA.updateRow("Accounts");
   accountA.close();
   accountB = bankConn.cursor("SELECT * from Accounts where AccountID='98765'", true);
   result += bankConn.majorErrorCode();
   accountB.next();
   accountB.balance += 100;  // Credit the account $100
   result += accountA.updateRow("Accounts");
   accountB.close();
if (result > 0)
   bankConn.rollbackTransaction();
else
   bankConn.commitTransaction();
```

The transaction handling in Listing 5.2 works by cumulatively adding the error code returned by each database operation to a variable called `result`. The methods `majorErrorCode`, `minorErrorCode`, and `updateRow` all return zero when database commands are successful, and they return nonzero values when an error occurs. Thus, if all operations are successful, these methods always return zero and the variable `result` still contains zero by the end of the update. If even a single error occurs, the value is added to the cumulative result, and, by the end of the update, `result` is greater than zero. When deciding whether to commit or roll back the transaction, the code checks `result`. If `result` is greater than zero, the code rolls back the transaction because it knows that an error must have occurred somewhere in the transaction. Otherwise, if `result` is zero, the transaction is committed. This method of checking for errors ensures that if either the debit from account A or the credit to account B fails, both transactions are rolled back and the account balances are restored to their previous states.

Even though some database servers support nested transactions, the SSJS database API does not support them, so you cannot have more than one transaction open at a time. Also, generally you should have transactions open only for one page. However, because Enterprise Server 3.0 allows `connection` objects to persist across pages and requests, it is also possible to keep a transaction open across pages and requests. In Chapter 6 we discuss multipage transactions, also called Web transactions.

Note   If you're using the `database` object instead of the `DbPool` and `connection` objects for database connections, you are not allowed to keep transactions open across multiple pages. Transactions must be committed or rolled back by the end of the page, or else the default `commit` or `rollback` flag set when you created the connection will commit or roll back the transaction automatically at the end of the page.

Earlier, when we discussed creating connections to databases, recall that you could choose whether you wanted SSJS to automatically commit or roll back updates made in a transaction if no commit or rollback was explicitly called for. The transactions referred to here are the same ones referred to in the connections section of the chapter. You can use explicit transactions anywhere in your code where you perform updates and not just when you're using updateable cursors. Let's look at another way you can perform updates with SSJS.

Pass-Through SQL

The SSJS `connection` object has a method called `execute` that lets you execute almost any command that is allowable on your database server, including `INSERT`, `UPDATE`, and `DELETE`. The only catch is that `execute` does not return any records to you if your statement returns records, although you can still catch and handle any error messages that the database server might generate. Fortunately, database modification statements do not generally return records, so `execute` should work well for modifying data.

If you're an SQL expert, using pass-through SQL will seem like old hat to you. Here's an example of inserting a record into a table:

```
var sql = "INSERT INTO Employee (Name, Title, Phone) VALUES " +
    " ('Jebediah Hibb, Jr.', 'CEO', '555-555-5555')");
myConn.execute(sql);
```

That's all there is to it. Just pass in your SQL, and the database executes it. As with most database operations, you can call one of the four built-in error methods of the `connection` object (`majorErrorCode`, `major ErrorMessage`, `minorErrorCode`, or `minorErrorMessage`) to check whether any errors occurred when the insert was performed.

A Complete Example

To illustrate how to work with databases using connections and cursors, performing updates in transactions, and generating HTML, we've contrived a complete sample application. The listings in this section revolve around the information systems needs of a fictional company, Hibb & Dringle Enterprises. All code related to this example can be found on the CD-ROM that accompanies this book.

Hibb & Dringle Enterprises is the world's oldest manufacturer of ice cream trucks. In fact, the (fictional) late Jebediah Hibb, Sr., is credited with originating the idea of playing obnoxious, repetitive music from the trucks at high volume to attract young children. The human resources database, which tracks employee information, is among the many databases Hibb & Dringle maintains to run its business. Suppose that we work in Hibb & Dringle's information systems department and our boss has asked us to create a small intranet application that will allow the Human Resources (HR) department to perform the following operations:

- List all employees by department.
- Allow users to sort the list by employee name or title.
- Update information on any employee.

The application will be used by a small department, so a light user load is expected. Figure 5.1 shows the data model we use for this example.

The application will consist of six pages, as shown in Figure 5.2.

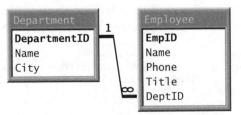

Figure 5.1 *Hibb & Dringle Enterprises data model*

Let's look at each page in some detail.

1. Initial page: The Initial page contains a small amount of initialization code for the application. Remember that initial pages are executed only when an application is started or restarted. The initial page for this application contains code to initialize a globally available `DbPool` object from which any page in the application can pull connections.

2. Lookup page: This is a simple HTML form that has a drop-down list containing all the departments in the company. A user can select a

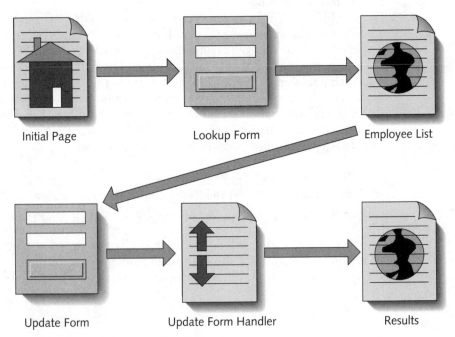

Figure 5.2 *Application page flow diagram*

department from the list and click the **Lookup Employees** button, causing the department name to be sent to the List page.

3. List page: Recall from Chapter 4 that SSJS puts all HTML form and query string data into the built-in `request` object. The name of the drop-down list on the Lookup page is `deptName`, so the List page can find the chosen department by looking in the `request.deptName` property. The page uses this name to create a list of all employees in that department.

4. Update form: From the List page, users can choose to update an employee record by clicking on the hyperlinked employee name, which takes them to the Update form. The page displays current employee information in an HTML form where users can modify the information and submit it to the database to update the record.

5. Update form handler: This form handler uses an updateable cursor to update employee information entered in the Update form.

6. Result page: This page displays the result of the update operation to the user.

The Initial Page

This page combines concepts of state management that you learned in Chapter 3 with the concept of `DbPool`s. Recall that the built-in `project` object can store both scalar and object data for the lifetime of an application and that data is accessible to all clients accessing the application. If it can hold objects, it can hold `DbPool` objects.

You can create a globally accessible pool of database connections by creating a `DbPool` and storing it in the `project` object. You don't have to do this on the Initial page, but it's generally a good place to do so because it's guaranteed to be executed when the application is started. Also, because the Initial page is executed before user requests are accepted, creating and storing the `DbPool` doesn't take up the time of any users who might otherwise have to wait for the `DbPool` to connect if it were created on a user-accessible page. When any page needs a database connection, it can request a connection from the `DbPool` object stored in the `project` object at the top of the page and can release the connection back into the pool at the bottom of the page. Listing 5.3 shows the code that makes up the entire Initial page of the application. For this example, we connect to a Microsoft Access database using an ODBC DSN on the Web server named "HRDSN".

Listing 5.3 *Hibb & Dringle HR application Initial page*

```
<SERVER>
// Create a pool of 5 connections to a Microsoft Access
// database through ODBC.  The ODBC DSN, "HRDSN", is used for
// the server name parameter.  Set commit flag to true.
project.appPool = new DbPool("ODBC", "HRDSN", "admin", "12345", "", 5, true);
</SERVER>
```

The Lookup Form

The Lookup form is a simple, static HTML form that contains only two form elements: a drop-down list and a submit button. It contains no SSJS code, although the ACTION attribute of the FORM tag on the page refers to the List page, which is an SSJS page. Figure 5.3 shows what the page looks like in a browser, and Listing 5.4 shows the HTML that constructs the page.

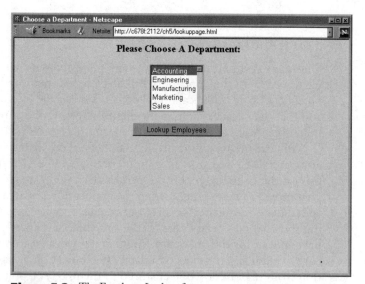

Figure 5.3 *The Employee Lookup form*

Listing 5.4 *The Lookup form page*

```
<HTML>
<HEAD>
<TITLE>Choose a Department</TITLE>
</HEAD>
<BODY BGCOLOR="#FFFFDE">
```

Listing 5.4 *The Lookup form page (Continued)*

```
<CENTER>
<FORM NAME="LookupForm" ACTION="ListPage.html" METHOD="post">
<H3>Please Choose a Department:</H3>
<SELECT NAME="DepartmentID" SIZE=5>
   <OPTION VALUE="1" SELECTED>Accounting
   <OPTION VALUE="2">Engineering
   <OPTION VALUE="3">Manufacturing
   <OPTION VALUE="4">Marketing
   <OPTION VALUE="5">Sales
</SELECT>
<BR>
<BR>
<INPUT TYPE="submit" NAME="Submit" VALUE="Lookup Employees">
</FORM>
</CENTER>
</BODY>
</HTML>
```

The List Page

The List page essentially loops through a cursor and displays all the information in a formatted HTML table. Additionally, we make the list more interactive by providing a way for a user to re-sort the list by employee name or employee title by clicking on the appropriate column header. Also, every employee name in the list is hyperlinked so that when the name is clicked, the user is sent to the Update form and the form contains information on the selected employee. First things first—let's construct the basic employee list, which is pared down from the entire company listing by filtering on the department name that's passed from the Lookup form.

The first task is to retrieve a connection to the database from the global pool. In case we need to debug the application later, we name the connection "ListPage" so that we know which connection might have the problem. Also, we set the connection timeout parameter to 10 seconds so that we don't keep the folks in HR waiting too long for a connection. If a connection isn't available after 10 seconds, we redirect to the Result page and report an error; we expect the application to have very few users, and the inability to grab a connection from the pool probably indicates a problem with the database rather than a busy system.

```
// Initialize local page variables
var listConn = null;
var msg = "";
// Grab a connection to the database from the global pool
listConn = project.appPool.connection("ListPage", 10);
if (listConn == null) {
   msg = escape("Error: Unable to connect to the database.");
   redirect("Result.html?msg=" + msg);
}
```

Notice that before we send the error message to the Result page, we URL-encode it using the top-level JavaScript function `escape`. When sending name-value pairs in the query string of a URL, you should always make sure to URL-encode the values so that illegal characters such as spaces are encoded for safe transport in the URL.

After a connection is retrieved, data can be retrieved by executing a SQL `SELECT` statement to retrieve the names of all the employees in the selected department. If the form parameter `deptName` is passed from the Lookup form in the `request` object, we filter the list of all employees to only those employees in the department whose names match `request.deptName`.

```
// Construct the cursor
var sql = "SELECT e.EmpID, e.Name, e.Title, e.Phone, d.Name AS DeptName " +
    " FROM Employee e, Department d WHERE d.DepartmentID=e.DeptID";
if (request.DepartmentID != null)
    sql += " AND d.DepartmentID=" + request.DepartmentID;
```

Note   Both the `Employee` and the `Department` tables have a column called `"Name"`. This duplication will cause an ambiguity when `empCursor.Name` is referred to. To avoid the ambiguity, use an SQL alias to change the name of one of the ambiguous fields. In the example shown, `Department.Name` was aliased with the SQL `AS` operator to `DeptName`. This field can subsequently be referred to as `empCursor.DeptName`.

Now we're ready to display the results in an HTML table. Listing 5.5 shows the complete code for generating the List page. It combines the code for generating the table with the previous code for creating the connection and the cursor.

Listing 5.5 *Dynamically generating an HTML table from a cursor*

```
<HTML>
<HEAD><TITLE>Employee List</TITLE></HEAD>
<BODY>
<SERVER>
// Initialize local page variables
var listConn = null;
var msg = "";
// Grab a connection to the database from the global pool
listConn = project.appPool.connection("ListPage", 10);
if (listConn == null) {
    msg = escape("Error: Unable to connect to the database.");
    redirect("Result.html?msg=" + escape(msg));
}
// Construct the cursor
var sql = "SELECT e.EmpID, e.Name, e.Title, e.Phone, d.Name AS DeptName " +
    " FROM Employee e, Department d WHERE d.DepartmentID=e.DeptID";
```

Listing 5.5 *Dynamically generating an HTML table from a cursor (Continued)*

```
if (request.DepartmentID != null)
   sql += " AND d.DepartmentID=" + request.DepartmentID;
empCursor = listConn.cursor(sql);
// Generate the HTML table that displays employee information
write("<TABLE BORDER=0 CELLSPACING=2 CELLPADDING=3>");
if (!empCursor.next())
   write("<TR><TH>No employees found.</TD></TR>");
else {
   // Write out a table caption such as:
   // Employees of the Accounting department.
   write("<CAPTION>Employees of the " + empCursor.DeptName +
      " department</CAPTION>");
   write("<TR><TH>Name</TH><TH>Title</TH><TH>Phone</TH></TR>");
   do {
   write("<TR>");
   write("<TD>" + empCursor.Name + "</TD>");
   write("<TD>" + empCursor.Title + "</TD>");
   write("<TD>" + empCursor.Phone + "</TD>");
   write("</TR>");
} while(empCursor.next());
write("</TABLE>");
empCursor.close();
listConn.release();
</SERVER>
</BODY>
</HTML>
```

At this point, we have all the code we need to construct the List page and display the query results in a dynamically generated HTML table. However, after this page is generated, it appears to be static to the user, who can take no actions from it. Let's add interactivity by modifying Listing 5.5 to let users sort the results by employee name and title.

Sorting a list in SQL is a trivial task. All that is required is the addition of an ORDER BY clause to the end of the SELECT statement followed by a comma-delimited list of fields on which to sort. For example, the statement SELECT * FROM Employee ORDER BY Name would return a list of all Employee records sorted alphabetically by Name in ascending order (A–Z). The seemingly tricky part is to generate the ORDER BY clause on-the-fly when the user clicks on a column header. As it turns out, generating tables that allow users to sort on certain columns is not very tricky. Follow these three steps and you'll get it right every time:

1. Modify your SQL statement to look for a custom property of the request object called orderby, which you'll construct in step 3. Use the value of this parameter to conditionally add an ORDER BY clause to your SELECT statement if the parameter was passed. If it was not passed, don't add the ORDER BY clause.

2. Make each column header that you wish to sort by a hyperlink pointing back to the same page. In our case, we hyperlink the `Name` and `Title` fields.

3. Add the parameter called `orderby` to the URL's query string and give it a value of the name of the database field you wish to sort by. This parameter is passed to the page and is picked up by the code you wrote in step 1. In addition to adding the `orderby` parameter to the query string, we must append the `DepartmentID` parameter again to this query string. If we don't, when the user clicks on a title to sort the list, the page will reload with all the names and not just the names from the previous query. As a rule, when using this trick you must always add the `orderby` parameter to whatever query came previously.

Listing 5.6 shows a version of Listing 5.5 that has been modified to follow the three steps. In addition, it shows the minor modification required to link each employee name displayed to the Update form. New or modified lines are highlighted in bold. Figure 5.4 (following the listing) illustrates what the page will look like when rendered in a browser.

Listing 5.6 *Complete code for the List page*

```
<HTML>
<HEAD><TITLE>Employee List</TITLE></HEAD>
<BODY BGCOLOR="FFFFE0">
<SERVER>
// Initialize local page variables
var listConn = null;
var msg = "";
// Grab a connection to the database from the global pool
listConn = project.appPool.connection("ListPage", 10);
if (listConn == null) {
    msg = escape("Error: Unable to connect to the database.");
    redirect("Result.html?msg=" + msg);
}
// Construct the cursor
var sql = "SELECT e.EmpID, e.Name, e.Title, e.Phone, d.Name AS DeptName " +
    " FROM Employee e, Department d WHERE d.DepartmentID=e.DeptID";
if (request.DepartmentID != null)
    sql += " AND d.DepartmentID=" + request.DepartmentID;

// Step 1: Add the ORDER BY clause
if (request.orderby != null)
    sql += " ORDER BY " + request.orderby;
empCursor = listConn.cursor(sql);

// Generate the HTML table that displays employee information
write("<TABLE BORDER=0 CELLSPACING=2 CELLPADDING=3>");
if (!empCursor.next())
    write("<TR><TH>No employees found.</TD></TR>");
```

Listing 5.6 *Complete code for the List page (Continued)*

```
else {
   // Write out a table caption such as:
   // Employees of the Accounting department.
   write("<CAPTION>Employees of the " + empCursor.DeptName +
      " department</CAPTION>");

   // Step 2: Hyperlink each column header back to this page
   // Step 3: Include the orderby parameter in the query string.
   write("<TR BGCOLOR=\"#DDAA44\">");
   write("<TH>" + "Name".link("ListPage.html?DepartmentID=" +
request.DepartmentID + "&orderby=e.name") + "</TH>");
   write("<TH>" + "Title".link("ListPage.html?DepartmentID=" +
request.DepartmentID + "&orderby=e.title") + "</TH>");
   write("<TH>Phone</TH>");
   write("</TR>");
   // Write out each row in the table.  Use a do/while loop
   // because we've already advanced the cursor to the first row.
   do {
       write("<TR BGCOLOR=\"#DDCCAA\">");
       // Link the employee name to the Update form.  Pass the
       // primary key of the Employee table, ID, so that Update form knows
       // which employee needs to be updated.
       var url = "UpdateForm.html?EmpID=" + empCursor.EmpID;
       write("<TD>" + empCursor.Name.link(url) + "</TD>");
       write("<TD>" + empCursor.Title + "</TD>");
       write("<TD>" + empCursor.Phone + "</TD>");
       write("</TR>");
   } while(empCursor.next());
} // end else
write("</TABLE>");

// Clean up the cursor and connections
empCursor.close();
listConn.release();
</SERVER>
</BODY>
</HTML>
```

Listing 5.6 shows the complete code for the List page, which renders an HTML form something like the one shown in Figure 5.4. With a couple of dozen lines of code, we've created a live connection to a database and can display live data to any user who requests it. Users see the latest, most up-to-date information whenever they perform a lookup and arrive at this page. This is only part of the power of the live database connectivity API that is part of server-side JavaScript. As discussed earlier, you can also give your users the power to add, modify, and delete data from any standard Web page.

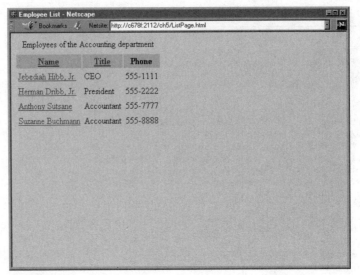

Figure 5.4 *The employee List page showing query results from the Lookup form*

The Update Form

This example illustrates techniques for building an HTML form using live data to provide default values for the form fields. By populating the input fields with the data from the selected employee record, we not only make it easy to update the record values but also provide a way to review the record so that users can be sure they have selected the right one. Because the update form lets users choose to either update or delete the record, it's a good idea to give them the opportunity to examine the record in detail before they make any permanent modifications to the database.

Building the update form involves three steps:

1. Connect to the database and create a cursor.
2. Populate each form field with the corresponding value from the cursor.
3. Close the cursor and database connection.

Sounds simple, right? That's because it is. First, let's create the database connection and the cursor, which should be familiar to you by now.

```
<SERVER>
// Initialize local page variables
var listConn = null;
```

```
var msg = "";

// Grab a connection to the database from the global pool
listConn = project.appPool.connection("ListPage", 10);
if (listConn == null || request.EmpID == null) {
   msg = escape("Database Error: Unable to connect or unspecified employee
ID.");
   // Release connection before redirecting
   if (listConn != null)
      listConn.release();
      redirect("Results.html?msg=" + msg);
}
```

Next, we write each form field and set the default value to the value of the corresponding field in the database. The form in this example contains only text input fields. Chapter 6 shows you how to set default values for other form elements and even how to generate them entirely from SSJS. Text input boxes have a VALUE attribute that sets the initial, default value that appears in the box. We could assign the value of the cursor field to the VALUE attribute and be done with it.

```
<INPUT TYPE="text" NAME="Phone" VALUE=`empCursor.Phone`>
```

But, what happens if that record doesn't have a value in the Phone field? What if that value is null? Because SSJS backquotes simply evaluate SSJS expressions into string values, it will evaluate the value of empCursor.Phone to null and then convert the value to a string. When converted to a string, the value null becomes the string "null". In keeping with user-friendly interface design principles, we shouldn't just blurt out the string "null" in a form field when a corresponding database field contains no value. It looks cleaner if we detect when the cursor value is null and set the form field's value to an empty string so that it appears blank. We do this using the Java-Script tertiary operator:

```
(expression) ? value1 : value2
```

The tertiary operator works like a simplified if-else statement. If the expression evaluates to true, value1 is returned; otherwise, value2 is returned. We use this operator to check for null values and return an empty string if the field value is null; otherwise, we return the entire VALUE attribute string, which assigns the cursor value to the input tag:

```
<INPUT TYPE=TEXT NAME="Phone" `(cursor.Phone == null) ? "" : ('VALUE="' +
cursor.Phone + '"')`>
```

Using this technique, we build all the form elements and populate them with live data, as illustrated in Listing 5.7. Figure 5.5 shows what the form looks like in HTML. Notice that we only display the unique identifier, EmpID, and do not allow the user to alter it. The EmpID field is an auto-incrementing field used to generate unique EmpID values because EmpID is the primary key of the Employee table. Because the field is an auto-incrementing field, we don't want to let users alter it. Even if it weren't an auto-incrementing field, it's generally not a good idea to allow users to modify primary keys of tables. If they do, and if the value they enter is not unique, the database will throw an error and the update will fail.

Listing 5.7 *Employee Update form*

```
<HTML>
<HEAD>
<META NAME="GENERATOR" Content="NetObjects ScriptBuilder 2.01">
<TITLE>Update an Employee</TITLE>
<SERVER>
// Initialize local page variables
var listConn = null;
var msg = "";

// Grab a connection to the database from the global pool
listConn = project.appPool.connection("ListPage", 10);
if (listConn == null || request.EmpID == null) {
   msg = escape("Database Error: Unable to connect or unspecified employee ID.");
      // Release connection before redirecting
   if (listConn != null)
      listConn.release();
   redirect("Results.html?msg=" + msg);
}

// Construct the employee cursor
sql = "SELECT * from EMPLOYEE WHERE EmpID=" + request.EmpID;
empCursor = listConn.cursor(sql);
empCursor.next();
</SERVER>
</HEAD>
<BODY BGCOLOR="#FFFFDE">

<CENTER>
<H3>Employee #<SERVER>write(request.EmpID);</SERVER></H3>
<FORM NAME="LookupForm" ACTION="UpdateFormHandler.html" METHOD="post">

<!-- Fill in this hidden field dynamically so that empID
     will be passed over to the form handler -->
<INPUT TYPE="hidden" NAME="EmpID" VALUE=`((request.EmpID != null) ? request.EmpID : 0)`>
<!-- Put the form in an HTML table for better alignment -->
```

Listing 5.7 *Employee Update form (Continued)*

```
<TABLE BORDER=0>
<TR>
<TD>Name:</TD>
<TD><INPUT TYPE="text" SIZE=30 MAXLENGTH=30 NAME="Name"
      `(empCursor.Name == null) ? "" : ('VALUE="' + empCursor.Name + '"')`></TD></TR>
<TD>Title:</TD>
<TD><INPUT TYPE="text" SIZE=30 MAXLENGTH=30 NAME="Title"
      `(empCursor.Title == null) ? "" : ('VALUE="' + empCursor.Title + '"')`></TD></TR>
<TD>Phone:</TD>
<TD><INPUT TYPE="text" SIZE=30 MAXLENGTH=30 NAME="Phone"
      `(empCursor.Phone == null) ? "" : ('VALUE="' + empCursor.Phone + '"')`></TD></TR>
</TABLE>
<INPUT TYPE="submit" NAME="Submit" VALUE="Update Employee">
<INPUT TYPE="reset" NAME="Reset" VALUE="Restore Defaults">
</CENTER>
</FORM>
<SERVER>
// Clean up the cursor and connection
empCursor.close();
listConn.release();
</SERVER>
</BODY>
</HTML>
```

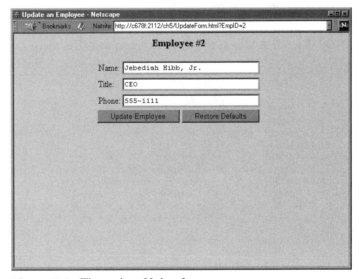

Figure 5.5 *The employee Update form*

The Update Form Handler

The Update form submits the values, whether or not a user has altered them, to the Update form handler, which updates the record in the database. The Update handler performs three operations:

1. Creates an updateable cursor on the Employee table
2. Updates the table with information from the form
3. Sends users to the Result page with a message indicating error or success

In addition to the operations this page performs, pay close attention to how we're managing database connections. Recall from earlier in the chapter that it's important that we clean up any cursors or connections before redirecting. For this reason, we've chosen not to redirect until the end of the page, where we first clean up any open connections before redirecting to the Result page. This is a simple way to ensure that you're always cleaning up connections and cursors before leaving a page. It also makes your code more readable in general by standardizing where your redirect calls occur. Redirects are essentially gotos, and gotos are notorious in the programming world for turning programs into spaghetti code. Use them sparingly.

Creating a Cursor

To create the cursor, we use the EmpID value (the one that was passed in a hidden field) from the form to select only the record we're trying to update.

```
<SERVER>
// Initialize local page variables
var listConn = null;
var msg = "";
var err = "";
var sql = "";
var result = 0;
// Grab a connection to the database from the global pool
listConn = project.appPool.connection("ListPage", 10);
if (listConn == null || request.empID == null) {
    msg = escape("Error: Unable to retrieve data from the database.");
    redirectURL = "Results.html?msg=" + escape(msg);
} else {
// Construct the updateable cursor
sql = "SELECT * from EMPLOYEE WHERE EmpID=" + request.EmpID;
listConn.beginTransaction()
    empCursor = listConn.cursor(sql, true);
    empCursor.next();
```

Updating the Employee Table

Next, we update each of the fields in the cursor with values from the corresponding form fields. When that is complete, we call `updateRow` to perform the update and assign the result to a variable in case any errors occurred.

```
empCursor.Name = request.Name;
empCursor.Phone = request.Phone;
empCursor.Title = request.Title
result = empCursor.updateRow("Employee");
```

Sending the User to the Result Page

Finally, we send users to the Result page so that they can find out whether the update succeeded or failed. You should always have some sort of confirmation message or page to let users know the results of an operation; otherwise, they may think that the operation succeeded when actually an error occurred. Depending on the success or failure of the update, we send the user a message indicating success or an error message containing detailed error information from the database.

```
if (result > 0) {
   msg = "Error updating database.";
   err = listConn.majorErrorCode() + ": " + listConn.majorErrorMessage();
   listConn.rollbackTransaction();
   redirectURL = "Results.html?msg=" + escape(msg) + "&err=" + escape(err);
} else {
   msg = "Employee updated successfully!";
   listConn.commitTransaction();
   redirectURL = "Results.html?msg=" + escape(msg);
}
// Don't redirect until the end of the page so we can release the connection
listConn.release();
redirect(redirectURL);
```

In Chapter 6 we discuss more-sophisticated error handling schemes. Listing 5.8 shows the complete code for the Update form handler for a database that supports updateable cursors, such as Microsoft SQL Server and Oracle. However, not all databases supported by SSJS can use updateable cursors. Listing 5.9 shows an alternative version of the form handler that uses pass-through SQL to perform updates for databases, such as Microsoft Access, for which SSJS does not support updateable cursors.

Listing 5.8 *Update form handler using updateable cursors*

```
<SERVER>
// Initialize local page variables
var listConn = null;
var msg = "";
var err = "";
var sql = "";
var result = 0;
// Grab a connection to the database from the global pool
listConn = project.appPool.connection("ListPage", 10);
if (listConn == null || request.EmpID == null) {
   msg = escape("Error: Unable to retrieve data from the database.");
   redirectURL = "Results.html?msg=" + escape(msg);
} else {
   // Construct the updateable cursor
   sql = "SELECT * from EMPLOYEE WHERE EmpID=" + request.EmpID;
   listConn.beginTransaction()
      empCursor = listConn.cursor(sql, true);
      empCursor.next();
      empCursor.Name = request.Name;
      empCursor.Phone = request.Phone;
      empCursor.Title = request.Title
      result = empCursor.updateRow("Employee");
      empCursor.close();
   if (result > 0) {
      msg = "Error updating database.";
      err = listConn.majorErrorCode() + ": " + listConn.majorErrorMessage();
      listConn.rollbackTransaction();
      redirectURL = "Results.html?msg=" + escape(msg) + "&err=" + escape(err);
   } else {
      msg = "Employee updated successfully!";
      listConn.commitTransaction();
      redirectURL = "Results.html?msg=" + escape(msg);
   }
   // Don't redirect until the end of the page so we can release the connection
   listConn.release();
   redirect(redirectURL);
} // end outermost else
</SERVER>
```

Listing 5.9 *Update form handler using pass-through SQL*

```
<SERVER>
// Initialize local page variables
var listConn = null;
var msg = "";
var err = "";
var sql = "";
var result = 0;
var empID = request.EmpID;
// Grab a connection to the database from the global pool
listConn = project.appPool.connection("ListPage", 10);
if (listConn == null || empID == null) {
   msg = escape("Error: Unable to retrieve data from the database.");
   redirectURL = "Results.html?msg=" + escape(msg);
```

Listing 5.9 *Update form handler using pass-through SQL (Continued)*

```
} else {
sql = "UPDATE Employee SET Name='" + request.Name + "'," +
      "Phone='" + request.Phone + "', " +
      "Title='" + request.Title + "' " +
      "WHERE EmpID=" + empID;
   result = listConn.execute(sql);
   if (result > 0) {
      msg = "Error updating database.";
      err = listConn.majorErrorCode() + ": " + listConn.majorErrorMessage();
      redirectURL = "Results.html?msg=" + escape(msg) + "&err=" + escape(err);
} else {
      msg = "Employee updated successfully!";
      redirectURL = "Results.html?msg=" + escape(msg);
}
   // Don't redirect until the end of the page so we can release the connection
   listConn.release();
   redirect(redirectURL);
} // end outermost else
</SERVER>
```

The Result Page

The Result page is the final page in our mini-application for Hibb & Dringle Enterprises. It informs the user of the result of the update operation. The SSJS code for this page is relatively light. If an error occurred, we display a graphic indicating an error and display the details of the error that were passed from the Update form. If the operation was successful, we display a decidedly happier graphic and output the message of success that was passed from the update form. Listing 5.10 shows the code, and Figure 5.6 shows a typical success page.

Listing 5.10 *The Result page*

```
<HTML>
<HEAD>
<!-- Dynamically generated page title -->
<TITLE>
<SERVER>write((request.err != null) ? "Error!" : "Success!");</SERVER>
</TITLE>
</HEAD>
<BODY BGCOLOR="#FFFFDE">
<CENTER>
<IMG SRC=`((request.err != null) ? "error.gif" : "success.gif")`>
<BR>
<FONT SIZE=+1>
<SERVER>
write(request.msg);
if (request.err != null) {
    write("<BR>");
    write(request.err);
```

Listing 5.10   *The Result page (Continued)*

```
}
</SERVER>
</FONT>
<BR>
<BR>
<A HREF="LookupPage.html">Return to Lookup Form</A>
</CENTER>
</FORM>
</BODY>
</HTML>
```

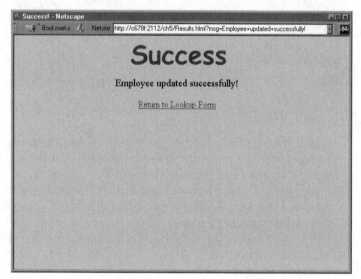

Figure 5.6   *A typical success page*

Working with Stored Procedures

Now that you've seen a complete example of how to work with cursor-based applications, let's talk about other parts of the SSJS API that can help you build scalable, heavy-duty SSJS applications. The ability to call stored procedures from SSJS is one of the most interesting and important features of the database API. Any client/server developer will tell you that stored procedures are the heart of the server end of most client/server database applications. Stored procedures are reusable, they run on the database server (freeing resources on your Web server), and they offer good performance. Because a stored procedure is compiled inside the database server, it executes faster than a comparable pass-through SQL query, which the database server must interpret before it can execute. Stored procedures are also well suited for automatically implementing integrity rules on the server. If you write SSJS applications to access legacy databases, you might run into databases that already have oodles of stored procedures implemented. With the SSJS database API, you can take advantage of them and do true client/server development for the Internet or intranets.

The hardest part about using stored procedures with SSJS is probably writing the stored procedures themselves. After you have the stored procedures, using them in server-side JavaScript applications is straightforward, provided that you follow the rules outlined in Chapter 9 of *Writing Server-Side JavaScript Applications*. Some of the rules for setting up the stored procedures and retrieving data from them change depending on the database server you're using, so make sure that you understand the requirements of your particular database server(s) before writing the code. Note that all our examples of stored procedures assume Informix as the database server.

Calling a Stored Procedure

To use any results from a stored procedure, you must first execute it. For stored procedures that return no data, this step is generally the only one required. Executing a stored procedure through SSJS is a simple process; all you need to know are the name of the stored procedure and the input parameters. The following code is all that is necessary to call the stored procedure `spGetEmployees` with parameters `departmentID` and `managerName`.

```
// dbconn is a valid connection object connected to an Informix database
departmentID = 7;
managerName = "JJ Kuslich";
spEmps = dbconn.storedProc("spGetEmployees", departmentID, managerName);
```

Note
Use the `storedProc` object for executing stored procedures that have return values or output parameters or that return result sets. For stored procedures that do not return any values (other than errors), use the `execute` method.

Note that data types matter when you pass parameters to the stored procedure. If you pass the string `"7"` instead of the number 7 for the `empID` value and if `empID` has an `Integer` data type in the stored procedure definition, you could receive an error from your database server reporting the data type mismatch. Some database servers forgive data type mismatches more than others. Informix gives an error message for mismatched data types; others might not care. In general, it's better to follow good programming practice and use the right data types. You should also pay attention to data types if there's a chance your application might need to switch database servers in the future or if you're accessing multiple database types in the same application.

Retrieving Data from a Stored Procedure

For stored procedures that return values during their execution, one or two more steps are necessary after you create the `storedProc` object to squeeze out all the information returned. There are three places you can look for returned values: return values, output parameters, and result sets.

The `resultSet` object is similar to the cursor object. Aside from the fact that result sets are read-only (that is, they aren't updateable), they behave exactly like cursors. You may think that the similarity makes them unusually boring because you already know everything about cursors; however, you'll probably find result sets very interesting if you consider the possibilities for writing routines that work for both cursors and result sets. Everyone knows that code reuse leads to shorter development cycles, lower costs, and happier programmers. After we describe exactly how result sets work, you'll see just how similar they are to cursors.

You create `resultSet` objects by calling the `resultSet` method of the `storedProc` object. For example, continuing with the preceding code snippet, suppose that the `spGetEmployees` stored procedure returns the names of every employee in the given department who works for a given manager. After creating the `storedProc` object, you could retrieve the results in a `resultSet` object with the following line of code:

```
rsEmployees = spGetEmps.resultSet();
```

After this statement is executed, any rows returned by the stored procedure will be stored in the `resultSet` object, `rsEmployees`. From this point on, you use the `resultSet` object in exactly the same way you would use a cursor:

- You use the `next` method to advance the `resultSet` object through the records.
- You must advance the `resultSet` object once to initialize it because, just after creation, it points to the position just before the first record in the set.
- When you reach the end of the set, `next` returns `false`.
- When you're finished with the `resultSet` object, you must call its `close` method and reclaim the resources it was using.

The `resultSet` object behaves exactly like a `cursor` object. The only real differences between the two are that they are created in different ways, and the `resultSet` object is read-only. You cannot assign values to any `resultSet` values. For example, the assignment statement `rsEmployees.empID = 7` would not assign the value 7 to the property `resultSet.empID`; instead, it would simply have no effect.

Depending on which database server you're using, you might find one more odd difference between `resultSet` objects and cursors. With Informix and DB2, you cannot refer to properties of the `resultSet` object by column name but instead must refer to them by their index. For these databases, the order of the returned columns matters, and it adds another potential source of bugs in your code that you must watch out for. Listing 5.11 illustrates the effects of this restriction. (With all other supported databases, you can use column names and ignore their order in the result set.)

Suppose that the stored procedure `spGetEmployees` returns a result set containing an employee's ID (`empID`), employee name (`empName`), and employee phone number (`empPhone`), in that order, for every employee in the given department who works for a given manager. If the procedure were written in Oracle, Microsoft SQL Server, or Sybase, you would use the code in Listing 5.11 to display the results.

Listing 5.11 *Working with stored procedures*

```
// Assume dbconn is a valid connection object created at some earlier stage
// Get all employees in department 7 who work for manager Joe Jackson
spGetEmp = dbconn.storedProc("spGetEmployees", 7, "Joe Jackson");
rsEmps = spGetEmp.resultSet();
while(rsEmps.next()) {
    write("ID: " + rsEmps.empID + "<BR>");
    write("Name: " + rsEmps.empName + "<BR>");
    write("Phone: " + rsEmps.empPhone + "<BR>");
}
rsEmps.close();
```

Suppose you want to perform exactly the same operation as in Listing 5.11 but for a stored procedure written for Informix. You would have to change the three boldface lines in the listing to the following:

```
write("ID: " + rsEmps[0] + "<BR>");
write("Name: " + rsEmps[1] + "<BR>");
write("Phone: " + rsEmps[2] + "<BR>");
```

We highly recommend that you create constants at the beginning of your code to represent the index values of the returned columns instead of

Databases 1

hard-coding each index. Using constants will make your code more readable by associating meaningful identifier names with meaningless column index numbers. Also, if a column ever changes positions because of a change in the stored procedure, you won't have to change every reference to that column if you refer to it through a constant. If you use constants instead, you need change the index value only once for the assignment of the index to the constant. Listing 5.12 shows how you can use constants to improve the code from the preceding snippet.

Listing 5.12 *Using constants for better maintainability*

```
// Create "constants" to represent column index values
var EMPID = 0;
var EMPNAME = 1;
var EMPPHONE = 2;
// dbconn is a valid connection object created at some earlier stage
// Get all employees in department 7 who work for manager Joe Jackson
spGetEmp = dbconn.storedProc("spGetEmployees", 7, "Joe Jackson");
rsEmps = spGetEmp.resultSet();

while(rsEmps.next()) {
    write("ID: " + rsEmps[EMPID] + "<BR>");
    write("Name: " + rsEmps[EMPNAME] + "<BR>");
    write("Phone: " + rsEmps[EMPPHONE] + "<BR>");
}
rsEmps.close();
```

Clearly, the code in this example is much more readable than the code that uses numbers to reference the columns. Were this a larger piece of code in which the return values were referred to several times, it should also be clear that if the positions of the columns were ever to change, it would be much more convenient and much less error-prone to simply replace the index values in the constants than to change the values at every reference point.

Note   JavaScript doesn't really have constants per se. We're applying the concept of constants to normal JavaScript identifiers. Using all capital letters visually differentiates our pseudo-constants from normal identifiers and lets us know that we should never change the value of those particular identifiers anywhere in the code other than where they are defined. It's not foolproof, but we've found that it works well as a way to introduce pseudo-constants into JavaScript.

Another limitation of LiveWire is that `resultSet` objects cannot be nested with some database servers; in other words, you cannot have more than one open at a time. So, for example, the code in Listing 5.13, which uses a nested `while` loop structure, would not work in LiveWire with Informix.

Listing 5.13 *Nested result set objects are not allowed*

```
// THIS CODE WILL NOT WORK WITH INFORMIX BECAUSE IT NESTS RESULTSET OBJECTS.
// Assume dbconn is a valid connection object created at some earlier stage
// Get all departments for the company Application Methods
spGetDept = dbconn.storedProc("spGetDepartments", "Application Methods Inc.");
rsDept = spGetDept.resultSet();

// Loop through all departments and display employee information for each
while(rsDept.next()) {
   // Get all employees in the particular department
   spGetEmp = dbconn.storedProc("spGetEmployees", rsDept.deptID);
   rsEmps = spGetEmp.resultSet();

   // Loop through and write out employee information
   while(rsEmps.next()) {
       write("ID: " + rsEmps.empID + "<BR>");
       write("Name: " + rsEmps.empName + "<BR>");
       write("Phone: " + rsEmps.empPhone + "<BR>");
   } // end inner while loop
   rsEmps.close();
} // end outer while loop
rsDept.close();
```

To work around this limitation, you could preload the data from the inner loop into an array structure and then loop through the array in the inner loop instead of the `resultSet` object. To be more efficient about it, you could better handle the case by simply using a different stored procedure that performs a join on the `Employee` and `Department` tables and returns a single result set that contains all the employees for a given department. In general, you should look for this type of workaround rather than try to implement a potentially inefficient kludge in server-side JavaScript.

Creating Tables

Now that we've shown you most of the specific tasks you can accomplish with the data in your database, we finish by stating that you can actually execute from SSJS any valid SQL, stored procedure, or other statement that your database server will accept. The `execute` method of the `connection` object allows you to pass through not only SQL statements but also other commands (including data definition language (DDL) statements) that allow you to create, alter, and drop tables.

Creating a table is a matter of passing through the proper DDL statements that your database server will accept. Listing 5.14 shows an example of how to create a table called `Contacts` from SSJS in a Microsoft Access 97 database. Assume that the variable `dbConn` is an instance of a database connection from a previously connected `DbPool`. You can try this query yourself,

provided that you first connect to a Microsoft Access 97 database through a
properly configured ODBC DSN. Make sure that you do not already have a
table named Contacts in your database. Also, keep in mind that if you try
this in another type of database, such as Oracle or Informix, you might have
problems because DDL syntax can be database-specific.

Listing 5.14 *Creating a new table from SSJS*

```
var ddl = "";
ddl += "CREATE TABLE Contacts ( ";
ddl += "CustomerID  INT          NOT NULL, ";
ddl += "Name         VARCHAR(55) NOT NULL, ";
ddl += "Phone        VARCHAR(18) )";
dbConn.execute(ddl);
```

Summary

Connecting to a database requires that you first create a pool of connections
through the DbPool object and then pull connections from the pool as they
are needed. After a connection object becomes available, you can retrieve
results through the use of cursors or stored procedures. You can update
databases uniformly using cursors, although there are limitations that may
require you to perform updates using pass-through SQL or more-efficient
stored procedures. You can use the execute statement to execute almost
any valid SQL or other statement that your database server recognizes,
although you cannot access any results that the operation may return. You
can even execute DDL statements and create tables on-the-fly. As we move
to advanced database topics, we build on the knowledge gained here to look
at broader database application design issues. If you missed anything in this
chapter along the way, don't be afraid to flip back and forth between chapters to fill in the gaps.

6

Advanced Database Application Techniques

In this chapter, we discuss advanced techniques you can use to build complex, real-world applications. Although we focus primarily on database applications, we also discuss several generic techniques. You should have no problems applying these generic techniques to other situations.

Application Design Strategies

Chapter 5 includes a significant discussion of the mechanics of interacting with databases through SSJS. Although understanding the database API is a must, the success of your database applications depends more on how you design them in the first place. As with building a house, if the blueprints (the designs) are flawed, no amount of raw materials (application code) will save you. In this section, we discuss the fundamentals of designing good database applications with SSJS.

Design Strategies with DbPools

The previous version of LiveWire provided only one way to connect to databases: through the `database` object. The `database` object was somewhat restrictive, allowing only one data source to be open at a time and never allowing connections to span requests. The new version of the LiveWire Database service includes a more powerful object, DbPool, for creating and maintaining pools of database connections that can coexist. There are a number of advantages to using the DbPool object, including improved performance. However, the real power of database pools comes from the ability they give you to address additional design problems, or scenarios, in your applications.

There are a few common strategies for connecting to databases using DbPool objects. Before you start to write a LiveWire application, you should think about how your users will access the application, what level of access they'll require, and how you will deal with other general security and data access issues. After you've outlined these scenarios, you can apply any of the strategies discussed here. Each strategy was derived from real-world approaches to design scenarios similar to ones you're likely to face. Table 6.1 maps design problems to recommended connection strategies. Don't forget that the real world often throws more than one scenario at you, so it's perfectly valid to use a combination of strategies to solve the problem at hand. We hope that these strategies will give you a good basis for creating good connection and database access designs for your applications.

Single Global Pool

This "one connection fits all" strategy uses a single DbPool object, usually created on the application's initial page, to service all database requests. After you create it, you make the DbPool object persistent by storing it in the project or the server object. Unlike earlier versions of server-side

Table 6.1 *Design problems and strategies*

Scenario	Strategy
■ You need a connection to a single data source, and all application users have the same level of access.	One global pool per application
■ You need to connect to more than one data source in the application. ■ Well-defined groups of users (for example, Marketing, Engineering) require different levels of access to the data. ■ Only a handful of users need connections.	Fixed set of global pools per application
■ Database access is rare and occurs only on a few pages in the application	One local pool per page

JavaScript, Enterprise Server 3.0 allows you to store objects in the `project` and `server` objects.

Use this strategy if your application connects only to a single data source and does not require different levels of user permissions. This strategy requires only one user account and set of permissions on the database server. Many Web applications do not use database server security for authenticating individual users of the application; instead, they use a custom solution or an LDAP server for user authentication. After being authenticated, all valid users have the same level of access to the data. Still other applications do not care who the users might be and don't have any user authentication process; the users are anonymous. In that case, you would create one generic account on the database server and use that account when creating the pool of connections.

Fixed Set of Global Pools

Some applications require more control over database access than the preceding scheme allows. Consider the common scenario of an application that has a few groups of users defined. For example, all Marketing users have the same set of rights over the data, but, as a group, Marketing has different permissions than Engineering has. Engineering may have only read-only access to customer data, whereas Marketing has read and write access to the same data. You could use server-side JavaScript to design a custom access-control scheme that implements the data access rights, but it's more common for such rules to be set at the database server level. This approach protects the data from any application that might try to access the data and not just a single application that has implemented the rules. It also eliminates the need to reimplement the rules in every application or to upgrade every application as the rules change.

There are two common ways to employ user groups for database access. The simplest way is to give all the users in a particular group, such as Human Resources, the username and password for the group account on the database server and use that account to validate users.

Another way is to set up a separate list of usernames and passwords for every individual user of the system and associate each individual user account with a group account on the database server. An individual user logs in with his or her own username and password, the application validates the user account, and, if successful, it then secretly logs in the user database server using the database server's group username and password. This second strategy is certainly more secure because average system users would never know the real username and password that access the database server. If such security is not necessary, simply giving the group username and password to each user in a group may be sufficient.

Table 6.2 *Database server accounts*

Username	Password	Group
loginOnly	pass000	Login
mktg	pass123	Marketing
engr	pass456	Engineering
ship	pass789	Shipping

We illustrate here how to implement the second strategy. In this scenario, we've created four database pools on the initial page of the application. Three pools are related to each account on the database server that represents the user groups: Marketing, Engineering, and Shipping. A fourth account has special privileges related to user validation, which are described later. Table 6.2 shows what the database accounts might look like and which groups they're associated with.

The connection pools are stored in an array in the **project** object and are referenced throughout the application to access data. The code in Listing 6.1 is used on the initial page to create the pools and store them in the **project** object, indexed in an array simply by their group name.

Listing 6.1 *Application initial page*

```
// Create an array of DbPool objects for use throughout the application.
project.poolArray = new Array();
project.poolArray["Marketing"] = new DbPool("INFORMIX", "ol_informix", "mktg", "pass123",
"applicationDB", 10);
project.poolArray["Engineering"] = new DbPool("INFORMIX", "ol_informix", "engr", "pass456",
"applicationDB", 20);
project.poolArray["Shipping"] = new DbPool("INFORMIX", "ol_informix", "ship", "pass789",
"applicationDB", 3);

// Create one pool for conducting user logins.
// This user account has only SELECT rights on tblUser.
project.poolArray["Login"] = new DbPool("INFORMIX", "ol_informix",
"loginOnly", "pass000", "applicationDB", 1);
```

The fourth pool belongs to a special user account on the database server that is used only for logging individual users in to the system. The account used with this pool has specific user rights on the database server, which allow it to execute only SQL SELECT statements (read-only) on a single table, tblUser. To be even more security-conscious, you could put the SQL

Table 6.3 *Data in* `tblUser`

Username	Password	Group
SallyR	sal1	Marketing
JoeB	joe2	Engineering
DaleS	dale1	Shipping

query that will look up usernames and passwords into a stored procedure and give the special login account only the rights to execute that one stored procedure. In this way, the LiveWire application calls the stored procedure and has no direct access to the tables until a user is validated. Table 6.3 contains a list of usernames and passwords for each of the individual users of the system along with the name of the group (for example, Marketing) to which each user belongs.

When individual users log in, the application looks in `tblUser` to find a matching username and password. If one is found, the application uses the associated group name to find the pool in the array of `DbPool` objects that has the matching connection and privileges for that user.

Listing 6.2 shows how the login process works. It uses two pages: `loginform.html` and `loginhandler.html`. The page `loginform.html` contains an HTML form that lets a user log in to the system. When the user clicks the **Submit** button, the username and password are passed to `loginhandler.html`, which conducts the login process. Using the configuration described, the `loginhandler.html` page uses the code in Listing 6.2 to perform user validation.

Listing 6.2 `loginhandler.html`

```
// Validate users using the "secret" account on the database server.
// Get a connection from that pool.
loginConn = project.poolArray["Login"].connection();

// Create a cursor on tblUser using the username and
// password entered by the user from loginform.html.
// If the username and password are valid, the cursor
// should contain one row. If either one is invalid,
// the cursor will contain no rows, indicating a failed
// login attempt.
var sql = "SELECT group FROM tblUser WHERE username='" +
          request.username +
          "' AND password='" +
          request.password + "'";
loginCursor = loginConn.cursor(sql);
```

Listing 6.2 `loginhandler.html` *(Continued)*

```
// If no record was found, the login was invalid so redirect to an error page.
// Otherwise, redirect to the application's main menu page.
if (!loginCursor.next())
   redirectPage = "Error.html";
else {
   // Assign group name to client property
   client.group = loginCursor.group;
   redirectPage = "MainAppForm.html";
}

// Clean up database connections
loginCursor.close();
loginConn.release();
loginPool.disconnect();

// Redirect based upon login attempt.
redirect(redirectPage);
```

The application then stores the group name retrieved from the secret login process in a property of the `client` object and uses it on any subsequent pages in the application as an index to find the appropriate connection pool in the `project` object. For example, for any given page in the application, grabbing a connection for previously validated Marketing user `SallyR` would set `client.group = "Marketing"`. The code would grab a connection from the database pool, as shown in Listing 6.3.

Listing 6.3 *Retrieving a database connection*

```
// Grab a connection to the database
pageConn = project.poolArray[client.group].connection();
custCursor = pageConn.cursor("select * from tblCustomers");

// … do things with the cursor
custCursor.close();
pageConn.release();
```

You could also employ the connection grouping strategy for applications that talk to multiple database servers, possibly even servers of different types (for example, Informix, Oracle, and so on). In such a scenario, you could establish one pool of connections for each database server, or you could choose to have groups of connections for each different database server. In either case, you could also employ a variation of the connection grouping strategy to support the multiple database server scenario.

One Local Connection per Page

Some applications might call for using a separate connection pool either for every user or for every page of the application. Perhaps each user of your system requires slightly different access rights on the database server, so you must make sure that each page of the application uses the account associated with the current user. Perhaps the application rarely accesses the database and, even then, only on a few pages. Rather than open a pool on the initial page and keep it open for the entire application, you can create a pool only on the pages that require a database connection.

For these scenarios, you create and disconnect the connection pool on every page that requires database access. The Netscape SSJS manual, *Writing Server-Side JavaScript Applications*, describes how to implement this scenario, so we don't rehash that material here. Listing 6.2, presented earlier, also uses this strategy in part to perform the secret login. Suffice it to say that implementing this strategy is fairly simple, although it's also the least efficient strategy in terms of performance. Repeating the creation of a connection pool every time a user enters a page requiring database access can be expensive. For this reason, you should avoid this strategy for heavily accessed pages when possible.

Connection Strategy Summary

These three connection strategies cover a number of scenarios you may come across when you design Web database applications. Don't forget that they can be applied in combination—and even with slight modifications—to cover other scenarios. For example, in the single global connection scenario, you need not create the pool on the initial page; you could create it on some other page in the application. Just be careful in such a case that you apply locking properly to avoid deadlock situations when multiple users try to access the same page simultaneously. When connecting on the initial page, you need not worry about locking because the initial page is fired only upon application or Web server initialization.

Data Security

Before we move on, we should point out one aspect of designing database applications that you must consider when building SSJS database applications. Data passed from the database through the SSJS engine and onto the browser is all passed in cleartext, which is to say that it is unencrypted. By default, any sensitive data in your databases that you pass to a browser will be sent over the wire unencrypted, and someone with sophisticated tools may be able to intercept and read the data. For some applications, such as an application that transmits private financial information, your design plans should include a plan for encrypting data before presenting it to the user in addition to validating user identity and privileges. Rather than write your own encryption routines or purchase expensive software, you can use standard Web security in the form of Secure Sockets Layer (SSL).

SSL is a standard protocol for encrypting data transmitted between browser and Web server. Most major browsers support it, as does Netscape Enterprise Server, even with SSJS applications. SSL is fairly simple to configure on the server end and requires no special configuration on the client end. However, because the URL for SSL pages differs from that of unencrypted pages (you must preface SSL pages with `https://` instead of `http://`), you'll need to consider SSL in your plans when constructing your site layout and when referring to other pages in your application. Refer to the Netscape Enterprise Server documentation for more information on configuring SSL on your Web server.

Advanced Implementation Techniques

We sneak in talk about good design practices throughout the book, but let's face the fact that if we don't write some code every once in a while, we'll all go crazy. Now it's time to look at some advanced implementation techniques.

Performing Database Operations Across Requests

To this point, all our database discussions have involved database operations performed on a single page, with the assumption that you should close database cursors, result sets, and connections at the end of each page. In general, this is exactly how you should write your database applications. However, in some situations you'll want to keep a connection or even a database transaction open across multiple pages so that you can perform lengthy database operations without having to open and close connections repeatedly. In this section, we show you how you can keep connections, cursors, and transactions open across multiple pages in an SSJS application.

Note   For release 3.x of Netscape Enterprise Server, you cannot keep connections or transactions open across requests if you use Informix as your database server. You must explicitly close all `cursor` and `resultSet` objects and release all `connection` objects at the end of each page.

In Chapter 5 we present a simple human resources application for a fictitious ice cream truck manufacturer, Hibb and Dringle Enterprises. The application consists of a page that generates a list of employees in any one department from the database. Suppose that each department in the company contains hundreds of employees. In this case, the list of employees on each page will be much larger than any user will want to sift through. You can try to solve the problem by providing comprehensive search tools that allow users to conduct specific searches. This is a good idea, but it may not solve the problem entirely. You could also solve the problem by showing only a few records at a time and allowing a user to navigate the list, much as Internet search engines allow you to navigate the results of a search. One way to implement such a solution is through the use of Web cursors.

First, we should offer some words of caution regarding Web cursors and Web transactions. Unlike traditional client/server applications, Web applications are usually nonlinear; a user can jump to any page in an application at any time, either by an explicit hyperlink or through saved bookmarks. Additionally, a user can leave an application simply by closing the browser, possibly leaving the application in an uncertain state. For these reasons, keeping connections, cursors, and transactions open can be risky in an environment where, almost by definition, users have short attention spans and are "trained" to jump on the first link that interests them. If a user leaves your application unexpectedly in the middle of a database transaction that spans several pages, it could leave the data in an uncertain state and needlessly keep a database connection open. Therefore, we advise you to avoid using Web cursors except when absolutely necessary.

Web Cursors

Web cursors are cursors that span more than one page or, more accurately, more than one page *request*. The SSJS database API allows you to create Web cursors so that you can maintain the cursor position and state across more than one request. If you can keep a cursor open for more than one request, you can navigate the cursor with each request and the current position will be remembered until it is closed.

Maintaining state information on a database cursor is no different from maintaining any other kind of state information. You must use the appropriate state maintenance objects that are built into SSJS, as explained in Chapter 3. Because each client navigates his or her own copy of the cursor, we should store the cursor in the `client` object. However, recall from Chapter 3 that the `client` object can hold only string values. We must use the `SuperClient` object we developed in that chapter because it can store and manage objects on a per-client basis. Using `SuperClient`, let's look at adding navigation capability to the employee list page of the Hibb and Dringle application (see Listing 5.6). We modify the listing in three ways to give users the ability to navigate the employee list 10 records at a time.

1. Store the `connection` and `cursor` objects in the `SuperClient` object.
2. Add code to display only 10 records at a time.
3. Add a link to advance the cursor to the next 10 records.

Listing 6.4 shows the Employee List page from Listing 5.6 with the required modifications highlighted in bold. First, we add code to retrieve our database connection and cursor from `SuperClient` instead of always generating them from scratch each time the page is accessed. In this way, the connection and cursor are saved and available for use across multiple pages. If the connection and cursor are not yet set in `SuperClient`—for example, if this is the first time a user opens the page—then we generate them. Next, we write the records as usual and dynamically generate (or not) a link at the bottom of the page that allows the user to view more records depending on whether there are more records left to view. This link refers to the same page and passes a parameter in the query string called `more` with a value of on. You can see that throughout the page, we check this value several times to see whether this is our first time on the page or whether we're in the middle of a sequence of records. Figure 6.1 shows what the modified page looks like in a browser.

Listing 6.4 *Modified Employee List page*

```
<HTML>
<HEAD><TITLE>Employee List</TITLE></HEAD>
<BODY BGCOLOR="FFFFE0">
<SERVER>
//Initialize a constant for the page
var MAXRECORDS = 2;

// Initialize local page variables
var listConn = null;
var empCursor = null;
var msg = "";
var noemp = false;
var moreRecords = false;
var sc = project.SuperClientCollection.getSuperClient();

// If this is the first page, reset the cursor
if (request.more != "on")
  sc.deleteProperty("empCursor");

// Initialize local variables
listConn = sc.getProperty("listConn");
empCursor = sc.getProperty("empCursor");
// If the connection is null, report an error
if (listConn == null) {
   msg = escape("Error: Unable to connect to the database.");
   redirect("Results.html?msg=" + escape(msg));
}
//Construct a new cursor if one isn't found in the SuperClient
if (empCursor == null) {

   // Construct the cursor
   var sql = "SELECT e.EmpID, e.Name, e.Title, e.Phone, d.Name AS DeptName " +
      " FROM Employee e, Department d WHERE d.DepartmentID=e.DeptID";
```

Listing 6.4 *Modified Employee List page (Continued)*

```
    if (request.DepartmentID != null)
       sql += " AND d.DepartmentID=" + request.DepartmentID;

    if (request.orderby != null)
       sql += " ORDER BY " + request.orderby;

    empCursor = listConn.cursor(sql);
    sc.setProperty("empCursor", empCursor, "cursor");
}

// Generate the HTML table that displays employee information
write("<TABLE BORDER=0 CELLSPACING=2 CELLPADDING=3>");

// If we're on the first page, check for an empty cursor
// and advance to the first record in the cursor
if (request.more != "on")
  if(!empCursor.next())
         noemp = true;

// If the cursor is empty, report that no records were found
// Else, write out the first set of employee records
if (noemp)
    write("<TR><TH>No employees found.</TD></TR>");
else {
    // Write out a table caption such as:
    // Employees of the Accounting department.
    write("<CAPTION>Employees of the " + empCursor.DeptName +
    " department</CAPTION>");

    // Hyperlink each column header back to this page
    // Include the orderby parameter in the query string.
    write("<TR BGCOLOR=\"#DDAA44\">");
    write("<TH>" + "Name".link("WCListPage.html?DepartmentID=" +
request.DepartmentID + "&orderby=name") + "</TH>");
    write("<TH>" + "Title".link("WCListPage?DepartmentID=" +
request.DepartmentID + "&orderby=title") + "</TH>");
    write("<TH>Phone</TH>");
    write("</TR>");
    // Write out each row in the table.  Use a do/while loop
    // because we've already advanced the cursor to the first row.
    var count = 0;

    do {
        write("<TR BGCOLOR=\"#DDCCAA\">");
        // Link the employee name to the Update Form.  Pass the
        // primary key of the Employee table, EmpID, so Update Form knows
        // which employee needs to be updated.
        var url = "updateform.html?empID=" + empCursor.EmpID;
        write("<TD>" + empCursor.Name.link(url) + "</TD>");
        write("<TD>" + empCursor.Title + "</TD>");
        write("<TD>" + empCursor.Phone + "</TD>");
```

Listing 6.4 *Modified Employee List page (Continued)*

```
     write("</TR>");
     count++;  // Only write out 10 records per page
  } while((moreRecords = empCursor.next()) && count < MAXRECORDS)
} // end else
write("</TABLE>");

//If there are more records, generate a link to let the user move on
if (moreRecords)
     write('<a href="WCListPage.html?more=on">More Employees</a><br>');

// DO NOT clean up the cursor and connections - leave them open
// empCursor.close();
// listConn.release();
</SERVER>
</BODY>
</HTML>
```

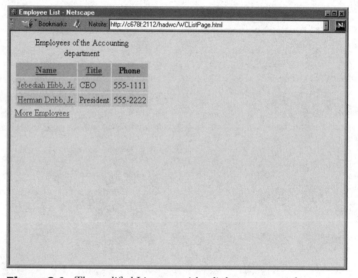

Figure 6.1 *The modified List page with a link to more records*

You may have spotted a problem with this example. We had to comment out the calls to close the cursor and release the connection because we need to keep them open as long as the user is moving forward and backward in the record set. However, we must close them at some point; we don't want to leave connections open indefinitely or occupy server memory needlessly by maintaining an open cursor. How do we know when to close them? You cannot rely on providing a "log off" feature for Internet sites or even an intranet application. With Web applications, there is no way to guarantee a linear process. Instead, we must rely on mechanisms, such as timers, and cleanup functions, such as the ones we built into the `SuperClientCollection` object in Chapter 3.

The `SuperClientCollection` object periodically cleans up old `Super Client` objects that have expired for the same reasons we must clean up Web cursors. Thus, by reusing the `SuperClient` object, we're halfway home to a solution for supporting Web cursors. To implement the cleanup functionality, we modify those methods to make sure that before they delete the connection and cursor properties, they first close the cursor and release the connection. Listing 6.5 shows the modified `SuperClient` object, and Listing 6.6 shows the modified `SuperClientCollection` object, with changes highlighted in bold. The new requirements force us to create a new object, called `Property`, and store it in the `SuperClient` object's properties array instead of simply storing the value because we must now store both a value and a property type to tell us what kind of value we're storing. We also modify `deleteSuperClient` of the `SuperClientCollection` object to take care of the new database cleanup operations before it deletes a `SuperClient` object from the collection.

In `setProperty` we add a type parameter so that we can identify those properties that are connections and cursors. We used this new parameter in Listing 6.4 earlier. Note that we now store the simple JavaScript object called `Property`, also shown in Listing 6.4, which holds two properties: `type` and `value`. Then we modify `deleteSuperClient` to first close any `cursor` or `resultSet` objects and release any `connection` objects that were properties of the `SuperClient` the method is deleting. We must loop through the `SuperClient` properties two times to find any properties of type `"cursor"`, `"resultSet"`, or `"connection"`. We must loop through the first time to close the `cursor` and `resultSet` objects. We must loop through a second time to close the `connection` objects. We must use a separate loop to ensure that we don't release any `connection` objects before we close all their `cursor` and `resultSet` objects. Attempting to close a cursor or `resultSet` on a released connection could generate an error.

Listing 6.5 *Modified portions of the* `SuperClient` *object*

```
function Property(value, type) {
    this.value = value;
    this.type = type;
} // End Constructor for Property object

function _sc_setProperty(name, value, type) {
    this.touch();
    this.properties[name] = new Property(value, type);
} // end _sc_setProperty
```

Listing 6.5 *Modified portions of the* SuperClient *object (Continued)*

```
function _sc_deleteProperty(name) {
        this.touch();
        if (this.properties[name]) {
            // If the property is a database object, close it.
            if (this.properties[name].type == "cursor" ||
                this.properties[name].type == "resultSet")
                this.properties[name].value.close();
            if (this.properties[name].type == "connection")
                this.properties[name].value.release();
            delete this.properties[name];
        } // end _sc_deleteProperty
```

Listing 6.6 *Modified* SuperClientCollection *method* deleteSuperClient

```
function _scc_deleteSuperClient(id) {
    if (this.elements[id]) {
    // Get a lock so that no others can access the collection
    // at the same time we're trying to delete an element.
    project.SuperClientCollectionLock.lock();
        for (var prop in this.elements[id].properties) {
            if (this.elements[id].properties[prop].type = "cursor" ||
                this.elements[id].properties[prop].type = "resultSet")
                this.elements[id].properties[prop].value.close();
        }
        for (var conprop in this.elements[id].properties) {
            if (this.elements[id].properties[conprop].type = "connection")
                this.elements[id].properties[prop].value.release();
        }
delete this.elements[id];
// If we just deleted the current client's SuperClient,
// then reset the pointer to it, client.__SuperClientID, to null.
if (id == client.__SuperClientID)
    delete client.__SuperClientID;
    //client.__SuperClientID = null;
    project.SuperClientCollectionLock.unlock();
    }
} // end  _scc_deleteSuperClient
```

Perfect, right? Well, not quite—one final problem remains. Let's analyze what we have so far and track down the final problem as if we were critiquing this in a design review. We've already told you there's a problem, but let's imagine that you're in a design review and you have a gut feeling that something is wrong.

Here's what we know so far.

- The page is no longer closing cursors or releasing connections; this allows users to navigate the record set *n* records at a time.

- We have modified the SuperClient object to close the Web cursor and connection when the SuperClient's cleanup timer expires.

- Imagine that we've set the cleanup timer for 10 minutes. This means that the user has 10 minutes of inactivity before the SuperClient closes the database connection. Whenever a user makes a new request to the page, the timer is reset for another 10 minutes. If the user leaves the terminal inactive for more than 10 minutes, the connection will be closed whether or not the user is in the middle of browsing the record set.

- If the connection is automatically closed by the SuperClient after the timer expires, what happens if the user comes back to the browser after 10 minutes and tries to start browsing again? The connection will be gone when the user makes a database request against a closed connection, and the application will return a confusing error message saying that the database connection has been lost.

To protect against these kinds of problems, Web cursors require extra checks that normal single-page cursors do not require. Fortunately, in the case of our Hibb & Dringle application, we need only modify the portion of the code that handles the connections at the start of the page to make sure that the connection in SuperClient is still valid before attempting to use it. This may have seemed obvious from the beginning, but we wanted to go through a detailed thought process to enforce the point that Web cursors, although useful, require extra validation checks and overhead code. To put it plainly, they can be helpful in certain situations, but they can also be a pain in the neck and may not save you as much time as you think. If you don't plan carefully from the beginning how and where you'll use them, you may wind up wasting the time they propose to save you in debugging limbo.

The modified listing is shown in Listing 6.7. Essentially, all we need to do is to check first to see whether we have a valid connection and cursor already stored in SuperClient. If we do, we don't want to create new ones. If we don't, we retrieve a new connection and cursor from scratch, assuming that this is the user's first visit to the page or the first visit since the last SuperClient object timed out. Modified or added lines are highlighted in bold.

Listing 6.7 *Modified Employee List page*

```
// Initialize local page variables
listConn = sc.getProperty("listConn");
empCursor = sc.getProperty("empCursor");
//Grab a connection to the database from the global pool
if (listConn == null) {
   listConn = project.appPool.connection("ListPage", 10) ;
   sc.setProperty("listConn", listConn, "connection") ;
}
```

Listing 6.7 *Modified Employee List page (Continued)*

```
//If it's still null, report an error
if (listConn == null) {
   msg = escape("Error: Unable to connect to the database.");
   redirect("Results.html?msg=" + escape(msg));
}
…<the rest of the code remains as-is>…
```

If you're thinking that all the management code required to use Web cursors looks like a workaround, you're right. There is no perfect way to clean up database connections using a timer in a manner that both guarantees efficiency and frees connections quickly. If you set the cleanup timer too short, your users' sessions will time out if they leave their computer for too long. If you set it for too long, you keep more connections open, leaving fewer for other application users. Because you cannot guarantee when your connections and cursors will be cleaned up, generally you should use Web cursors only under the following conditions.

- You have a light user load or adequate database connection licenses to support larger numbers of simultaneous users.
- You need Web cursors only for a small portion of your overall application.

Summary

Web cursors can help you build complex interactions across several pages. You can keep connections open longer than one page if you need to, but it requires that you write additional code to manage the connections. Because Web applications are nonlinear, managing open connections and cursors can be tricky.

When you design database applications for the SSJS platform, there are many considerations, including the allocation of database connections as well as performance and maintainability concerns. Knowing how to use the objects in the SSJS database API doesn't guarantee that you'll be able to build the most efficient or stable application. A good design will take you further than fancy code any day of the week and twice on Sunday.

File System Access

Although most SSJS applications access databases, you'll occasionally find that you need to interact with the local file system. You may wish to avoid using a database and instead store data in files, or you may want to update data in existing files. You may also want to enable users to upload files (such as resumes, images, and HTML documents). In this chapter we show you how to manipulate files on the server using SSJS. Unlike most SSJS books, this one doesn't tread lightly here. We address the things you'll want to do most with files.

We show you how to manipulate files on the server so that you can read from and write to them. We also show you how to upload files from the client to your server. This means that you can create job-listing applications and your users can upload their resumes in any format they like. We even use LiveConnect to show you how to delete files on the server, get directory listings, and so forth. Figure 7.1 shows the sample application included on the CD-ROM.

The SSJS `File` Object

The `File` object in SSJS gives you the ability to manipulate files on the server. The object provides the basic functionality of reading from and writing to files, but little else. (It's simply a thin layer on top of the C runtime library buffered I/O routines.) Fortunately, the `File` object can be extended to provide additional functionality (such as deleting files and getting directory listings), as you will see later in this chapter.

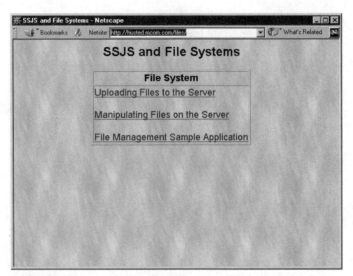

Figure 7.1 *Sample application*

For now, let's talk briefly about the syntax required to use the `File` object. Then we'll talk about the properties and methods associated with it.

The syntax required for implementing and using the `File` object is simple: create a new instance of the `File` object.

```
var myFile = new File("/full_path/filename.ext");
```

Here `"full_path"` is the fully qualified path to the file on the server (and *not* a URL); remember to include drive letters on Win32-based machines (`"c:/full_path/filename.ext"`). If you create the `File` object without any path information, it is generally created in `<server-root>/config`. The `File` object can be used only on the server; you cannot read or manipulate files on a client machine using this object. An SSJS application can read or write files anywhere the operating system allows. This means that you could overwrite sensitive system files or corrupt configuration files, so exercise caution when accessing the server's file system.

Table 7.1 shows all the methods associated with the `File` object. These methods enable you to manipulate files on the server's file system (read, write, append, and so on). Unfortunately, they do not allow you to get a directory listing, create directories, or delete files; later in the chapter we show you how to do these things using LiveConnect and Java.

Table 7.1 File *object methods*

Method	Description
byteToString(num)	Static method converts num (0–255) to its ASCII equivalent.
clearError()	Clears the error code and clears the value of eof().
close()	Closes the file.
eof()	Returns true if the file pointer is at the end of the file; otherwise, it returns false.
error()	Returns a number representing the error status, or –1 if the file is not open or cannot be opened, or 0 if there is no error. The error status codes returned by error() are platform-specific.
exists()	Returns true if the file exists or returns false if it does not.
flush()	Writes the buffer to the file on disk.
getLength()	Returns the number of bytes in the file. On Windows systems, this method returns the number of *characters* in a text file or the number of *bytes* in a binary file. On UNIX systems, binary and text files are the same, so the number returned represents the number of bytes in the file.
getPosition()	Returns the current position of the file pointer.
open(mode)	Opens the file in the specified mode (r,w,a,+,b). See Table 7.2 for details.
read(num)	Reads num bytes from the file and returns a string value.
readByte()	Reads a single byte from your file and returns the numeric value of the byte (0–255) or –1 if an error occurs.
readln()	Reads from the current position of the file pointer to the next line-separator character and returns a string.
setPosition()	Sets the current position of the file pointer.
stringToByte(str)	Static method returns a number (the ASCII equivalent [0–255]) corresponding to the first character in str.

Files

Table 7.1 File *object methods (Continued)*

Method	Description
write(str)	Writes str to the file, starting at the current position of the file pointer.
writeln(str)	Writes str to the file, starting at the current position of the file pointer, and writes a trailing linefeed/carriage-return character.
writeByte(num)	Writes a single byte to the file.

Creating a File Object

Following is the syntax for creating a File object.

```
var myFile = new File("path/filename.ext");
```

Before you can access a file, you must use the file constructor to create a new File. Calling "new File(path)" returns a File object that points to the file specified by path (where path is the full pathname and filename of the file you want to access). "C:/myPath/myFile.ext" and "C:\\myPath\\myFile.ext" work equally well on Win32, but you must always use forward slashes on UNIX: "/myPath/myFile.ext". (Note that you must use two consecutive backslash characters on Win32 systems because \ is the escape character in JavaScript.) The examples in this chapter generally follow the Win32 style for filenames (drive:\directorypath\filename.ext) because most readers will not be fortunate enough to develop their applications on robust and reliable UNIX systems.

Listing 7.1 is an example of creating a new File object.

Listing 7.1 *Creating a new* File *object*

```
var myFile = new File("c:\temp\ssjsFiles\data.txt");
```

When you use the syntax shown in Listing 7.1, the value returned is a new File object that points to the file you specified. To display the filename assigned to the new File object, you use it in a write statement, as shown in Listing 7.2.

Listing 7.2 *Displaying the name of the file*

```
write("The filename is: " + myFile);
```

In Listing 7.2, the filename would be displayed like this:

```
The filename is c:\temp\ssjsFiles\data.txt
```

Now that you have created a new File object, you can manipulate the file using any of the methods shown earlier in Table 7.1.

Opening and Closing a File

Following is the syntax for opening and closing a file.

```
if (myFile.open(mode)) { . . . }
myFile.close();
```

After creating a File object, you use the open() method to open the file so that you can read from it or write to it. The open() method returns true if the file was opened successfully. Listing 7.3 shows the syntax for the open() method. The string "mode" should be one of the modes by which a file can be opened, as shown in Table 7.2.

Listing 7.3 *Opening a file*

```
myFile.open(mode);
```

Table 7.2 *Modes by which a file can be opened*

Mode	Description	Returns False If...
r	Opens the file for reading (file pointer is positioned at beginning of file).	The file does not exist or is unreadable.
w	Creates an empty file (overwrites any existing files).	SSJS cannot write to the specified directory.
a	Opens an existing file for writing. The file pointer is positioned at the end of the file, and the file is created if it does not already exist.	SSJS cannot write to the existing file or cannot write to the specified directory.

Files

Table 7.2 *Modes by which a file can be opened (Continued)*

Mode	Description	Returns False If...
r+	Opens the file for reading and writing (the file pointer is positioned at the beginning of the file).	The file does not exist or is not readable.
w+	Creates an empty file for reading and writing (overwrites any existing file).	SSJS cannot write to the specified directory.
a+	Opens the file for reading and writing (the file pointer is positioned at the end of the file).	SSJS cannot write to the existing file or cannot write to the specified directory.
b	Windows only: opens the file as a binary file. (Can be used with any of the previous six modes.)	N/A

So to open an existing file so that you can read from it, write to it, and position the file pointer at the end of the file, you would use code similar to that shown in Listing 7.4.

Listing 7.4 *Opening a file in read/write mode*

```
if(myFile.open("a+")) . . .
```

When you are finished with the file, you can close it using the `close()` method as shown in Listing 7.5. This method returns `true` if the file was previously open and has successfully been closed. If you forget to close a file, SSJS will flush any open buffers and close that file when your SSJS page is completely executed and returned to the requesting client. However, it's always best to explicitly close the file yourself.

Listing 7.5 *Closing a file*

```
if(myFile.close()) . . .
```

Reading from a File

Following is the syntax for reading from a file.

```
var myData = myFile.readByte();
var myData = myFile.read(numBytes);
var myData = myFile.readln();
```

The two most common uses of a file are to read and to write data. The SSJS File object has three methods for reading data from a file, and that gives you flexibility in how you retrieve data. The readByte() method lets you read a single byte from the file. This is useful if you don't know the format of the file or if you want to access the file one byte at a time (see Listing 7.6). This method returns the numeric value of the byte (0–255) or returns –1 if an error occurs.

Listing 7.6 *Reading and displaying a file one byte at a time*

```
while (!eof()) {
    var aSingleByte = myFile.readByte();
    if (aSingleByte != -1) {
        write(File.byteToString(aSingleByte));
    }
{
```

Note that in Listing 7.6 we use the static byteToString() method of the File object. We explain this method later in the chapter. For now, it suffices to say that the method converts a byte (a number from 0 to 255) into its ASCII character equivalent.

If your data is stored in fixed-length records (for example, 20 characters for the last name, 20 characters for the first name, and 10 characters for an identification number), you can either read the entire record at once or read each part of the record using the read(numBytes) method, where numBytes is the number of bytes you want to read. Listing 7.7 shows you how you would read each value from the file. The read() method reads the specified number of bytes from the file and returns a string value. If the number of bytes requested exceeds the number of bytes left in the file, the number of bytes left in the file is returned and the file pointer is positioned at the end of the file.

Listing 7.7 *Reading fixed-length records in a file*

```
var lastName = myFile.read(20);
var firstName = myFile.read(20);
var idNum = myFile.read(10);
```

Files

If you are reading a text file, the data is generally stored as string values, which are terminated by a carriage-return/linefeed character. You can use the `readln()` method to read an entire string of data, as shown in Listing 7.8. The `readln()` method reads from the current position of the file pointer to the next line-separator character and returns a string. (The returned string does not include the line separator; that character is ignored, and the file pointer is positioned at the next character following the line separator.) Windows recognizes the \r\n combination as a line separator, whereas on UNIX and Macintosh the \n character is the line separator that is recognized by the `readln()` method.

Listing 7.8   readln(): *Reading a line of text from a file*

```
var myDataString = myFile.readln();
```

Writing to a File

Following is the syntax for writing to a file.

```
myFile.write(string);
myFile.writeln(string);
myFile.writeByte(number);
myFile.flush();
```

The `write()` method writes a string to the file starting at the current position of the file pointer. The method returns `true` if successful and returns `false` otherwise. Note: `write()` does not add a linefeed character after writing the data.

The `writeln()` method writes a string to the file, followed by a \n line-separator character (a\r\n combination on Windows platforms). This method returns `true` if the write was successful and returns `false` otherwise.

The `writeByte()` method writes a single byte (ASCII value from 0 to 255) to the file. The method returns `true` if successful and returns `false` otherwise.

When you use either the `write()`, the `writeln()`, or the `writeByte()` method, the file contents are buffered internally by the server for efficiency. The `flush()` method forces the server to write the buffer to the file. The `flush()` method is called before the file is closed, but if you are doing several writes or writing large amounts of data, you should use `flush()` periodically to ensure that the contents of the buffer get written to the file. If an

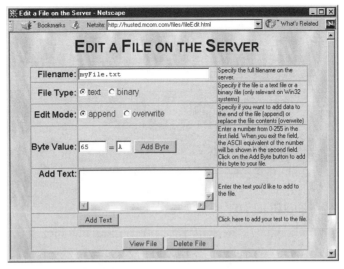

Figure 7.2 *Editing a file on the server*

error occurs, you can be certain that at least part of your data was saved. This method returns **true** if successful and returns **false** otherwise.

Always remember to reserve the file for exclusive use by locking the **project** or **server** object and then opening the file for writing. After closing the file, remember to unlock the **project** or **server** object so that others can then access the file.

Figure 7.2 shows the sample application, which writes to the specified file on the server.

Locking a File

Following is the syntax for locking a file.

```
if(project.lock()) { . . . }
```

An application might be accessed by several users simultaneously. To prevent possible errors, it's a good idea to lock the file before writing to it. To reserve the file for exclusive use, you can use either the **project** object or the **server** object. Technically, you're not locking the file, but you are locking the **project** or **server** object, effectively locking all users out of the file until you're finished writing to it. (Use the **project** object if only one application will access the file; otherwise, use the **server** object.) Listing 7.9 demonstrates how you would lock the **project** object; open the file to write to it; close the file; and finally unlock the `project` object. This method of locking ensures that only one user can access the file at any given time.

Listing 7.9 *Locking a file for exclusive use*

```
if ( project.lock() ) {
    myFile.open("r+");
    // "use the file as needed"
    myFile.close();
    project.unlock();
}
```

Positioning in a File

Following is the syntax for positioning in a file.

```
var currentPosition = myFile.getPosition();
myFile.setPosition(42);
if (myFile.eof()) { . . . }
```

A file pointer points to the current position in a file where the next read or write will occur. You can get the current location of the file pointer by using the `getPosition()` method, or you can move the file pointer to a specific place in the file by using the `setPosition()` method, and you can check to see whether you are at the end of the file by using the `eof()` method. These three methods allow you to move anywhere in your file where you wish to begin a read or write operation.

The `getPosition()` method always starts at byte 0 (the first byte) in the file and returns a number that represents the current position of the file pointer in the file (see Listing 7.10). This helps you know where the file pointer is positioned and where in the file the next read or write will occur. This method returns −1 if an error occurs.

Listing 7.10 `getPosition()`: *Getting the current position of the file pointer*

```
if( (myPosition = getPosition()) != -1) { . . .}
```

The `setPosition()` method moves the file pointer to a specific location in a file so that you can begin reading or writing at that location. The `setPosition()` method takes one argument (`position`) and an optional second argument (`reference`), as shown in Listing 7.11, where `position` is a number representing the byte in the file to which you wish to move (for example, 1057) and `reference` is one of the values listed in Table 7.3. This method returns `true` if it successfully moved the file pointer to the location in the file you specified. Otherwise, it returns `false`.

Listing 7.11 `setPosition()`: *Setting the position of the file pointer in a file*

```
myFile.setPosition(position);
myFile.setPosition(position, reference);
```

Table 7.3 *Optional reference values for the* `setPosition()` *method*

Reference	Position Is Relative To:
0	The beginning of the file (byte 0). This is the default.
1	Current position (wherever the file pointer is currently located in the file).
2	The end of the file.
n	A specific place in the file relative to the beginning (byte 0). So a `reference` value of 1000 would position the file pointer at byte 1000 in the file and then move it forward the number of bytes specified by `position`.

The `eof()` method returns true if the file pointer is at the end of the file; otherwise, it returns false. Use this method in read operations to ensure that you haven't moved to the end of the file, as shown in Listing 7.12.

Listing 7.12 *Using the* `eof()` *method to test for end of file*

```
if (!myFile.eof()) { . . . }
```

As you can see, in SSJS you can easily position the file pointer anywhere in a file. You can get the exact position of that pointer, and you can test to see whether the end of the file has been reached. If you're storing data in a file, you can use a fixed record length (for example, the first 20 characters are the last name, the next 20 are the first name, the next 10 are the identification number, and so on). This makes it possible to quickly jump to record number 15 in your file, as shown in Listing 7.13. Storing data in this manner is generally inefficient in file size; if a last name has fewer than 20 characters, the remaining characters contain spaces. This storage method is also inflexible in regard to field length; the last name would be limited to 20 characters, and anything longer than that would need to be truncated. However, fixed-length records allow for faster and easier access to the data.

Listing 7.13 *Positioning the file pointer using fixed-length records*

```
var recordSize = 50;
var recordNum = 15;
myFile.setPosition(0, recordNum * recordSize);
```

You can also store your data in a character-delimited format in which each field is separated by a character, perhaps a comma (,) or a pipe symbol (|). This makes data storage more efficient because you don't have to pad fields with blank spaces. However, you cannot easily grab the data you need; you must loop through each line of the file until you get to the record you want. Then you must parse the data yourself to extract individual fields. You must also check the data before storing it to ensure that the delimiter character does not appear in the data you are storing.

Converting Data

Following is the syntax for converting data.

```
File.byteToString(number);
File.stringToByte(string);
```

When writing data to a file, you may find it necessary to convert the data to a byte value (ASCII value from 0 to 255) or to a string value. You can use the `byteToString()` or `stringToByte()` method to accomplish this. These methods are static methods of the `File` object, so you should use the correct syntax shown in Listing 7.14 and not the incorrect syntax shown in Listing 7.15.

Listing 7.14 *Correct syntax for static methods of the* `File` *object*

```
File.byteToString(myNumber);
File.stringToByte(myChar);
```

Listing 7.15 *Incorrect syntax for static methods of the* `File` *object*

```
myFile.byteToString(myNumber);
```

The `byteToString()` static method takes a number (0–255) as an argument and converts that number to its ASCII equivalent. You would likely use this method with the `write()` and `writeln()` methods (see Listing 7.16). This is a static method of the `File` class, so use the `File` class itself, and not an instance of the class (an "object"), to call this method. If the argument is a number, the ASCII equivalent is returned; otherwise, the method returns an empty string.

Listing 7.16 *Using the* byteToString() *static method*

```
myFile.write(File.byteToString(myChar));
```

The `stringToByte()` static method takes a string and returns a number corresponding to the first character in the string you pass to it, or 0 if the string contains no characters (see Listing 7.17). Use this method to convert the first character of a string to a corresponding ASCII numeric value (0–255).

Listing 7.17 *Using the* stringToByte() *static method*

```
myFile.writeByte(File.stringToByte(myChar));
```

Getting File Information

To get information about the file you have opened, you can use the methods shown in Table 7.4. Later in this chapter we show you how to extend the SSJS `File` object using LiveConnect and Java to get additional file information. For now, these methods will help you get basic file information.

Figure 7.3 shows a screenshot from the sample application. The sample app lets you upload a file to the server and then store information about the uploaded file, using some of the methods previously covered. Now we'll show you how to upload files to the server.

Table 7.4 *Methods used to get file information*

Method	Description
eof()	Returns true if the file pointer is at the end of the file; otherwise, it returns false.
exists()	Returns true if the file exists or false if it does not.
getLength()	Returns the number of bytes in the file. On Windows systems this method returns the number of characters in a text file or the number of bytes in a binary file. On UNIX systems, binary and text files are the same, so the number returned simply represents the number of bytes.

Table 7.4 *Methods used to get file information*

Method	Description
getPosition()	Returns the current position of the file pointer.
error()	Returns a number representing the error status, −1 if the file is not open or cannot be opened, or returns 0 if there is no error. The error status codes returned by the error() method are platform-specific.
clearError()	Clears the error code and the value of eof().

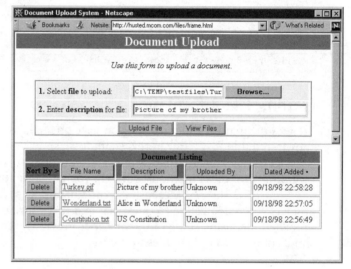

Figure 7.3 *Second sample application: uploading files (author: Willy Mena)*

Uploading Files

If you upload files to the server (not an easy task, for reasons we explain shortly), you use the File object to save them. The tricky part is to extract the file contents from the uploaded form data. We got a call from a developer who was trying to create an application that would accept resumes—not boring ASCII text resumes, but Word Perfect and Word documents that would have nice formatting, cool fonts, and maybe even a background or watermark. How would you do this?

To upload a file you must first include in your form an input field of TYPE=FILE. Listing 7.18 shows a form that contains a file field that enables users to upload a file.

Note   The ENCTYPE (encoding type) for the form in Listing 7.18 is "multipart/form-data". When you specify this encoding type, the file is encoded anad uploaded to the server. Otherwise, only the name of the file is sent, and generally that's not what you want. On the server, you need to unencode the file and save the contents. The **request** object does not parse the input from the form—you must do all this yourself—and that's why file uploads can be tricky. However, we'll try to make it easier for you.

Listing 7.18   *Form for uploading a file from the client browser to a remote server*

```
<FORM NAME="uploadForm" ACTION="saveFile.html" METHOD="get" ENCTYPE="multipart/form-data">
File to Upload: <INPUT TYPE="FILE" SIZE=30 NAME="fileUpload">
Directory on Server: <INPUT TYPE="TEXT" SIZE=30 NAME="serverDirectory" VALUE="">
File Name: <INPUT TYPE="TEXT" SIZE=30 NAME="filename" VALUE="">
<INPUT TYPE="submit" NAME="sendFile" VALUE="Upload File to the Server">
</FORM:>
```

Listing 7.18 shows the form we'll use to upload the contents of a file on our local client machine. The most important things to notice are the value of ENCTYPE and the TYPE of our INPUT field called "fileUpLoad". After the file is uploaded properly, we start parsing the data we need.

Listing 7.19 shows the code required to unencode the multipart form data you receive on the server side. Unfortunately, the **request** object does not parse input for multipart/form-data form submissions; you must do this manually. Luckily, this task is made easier with the use of regular expressions, which are supported in JavaScript 1.2. We show you all the code first, and then we step through it line by line to show you what's happening. At the end of this section you should have a clear idea of how multipart forms work and how you parse them in SSJS.

Listing 7.19   *Parsing a* multipart/form-data *upload*

```
//Author: Unknown - LiveWire Newsgroup Contributor, 1998
function getUploadedData(){
   var header=request.httpHeader();
   data = request.getPostData(0);
   var inputFields = null;
   var re = new RegExp("multipart\/ form-data,*boundary=(.*)$");
   if (re.test(header["content-type"])){
      var boundary = RegExp.$1;
      re.compile("\r{0,1}\n{0.1}&*-*"+boundary+"-*\r{0,1}\n{0,1}",'');
      var dataParts = data.split(re);
```

Files

Listing 7.19 *Parsing a* multipart/form-data *upload (Continued)*

```
        re.compile("\\r\\n\\r\\n","");
        RegExp.leftContext
        var nameRE = new RegExp(' name="(['"]+)"',"");
        inputFields = new Object();
        for (i = 0; i < dataParts.length; i++){
          dataParts[i].search(re);
          value = RegExp.rightContext;
          nameRe.test(RegExp.leftContext);
          name = RegExp.$1;
          inputFields[name] = value;
        }
    }
    return(inputFields);
}
```

The function in Listing 7.19 comprises 23 lines of code. The function grabs all the form data, creates an object, and creates new properties of the object. Each property is named after an uploaded field and has a value corresponding to the uploaded value from the form. The name of each property of the new object corresponds to the field name on the submitted form, and the value of that property corresponds to the uploaded value (the value entered in the form field, or the uploaded file). The inputFields object we create makes it easy to reference the uploaded values (including the uploaded form).

Figure 7.4 shows the header values that accompany a file upload. The name-value pairs from the form are packed together with the contents of

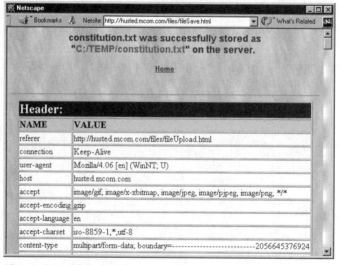

Figure 7.4 *Uploading files to the server*

the uploaded file. Now we show you how to extract the name-value pairs and file content.

As shown in Listing 7.20, the first thing we do in `getUploadedData()` function is to grab the `httpHeader` information from the `request` object. This returns an object containing all the name-value pairs that are sent with the `request` header, including the referring page, user agent, host name, content type, content length, and so on.

Next, we call the `getPostData()` method of the `request` object to get all the uploaded information from the file. (Again the ENCTYPE of our form is `"multipart/form-data"`, so the `request` object does not parse the information for us. We must do it ourselves.) We pass the `getPostData()` method an argument of 0 so that it will return all the uploaded data. (If you specify another number in your call to `getPostData()`, you can get portions of the uploaded data, but we just grab all of it.) We also create the `inputFields` variable, which will eventually be an object that contains an array of objects. This mimics the `request` object; it allows us to separate all the name-value pairs from our uploaded form so that we can more easily reference the names and values.

Listing 7.20 *Getting header and posted data from the* request *object*

```
function getUploadedData(){
    var header=request.httpHeader();
    data = request.getPostData(0);
    var inputFields = null;
```

In Listing 7.21 we create a regular expression that will match `"multipart/form-data"` and then any number of characters before the string `"boundary="`. In this way, we ensure that the uploaded data is ENCTYPE=`multipart/form-data` and that a boundary exists to separate the data from the contents of the uploaded file. We then test the `"content-type"` property of the header object (which is the `httpHeader` property of the `request` object) to ensure that `"multipart/form-data"` and `"boundary="` exist in the `"content-type"` property. The `content-type` string will look something like this:

```
multipart/form-data; boundary=---------------------------192512200717982
```

Then, we strip off the boundary from the string; this boundary separates the file contents from the uploaded data. Now the data looks like this:

```
----------------------------66192697815072 Content-Disposition: form-data;
name="fileUpload";
filename="C:\www\backgrounds\bluepattern.gif" Content-Type:image/gif
GIF89a□ Lö...----------------------------66192697815072 Content-Disposition: form-data;
name="sendFile"...
```

Each name-value pair from the form is separated by the boundary (----------------------------66192697815072). We compile another regular expression that searches for boundaries and linefeed characters to separate all the name-value pairs (including the file contents) and packs the separate pieces of data into an array called `dataParts`. After the code shown in Listing 7.21 is executed, `dataParts` contains all the uploaded data as array elements.

Listing 7.21 *Getting the boundary that separates the uploaded data*

```
var re = new RegExp("multipart\/ form-data.*boundary=(,*)$");
    if (re.test(header["content-type"])){
        var boundary = RegExp,$1;
        re.compile("\r{0,1}\n{0,1}&*-*"+boundary+"-*\r{0,1}\n{0,1}","");
    var dataParts = data.split(re);
```

Now we have an array called `dataParts`, and all the data is separated. However, it's still messy. All our form values contain extra information we don't need.

```
dataPart[0]: Content-Disposition: form-data; name="fileUpload";
filename="C":\www\backgrounds\bluepattern.gif" Content-Type: image\gif
GIF89a ...
dataPart[1]: Content-Disposition: form-data; name="serverDirectory"
c:/test/
dataPart[2]: Content-Disposition: form-data; name="filename"
pattern.gif
dataPart[3]; Content-Disposition: form-data; name="sendFile"
Upload File to the Server
```

So the uploaded file appears in the first element of the array, but it has lots of additional data that we don't need (the actual file contents start at GIF89a. . .). Next is each of the field elements in our form, but they also have extra data we don't need. What we do is grab the data that's in quotes after `"name="`—this will be the name of the new object we'll create to put into the `inputFields` array of objects. The data following the `name="..."`

portion of the string and preceded by two linefeed characters (/r/n) is the corresponding value. We create two regular expressions:

- nameRE, which matches any value that comes after "name=" and is surrounded by quotes
- re, which matches two consecutive linefeed characters

All this is shown in Listing 7.22. We create two new regular expressions (nameRE and re) and a new object that will hold the uploaded data.

Listing 7.22 *Creating two regular expressions (*re* and* namere*) to parse the uploaded data*

```
re.compile("\\r\\n\\r\\n","");
var nameRE = new RegExp(' name="(['"]+)"','');
inputFields = new Object();
```

In Listing 7.23, we loop through the dataParts[] array so that we can parse each name-value pair. We use the regular expression, re, to search for two consecutive linefeed characters that precede the value. The search automatically creates a RegExp object, which has several properties; we work with only three of those properties ($1, leftContext, and right Context). RegExp.$1 contains our match (two consecutive linefeed characters), RegExp.leftContext is everything to the left of the match, and RegExp.rightContext is everything to the right of the match (the value). We therefore assign RegExp.rightContext (the value portion of this part of our uploaded data) to the variable value.

Listing 7.23 *Extracting and assigning name-value pairs to properties of input fields*

```
for (i = 0; < dataParts.length; i++){
        dataParts[i[.search(re);
        value = RegExp.rightContext;
        nameRE.test(RegExp.leftContext);
        name = RegExp.$1;
        inputFields[name] = value;
    }
}
return(inputFields);
}
```

So given the value

```
Content-Disposition: form-data; name="filename"
pattern.gif
```

re matches the /r/n/r/n linefeed characters following name="filename".
So RegExp.$1 contains "/r/n/r/n", RegExp.leftContext contains
"Content-Disposition: form-data; name="filename"", and
RegExp.rightContext contains "pattern.gif". Because RegExp.right-
Context contains what we want (the value), we assign it to the variable
value.

We apply the next regular expression to RegExp.leftContext, which
contains the name of the uploaded field. The regular expression nameRE
searches for whatever follows "name=" and is surrounded by quotes. So
RegExp.$1 contains "filename", RegExp.leftContext contains
"Content-Disposition: form-data; name="", and RegExp.rightCon-
text contains a single quote character. Because RegExp.$1 contains what
we want (the name), we assign it to the variable name.

Now that we've assigned the name-value pair to the corresponding variables name and value, we create a new property of the input fields object
and call it name, and give it the value stored in the variable value. So if our
name-value pair was "filename/pattern.gif", then we now have a new
property in the inputFields object called "filename" with a value of
"pattern.gif".

After we've assigned all the name-value pairs to inputFields, we pass
the new object back to the calling function. You can then reference any of
the name-value pairs in the same way you reference them in the request
object, as shown in Listing 7.24. The code prints the filename and the contents of the file.

Listing 7.24 *Referencing the uploaded name-value properties*

```
var requestII = getUploadedData();
write(" <BR>Filename: " + requestII.filename);
write( " <BR>File Contents: " + requestII.fileUpload);
```

Listing 7.25 shows how to write the file contents to the server. The code
calls getUploadedData(), which returns an object and assigns it to the
variable uploadData. We then reference the name-value pairs we want by
referencing the properties of uploadData. Then we open the file and write
the contents of the uploaded file, which were assigned to the fileUpload
property of the uploadData object. Figure 7.5 shows the fileUpload
property that contains the contents of the uploaded file.

Listing 7.25 *Writing the uploaded file to the server*

```
uploadData = getUploadedData();
var myFileName = uploadData.filename;
var myDirectory = uploadData.serverDirectory;
var myFilePath = myDirectory + myFileName;
var myFile = new File(myFilePath);
if (myFile.open("wb")) {
   myFile.write(uploadData.fileUpload);
   myFile.close();
}
```

And that's it. We've successfully uploaded a file from the client browser to the server. We've even created our own `request` object (`uploadData` in Listing 7.25) and used it to reference the field names and associated values from the uploaded form. Now our users can upload all kinds of data to the server.

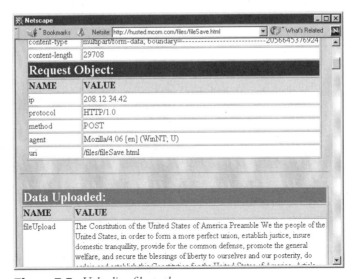

Figure 7.5 *Uploading files to the server*

Extending the SSJS File Object

The `File` object allows you to manipulate a single file on the server, but what happens when you want to get additional information about the file, create a directory on the server, or get a directory listing? You can't do that with JavaScript—the original idea behind JavaScript was to keep it simple.

However, there is a way to extend JavaScript using LiveConnect and Java. As explained in Chapter 9, LiveConnect is the glue that ties JavaScript to Java.

If you use Java you must create classes and then inherit from them to form supersets of the class. Does that sound complex? JavaScript makes it easier by letting you simply add functionality to an existing object. In this way, you can avoid much of the intricacies of object-oriented programming (OOP) syntax and simply add functionality without worrying about base classes, superclasses, and so forth.

When you create a `File` object in SSJS, you use syntax similar to that in Listing 7.26 to create a new `File` object that points to a specific file. The `File` object has certain methods that you can call to manipulate your file (`open()`, `read()`, `write()`, `close()`, and so on). After creating an instance of the `File` object, you can add your own methods and thus extend the `File` object.

Listing 7.26 *Creating a* `File` *object*

```
var myFile = new File(" path/filename.ext );
```

To create an easily extensible instance of the `File` object, we create a JavaScript function that accepts a filename, creates a new `File` object, and then returns the new `File` object, as shown in Listing 7.27.

Listing 7.27 *Creating a prototype of the* `File` *object: the* `SuperFile` *object*

```
function SuperFile(filename)
{
    var f = new File(filename);
    return f;
}
```

All we are currently doing in the `SuperFile()` function is to create an instance of the `File` object and return it. However, we'll soon add more to this function to extend the capabilities of the `File` object. Listing 7.28 shows how we use the `SuperFile()` function to create a new `File` object.

Listing 7.28 *Creating an instance of the* `SuperFile` *object*

```
var myFile = SuperFile("c:/temp/text.txt");
```

The syntax is similar to that used to create a regular SSJS `File` object, so what's the difference between `SuperFile` and `File`? Aside from having a

JavaScript wrapper around a JavaScript object, nothing. But now we add functionality to SuperFile that will truly make it different. We do the following:

- Create a function that returns the entire contents of a text file.
- Add the new function's name as a property of the SuperFile object (this is how we assign a JavaScript function to be a method of the SuperFile object).

First, we create a function that gets the entire contents of a file, as shown in Listing 7.29. We simply read a text file line by line, pack the data into the variable contents, and then return that string variable. We reference this, which at present refers to nothing. In a moment, however, it will refer to the File object that SuperFile points to (after we add the function as a method of SuperFile). Note that we append SuperFile_ to the beginning of the name of our function. This naming convention helps us remember that the function is meant to be a method of the SuperFile object.

Listing 7.29 *A function that returns the entire contents of a text file*

```
function SuperFile_getTextContents() {
    var contents="";
    var line="";
    // READ FILE LINE BY LINE UNTIL END OF FILE IS REACHED
    while (! this.eof())
    {
        if ((line = this.readln()) && ! this.eof())
    contents += line;
    }
    return contents;
}
```

Now that we have a function that returns the entire contents of a text file, how do we link it to the SuperFile object? It's simple. We define this function as a method of the SuperFile object we created in Listing 7.27: we assign the name of the function to a property of the SuperFile object (see Listing 7.30).

Listing 7.30 *Creating the* getTextContents *method of the* SuperFile *object*

```
function SuperFile(filename)
{
    var f = new File(filename);
    f.getTextContents = SuperFile_getTextContents;
    return f;
}
```

Notice that f.getTextContents is a property that points to the name of the SuperFile_getTextContents() function, which is simply "SuperFile_getTextContents" without the trailing parentheses. When we call getTextContents() as a method, we include the parentheses and any arguments the function might take, as shown in Listing 7.31. However, when we assign the SuperFile_getTextContents() function to a property of the SuperFile object (which makes it a method of the SuperFile object), we do not include the parentheses. This is an important point to remember as you create your own prototype objects. You can call the getTextContents() method of the SuperFile object as shown in Listing 7.31. This method call places the entire contents of the text file referenced by myFile into the JavaScript variable contents.

Listing 7.31 *Calling the* getTextContents() *method of the* SuperFile *object*

```
var myFile = SuperFile("C:/temp/test.txt");
var contents = myFile.getTextContents();
```

Using Java to Extend the SuperFile Object

You've seen how to create a new method from a JavaScript function, but how do you use Java? Java also has a File object, one that provides more methods and properties than the basic SSJS File object. To access a Java File object from within SSJS, you do the following.

1. Create a Java File object and assign it to a property of the Super-File object.

2. Create a JavaScript function that references a property or calls a method of the Java File object.

3. Add the JavaScript function as a method to the SuperFile object.

To create a Java File object when we create the SuperFile object, we assign a Java File object to a property of SuperFile as shown in Listing 7.32. All we do is create SuperFile object as shown previously in Listing 7.28. In this way, we have a JavaScript File object with a getText-Contents() method (in addition to all the standard SSJS File object methods), and we have a new property called "JavaFile" that is a Java File object and points to exactly the same file.

Listing 7.32 *Assigning a Java* File *object to a property of* SuperFile()

```
function SuperFile(filename)
{
    var f = new File(filename);
    f.getTextContents = SuperFile_getTextContents;
    f.javaFile = new java.io.File(filename);
    return f;
}
```

Now we can reference any method of the Java File object by referencing the javaFile property of the SuperFile object. In Listing 7.33 we get the date the file was last modified by referencing the Java File object's lastModified() method.

Listing 7.33 *Directly calling a method of the Java* File *object in* SuperFile()

```
var myFile = SuperFile("C:/temp/test.txt");
var modifiedTimeinSeconds = myFile.javaFile.lastModified();
```

Note The lastModified() method throws a security exception if the file cannot be examined. Enterprise Server 3.x supports JavaScript version 1.2, which does not support handling Java exceptions. Therefore, you should not call these methods directly but rather should call a Java wrapper and pass the javaFile property (a reference to a Java File object) as an argument. This "wrapping" is explained in Chapter 9, so we don't go into it here.

To avoid calling myFile.javaFile.lastModified(), you can create a JavaScript function that does it and then assign the function as a method of SuperFile, as shown in Listing 7.34. The function returns a JavaScript Date object corresponding to the date the file was last modified. Again, you should avoid calling the Java File object's lastModified() method directly and instead use a wrapper and thereby avoid the possibility of crashing your SSJS application if a Java exception gets thrown. (You need to do this only if you think that SSJS won't have proper access to the specified file at runtime.)

Listing 7.34 *The* lastModified() *function returns a JavaScript* Date *object*

```
function SuperFile_lastModified()
{
    return new Date(this.javaFile.lastModified());
}
```

You can then assign the `SuperFile_lastModified()` function name to a property of the `SuperFile` object as shown in Listing 7.35.

Listing 7.35   *Creating the* `lastModified()` *method of* `SuperFile`

```
function SuperFile(filename)
{
    var f = new File(filename);
    f.getTextContents = SuperFile_getTextContents;
    f.javaFile = new java.io.File(filename);
    f.lastModified = SuperFile_lastModified;
    return f;
}
```

Now you can call the `lastModified()` method of the `SuperFile` object as shown in Listing 7.36. In this way, the developer who creates the `SuperFile` object never even has to know that you're using a Java `File` object or calling methods of that object.

Listing 7.36   *Calling the* `lastModified()` *method of* `SuperFile`

```
var myFile = SuperFile("C:/temp/test.txt");
var fileModificationDate = myFile.lastModified();
```

You can add methods to the `SuperFile` object as you see fit. The sample application for this chapter also uses the `SuperFile` object, so you can see it in action.

Deleting Files in SSJS

Sometimes you may want to delete a file in your applications, but the native SSJS `File` object does not allow you to do this. To add this capability, you must add a method to SuperFile that calls the `delete` method of a Java `File` object. Earlier we added a Java File object as a property of SuperFile and called it "javaFile". Both SuperFile and the `javaFile` property point to the same file on the server.

Since Java provides more methods for file manipulation than SSJS, we can simply call one of the Java methods to delete our file. The following SSJS code shows how to call the `delete` method of the Java `File` object.

```
function SuperFile_delete()
{
    // delete is a reserved word in JavaScript, so use array syntax
    return this.javaFile['delete']();
}
```

We've created a JavaScript function called `SuperFile_delete` that we can call whenever we want to delete a file on the server. We call our new method "remove" because the word "delete" is a keyword in JavaScript and will cause conflicts. Therefore, we have to use a different word for our new method. The following code shows how to add `SuperFile_delete` as a method of our `SuperFile` object.

```
function SuperFile(filename)
{
    . . .
    // a reference to the Java version of our file
    f.javaFile = new java.io.File(filename);
    . . .
    f.remove = SuperFile_delete;    . . .
    return f;
}
```

After creating the `SuperFile` object in our SSJS application, we can call the remove method to delete the file. The following code shows how to create a `SuperFile` object and delete the specified file.

```
var myFilename = "/path/myFile.ext";
target = new SuperFile(myFilename);
target.remove();
```

Note   The delete method of the Java File object will throw a securityException if the file cannot be deleted for security reasons. Therefore, you should place the call to the delete method of the Java File object inside of a Java wrapper before using it. We show you how to create Java wrappers in Chapter 9.

You can add methods to the `SuperFile` object as you see fit: you may want to determine if a given file is a directory; you may want to get directory listings; you may want to create subdirectories; and so forth. Simply add the necessary methods to the `SuperFile` object and you can call them from JavaScript without ever knowing you're using Java. The sample application for this chapter also uses the `SuperFile` object, so you can see it in action.

Summary

You can manipulate files on the local server by using the built-in methods of the `File` object and by extending the `File` object. You can use LiveConnect and Java to get additional file information, and you can upload files from the client to the server. There's almost nothing you can't do with files on the server's file system using SSJS.

Enabling Messaging in SSJS Applications

E-mail has been called the "killer app" of the Internet. Not only does it allow us to keep in close contact with friends and family, but it also lets us write for technical support, meet new and exciting people, and even write to the occasional billionaire (for example, `billg@microsoft.com`). E-mail seems to be in use everywhere except where it's needed most: in Internet, intranet, and extranet applications. Netscape's Inbox-Direct program is only one example of what HTML e-mail can do—it's the tip of the iceberg. But we're getting ahead of ourselves. Let's start simple.

The SendMail Object

One of the best improvements to SSJS occurred in Enterprise Server 3.0 with the introduction of the `SendMail` object, which enables you to send e-mail (plain text and HTML) directly from an application. This means that you can easily do any of the following.

- Send e-mail messages if errors occur in your application.
- Send security alerts if someone tries to access your application from an unsupported IP address or fails to log in successfully.
- Send daily or weekly reports by querying a database, building the report as an e-mail message, and sending it to all interested managers.

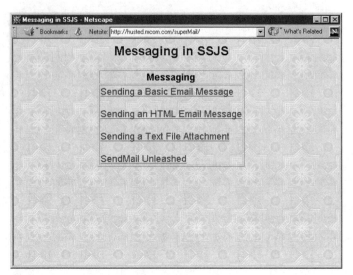

Figure 8.1 *Sample messaging application on the CD-ROM*

- Send users the login screen of an SSJS application (for apps that are meant to be used periodically, such as status updates, time cards, and so on).
- Send surveys (HTML forms that users can fill out while reading their e-mail).
- Use forms with user data that needs to be updated regularly (such as employee benefits information).
- Create automated workflow-style applications, such as vacation requests, purchase orders, and so on, in which HTML forms are sent rather than paper documents.

This innovation greatly expands the scope and power of JavaScript. If you're not currently using e-mail in your applications, it's time to start.

In this chapter we talk about the basic `SendMail` object (just as all the other books do), and then we expand on that. We show you how to send rich-text (HTML) e-mail to automate many tasks in your company. We show you how to send file attachments and even how to send multiple file attachments in a single e-mail message. The sample application shown in Figure 8.1 is included on the CD-ROM and helps you learn how to send plain-text e-mail, rich-text e-mail, file attachments, and so forth. One important note: we would be saddened to learn that the material in this chapter was used for spamming (the sending of unsolicited bulk e-mail). Please, e-mail responsibly.

Using the SendMail Object

To send an e-mail message from within an application, follow these steps.

1. Ensure that the MTA Host server setting is correctly specified in your Web server (see Figure 8.2). Please see your user's manual or talk with your system administrator if you need additional information on setting up your Web server to communicate with a messaging server.
2. Create a SendMail object.
3. Set the properties of the SendMail object (To and From at a minimum, but generally you'll set at least the To, From, Subject, and Body properties).
4. Call the send() method of the SendMail object.

Listing 8.1 shows the syntax for creating an instance of the SendMail object, and Table 8.1 shows a list of the properties available in the SendMail object.

Listing 8.1 *Creating a* SendMail *object*

```
var msg = new SendMail();
```

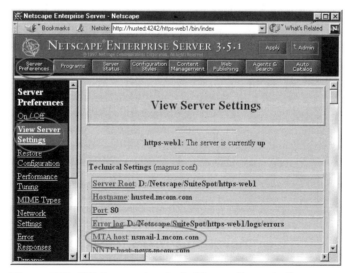

Figure 8.2 MTA host *settings in the Netscape Enterprise Server preferences*

Later in this chapter we show you how to extend the SendMail object. For now, simply note that the SendMail object has only three methods, only one of which you'll generally use: send(). The send() method copies all the properties you've set for the SendMail object into the message header and copies only the body property into the message body. You can add any properties you wish by using the syntax in Listing 8.2; all your properties will be sent in the header of your e-mail message.

Listing 8.2 *Setting the properties of a* SendMail *object*

```
var myMail = new SendMail();
myMail.Group = "netscape.public.mozilla.general";
myMail.TVShows = "Seinfeld";
myMail["New Car"] = "Porsche";
```

All the properties you've added to the instance of SendMail in Listing 8.2 will be sent with your e-mail message. If your mail client (Messenger, Eudora, and so on) recognizes a property as being important (such as "Reply-To"), it will use it. Otherwise, it's simply included in the message header by SSJS and ignored by the mail client.

Table 8.1 SendMail *object methods and properties*

Method	Description
errorCode()	Numeric value representing the error.
errorMessage()	Text string that briefly explains the error.
send()	Sends the e-mail message

Property	Description
To	The primary recipient(s) of the e-mail message. If there is more than one recipient for the To, From, Cc, or Bcc field, you must separate each e-mail address with a comma. Required.
From	The e-mail address of the person or entity sending the e-mail message. Required.
["Reply-To"]	If the mail recipient presses the **Reply** button, the address shown in the To field will be this address rather than the From address. Optional.

Table 8.1 `SendMail` *object methods and properties (Continued)*

Method	Description
Cc	"Carbon copy"—a copy of the message is sent to the specified person(s), and their names appear in the message header. Optional.
Bcc	"Blind carbon copy"—a copy of the message is sent to the specified person(s), but their names do not appear in the header. No one will know that they received a copy. Optional.
Group	Sends your e-mail to the specified newsgroup(s). Optional.
Subject	The subject of your message. Optional.
Body	The body of your e-mail message, comprising plain ASCII text, HTML code, and/or file attachments. Optional.
["Content-Type"]	Specifies the type of e-mail message you are sending. "text/plain" sends a standard plain-text e-mail message. "text/html" sends an HTML e-mail message. Optional. Default is "text/plain".
Organization	The name of the organization from which this e-mail originated. Optional.
Smtpserver	The mail (SMTP) server name. This property specifies the SMTP server that will be used to send your message; it defaults to the MTA Host property. Optional if the MTA Host property is set in your Enterprise Server under Server Preferences | Network Settings in Server Administration. (Figure 8.2)

Mail

All the properties shown in Table 8.1 are valid. You can include any desired MIME header information in your headers. If your application sends e-mail messages or application forms, you might want to include additional properties in the header to help you track which application sent the e-mail, whether the e-mail was triggered by a server agent or a user, and so forth.

Listing 8.3 demonstrates how to create and send a mail message in SSJS. Start by creating an instance of the `SendMail` object; set the desired properties (`To`, `From`, `Subject`, `Body`); then send the e-mail message. If the message is not sent, the `send()` method returns `false`, so you might want to write a message in the debug window showing the error code and textual error message (using the `errorCode()` and `errorMessage()` methods of the `SendMail` object).

Listing 8.3 *Sending a basic e-mail message*

```
var msg = new SendMail();
msg.To = 'president@whitehouse.com';
msg.From = 'husted@netscape.com';
msg.Subject = 'Dinner Cancellation';
msg.Body = 'Sorry Bill, but something came up -- the Niners are playing ' +
          'at home tonight.  Can I take a rain-check?';
if (!msg.send()) {
    debug("Error: <B>" + msg.errorCode() + "</B> " + msg.errorMessage() + "\n");
}
```

Message Headers

When creating your message, you can select from the list of predefined header fields in Table 8.1, or you can create your own. Request for Comments (RFC) 822 directs that e-mail messages can contain unique user-defined fields that do not conflict with published extensions. (RFCs are documents that are used to define standards such as MIME, HTTP, HTML, LDAP, and so on. The RFC proposals are updated until a standard is agreed upon and approved by a standards body such as the W3C, ECMA, IETF, and so on.) Refer to RFC 822 (the link is listed in Resources) to get more information on which header fields are predefined in the MIME standard.

Header fields do not have to appear in any particular order in an e-mail message, except that all of them must precede the message body. You can create additional properties in the header, and all of them will be sent with your e-mail (as shown in Listing 8.2), but each property should appear on its own line with no lines between them. The first blank line in the e-mail begins the body of the message.

Sending HTML Messages

Plain-text e-mail messages are sent by default (`Content-Type="text/plain"`) when you use the `SendMail` object. If you want to send HTML messages, simply set the `"Content-Type"` property to `"text/html"`, as shown in Listing 8.4. You can include as much HTML code in the body of your message as you like, including HTML pages, forms, and so on. So if you want to remind people to log in to your application every morning, send them e-mail every night with the login form in the body of your message.

Listing 8.4 *Sending an HTML e-mail message*

```
var msg = new SendMail();
msg.To = 'rhall@netscape.com';
msg.From = 'husted@netscape.com';
msg['Content-Type'] = 'text/html';
msg.Subject = 'Open Studio';
msg.Body = 'Netscape Open Studio <FONT COLOR=RED SIZE=+3>ROCKS!</FONT>';
if (!msg.send()) {
    debug("Error: <B>" + msg.errorCode() + "</B> " + msg.errorMessage() + "\n");
}
```

The `SendMail` class enables you to send either simple text messages or complex MIME-compliant messages, which might include attachments. Let's say you want to send a graphic image as your message. You simply set the `Content-Type` property to `"image/gif"` (this tells the e-mail client that it's receiving an image instead of plain text). Then set the `Content-Transfer-Encoding` property to `"base64"`. Last, set the `Body` property of the `SendMail` object to the file contents of a GIF image that has been converted to base64 encoding (using `uuencode`, `mmencode`, and so on). Listing 8.5 shows how to send a GIF image as the contents of an e-mail message.

Listing 8.5 *Sending a GIF image*

```
<SERVER>
msg = new SendMail();
msg.To = "husted@netscape.com";
msg.From = "myApp@netscape.com";
msg.Subject = "A GIF Image For You";
msg["Content-Type"] = "image/gif";
msg["Content-Transfer-Encoding"] = "base64";
myFile = new File("/tmp/hansolo.gif");
if ( myFile.open("r") ) {
    msg.Body = myFile.read(myFile.getLength());
    msg.send();
}
</SERVER>
```

Mail

The file used in Listing 8.5 must be a base64-encoded file. If it's a binary file, the message will not be sent properly. (Remember that all e-mail messages are text-based and not binary, so your attachments must be converted to a text form before they can be sent.) You can also send a text or HTML e-mail message with an attached file. That's a bit more complicated.

Sending Attachments

A MIME-compliant e-mail message is somewhat like an HTML page in that it consists of a header and a body. The header contains all kinds of routing information (to, from, cc, bcc) and other useful information that the mail client uses when displaying information about your message (see Listing 8.6). The body contains the actual message (see Listing 8.7). The body can optionally be divided into sections, each one of a different MIME type (a Word Perfect document, JPG file, Excel spreadsheet, and so on).

Listing 8.6 *Sample MIME message header*

```
. . .
Message-ID: <35F9F62A.E599627E@netscape.com>
Date: Fri, 11 Sep 1998 21:18:50 -0700
From: husted@netscape.com (Robert Husted)
Organization: Netscape Communications
X-Mailer: Mozilla 4.06 [en] (WinNT; U)
MIME-Version: 1.0
To: husted@netscape.com
Subject: test
Content-Type: multipart/mixed; boundary="mime-boundary "
X-Mozilla-Status: 8001
```

Listing 8.7 *Sample MIME message body*

```
--mime-boundary
Content-Type: text/html; charset=us-ascii
Content-Transfer-Encoding: 7bit

<HTML>
<H1>Hello World!</H1>
</HTML>
--mime-boundary
Content-Type: application/octet-stream; name="myFilename.ext"
Content-Transfer-Encoding: base64
Content-Disposition: attachment; filename="myFilename.ext"

--mime-boundary
Content-Type: image/gif; name="myImage.gif"
Content-Transfer-Encoding: base64
Content-Disposition: inline; filename="myImage.gif"

--mime-boundary--
```

Notice that the Content-Type is "multipart/mixed". This means that your message will contain multiple content types. Each section of your message is separated by a boundary. (The same boundary is used throughout the message unless you're doing nested multipart/mixed messages. That's left as an exercise for the reader—we don't want to get too complicated here.) Following the boundary, you might have a few additional comments describing the `content-type`, `content-transfer-encoding`, and `content-disposition`, all of which tell the mail client how to handle each section of your message.

The boundary that divides each section of the mail message is described in the message header. In Listing 8.6, the MIME boundary is defined. When you actually *use* the MIME boundary in the body to separate parts of your message, you must start with two hyphens (--). So if your boundary is "`-boundary`", you would use "`---boundary`" to separate each part of your message. The final line of the message contains a closing boundary, which starts with two hyphens and ends with two hyphens: "`---boundary--`".

If you attach a file to the body of your message, it must be text-based. Therefore, if you have a binary file that you want to attach, first convert it to base64 encoding (a text-based encoding that converts binary data into a text format). If the e-mail client recognizes MIME-formatted messages, it will be able to unencode the base64-encoded data. (Eudora and Messenger can do this.)

When you are encoding binary data, remember to remove any extra lines from the resulting file. For example, `uuencode` adds one line to the beginning of the file and one line to the end. Delete both lines before attaching the file contents to your message body. Several programs are available on both Win32 and UNIX systems for doing base64 encoding. The only gotcha are those pesky extra lines that the encoding programs sometimes add.

We do not go into detail regarding base64 encoding. However, you can download the Netscape Messaging SDK (the URL is listed in Resources) and use it to encode your files. Table 8.2 shows a binary file on the left and the base64-encoded version on the right. This should give you a better idea of the difference between binary files and base64 files. Remember, base64 is simply a text representation of binary data.

Table 8.2 *GIF file and base64 equivalent*

GIF File `calendar.gif`	Base64-encoded file `Calendar.mme`
GIF89a□ □ ³ÿ ÿÿÿÿÿ 333	Content-Type: application/octet-stream; name="calendar.gif"
™ÿ ™Ì ÿ îÀÀÀˆˆˆDDD	Content-Transfer-Encoding: Base64
!ù□□ □ , □ □	Content-Disposition: attachment; filename="calendar.gif"
@□LðÈI«□□è□	
□Ãu□ˆ(□G□¯•÷íJ"°ô™jxÈz	R0lGODlhFAAUALP/AP//////ADMzMwCZ/wCZzAAA/wAA7sDAwIiIiE

Table 8.2   *GIF file and base64 equivalent (Continued)*

GIF File calendar.gif	Base64-encoded file Calendar.mme
x‡Ç4A□¨□□H□é¨D□|°]àõ	RERAAA
□□v8□□ 8□^¿DxTøÂdGÏ¡	AAAAAAAAAAAAAAAAAAAACH5BAEAAAcALAAAAAAUABQAQ
^I·# ;ÿÎ™ÎÎ™™™Î™fÎ™3Î™	ARM8MhJq50B6AIK

Extending the SendMail Object

It would be a shame to have to manually open files, add them to your message body, and finally send your e-mail messages. A library of JavaScript functions might help, but it would be even better to use the concepts you learned in Chapter 7 to extend the SendMail object. We simply add methods that will take care of the MIME boundaries, MIME types, and so on.

There's only one problem: Because all the properties of the SendMail object are copied into the header of the outgoing mail message, we can't assign functions as properties of the SendMail object. Not to worry—we simply add methods differently this time around. Instead of modifying an instance of the SendMail object, we modify the SendMail prototype on the server so that all instances of SendMail will have access to our JavaScript functions. We do this by using object prototypes.

Adding Properties and Methods to SendMail

Let's look at the functions that will make up our extended SendMail object before we look at how to add them as methods. Table 8.3 shows a listing of all the methods that we will eventually add to the SendMail object. However, first we show you each function and describe what it's doing. In that what way, you can see that the added methods are simply JavaScript functions.

Let's start simple. We create a function called SuperMail that extends the SendMail prototype on our server (so all SendMail objects will have the new methods we create). Afterward we show you the JavaScript functions that we've added as SendMail methods.

JavaScript prototypes are objects—such as Array, Date, File, Send-Mail, and so on—that are created using the new operator. All prototypes have constructor methods that are used to create an instance of the object. The constructor has a property called prototype that points to an object. By adding properties or functions to the object pointed to by prototype, you effectively add properties and methods to the prototype for a given object. So every object you create from the class prototype will have access to the properties and methods you've added.

Table 8.3 *New methods added to the SSJS* `SendMail` *object*

Method Name	Description
`Send()`	Adds all attachments to the outgoing e-mail message and then calls the `send()` method of the `SendMail` object.
`setHTML()`	Changes the `"Content-Type"` property to `"text/html"` so that the outgoing message will be interpreted by an e-mail client as HTML text.
`setPlainText()`	Changes the `"Content-Type"` property to `"text/plain"` so that the outgoing message will be interpreted by an e-mail client as plain text.
`attachTextFile(filename)`	Reads the contents of a text file into the attachments array. The file contents are added to the outgoing message before it is sent.
`attachMIMEFile(filename,mimeType)`	Reads the contents of a base64-encoded file into the attachments array. The file contents are added to the outgoing message before it is sent.
`addAttachments()`[*]	All file attachments are in the attachment array. If files were added (via the `attachTextFile()` or `attachMIMEFile()` method), they are added to the outgoing message.
`generateBoundary()`[*]	Creates a unique MIME boundary that is used to separate each file in the outgoing message.

[*] Indicates a private method. You should not need to call this method directly. It is called by other methods when attachments are added to the outgoing message.

Let's put this in simpler terms so that it's clear what we're doing. A JavaScript prototype is like a blueprint of a house, and an instance is like a house built from the blueprint. You can modify the house, perhaps by adding a room. However, you can also change the blueprint so that every new house built from it will have the additional room. (The way JavaScript works, even the older houses we've already built from the blueprint will suddenly have the additional room.)

Listing 8.8 shows the `SuperMail()` function, in which we assign new properties and JavaScript functions to the `SendMail` prototype. If we add a variable or an array, it becomes a new property of `SendMail`. If we add a JavaScript function (by referencing its name), it becomes a new method of `SendMail`.

Mail

Listing 8.8   *Extending the SSJS* SendMail *class prototype*

```
function SuperMail() {
    // PROPERTIES
    SendMail["Content-Type"] = "text/plain";    // DEFAULT CONTENT TYPE IS TEXT
    // METHODS
    SendMail.prototype.setPlainText      = SuperMail_setPlainText;
    SendMail.prototype.setHTML           = SuperMail_setHTML;
    SendMail.prototype.attachTextFile    = SuperMail_attachTextFile;
    SendMail.prototype.attachMIMEFile    = SuperMail_attachMIMEFile;
    SendMail.prototype.Send              = SuperMail_send;
    // PRIVATE METHODS
    SendMail.prototype.addAttachments    = SuperMail_addAttachments;
    SendMail.prototype.clearAttachments  = SuperMail_clearAttachments;
    SendMail.prototype.generateBoundary  = SuperMail_generateBoundary;
}
```

That's all there is to it. We've just extended the SSJS SendMail prototype, so now every instance of the SendMail object on the server will have
these new properties and methods. Now all we need to do is to create the
JavaScript functions we've referenced in Listing 8.8. We show the code for
each of the new methods (including the private methods) to help you understand what kind of functionality we've added. (We make it easier for you to
easily set the content-type [text or HTML] and attach text and MIME-
encoded files to your e-mail messages.)

Setting the Message Type

We start with the setPlainText() and setHTML() functions shown in
Listing 8.9. If you call the setPlainText() method, it will set the content
type of your message to plain text. If you call the setHTML() method, it will
set the content type of your message to HTML so that you can send
HTML documents or forms inline with your e-mail message. Users will see
HTML in the message (assuming that they're using a mail client that supports HTML e-mail, such as Netscape Messenger).

Listing 8.9   *Setting the* content-type *of a message*

```
// SET THE CONTENT-TYPE TO HTML
function SuperMail_setHTML() {
    this["Content-Type"] = "text/html";
}
// SET THE CONTENT-TYPE TO PLAIN TEXT
function SuperMail_setPlainText() {
    this["Content-Type"] = "text/plain";
}
```

Creating Text File Attachments

Figure 8.3 shows the form in the sample application that lets you practice sending e-mail attachments. Listing 8.10 shows the entire contents of a function that adds a text file as an attachment to the outgoing message. We break the code into sections and explain each section so that you can better understand what's going on. However, we thought you'd want to see all the code in one block to get an overall idea about what the code is doing.

Listing 8.10 *Creating a text file attachment*

```
function SuperMail_attachTextFile(fullFilename) {
  // CREATE FILE ATTACHMENT ARRAY IF IT DOES NOT EXIST
  if (this.attachments == null) {
    this.attachments = new Array();
  }
  var filename = fullFilename;
  var contentType = "text/plain";
  if (filename.indexOf(".htm") != -1) {
    contentType = "text/html";
  }
  if (filename.indexOf("/")) {
    filename = filename.substring(filename.lastIndexOf("/")+1,file name.length);
  }
  if (fullFilename.indexOf("\\")) {
    filename = filename.substring(filename.lastIndexOf("\\")+1,file name.length);
  }
  var inFile = new File(fullFilename);
  var contents = "";
  if (inFile.open("r")) {
    contents = "Content-Type:" + contentType + "; charset=us-ascii name=\"" +
               filename + "\"\n" + "Content-Transfer-Encoding: 7bit\n" +
               "Content-Disposition: inline; filename=\"" + filename + "\"\n\n";
    contents += inFile.read(inFile.getLength());
    this.attachments[fullFilename] = contents + "\n";
    inFile.close();
    return true;
  }
  else {
    return false;
  }
}
```

In Listing 8.11 we start by creating an array to hold the file attachments (if one does not already exist). Next, we get the name of the file and check to see whether it has the `.htm` extension (which matches `.htm` and `.html`). If the file has this extension, we set the content type of this file to `"text/html"`. Otherwise, we assume it's a standard ASCII text file and set the content type to `"text/plain"`.

In Listing 8.12 we parse the filename to remove the path information so that we can use only the filename in the descriptive header that always fol-

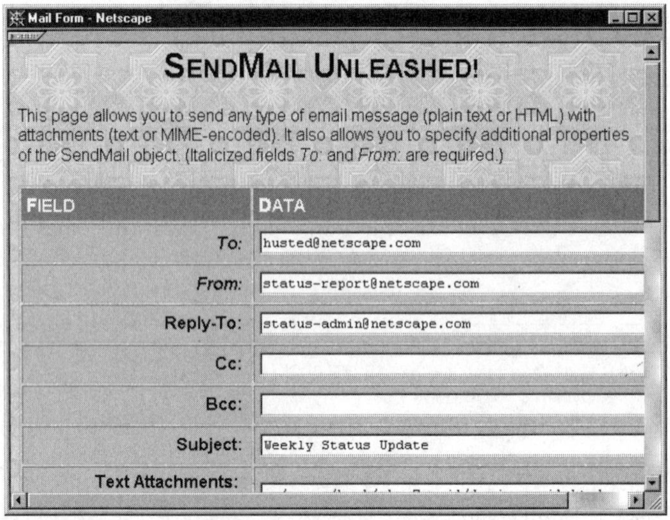

Figure 8.3 *Sending e-mail attachments*

Listing 8.11 *Setting the file type*

```
// CREATE FILE ATTACHMENT ARRAY IF IT DOES NOT EXIST
  if (this.attachments == null) {
    this.attachments = new Array();
  }
  var filename = fullFilename;
  var contentType = "text/plain";
  if (filename.indexOf(".htm") != -1) {
    contentType = "text/html";
  }
```

lows a MIME boundary and precedes the contents of a file. The filename
appears in the MIME header, so we want only the name of the file and not
all the extra path information. The header tells the mail client what type of
file is attached, what the name of the file is, and what the content disposition
is (how it's supposed to appear). If you set the disposition to `"attachment"`,
it's treated as a standard attachment. If you set the disposition to `"inline"`,
some mail clients will try to display the file as part of the body of the e-mail
message.

Listing 8.12 *Extracting the filename from the path*

```
if (filename.indexOf("/")) {
  filename = filename.substring(filename.lastIndexOf("/")+1,filename.length);
}
if (fullFilename.indexOf("\\")) {
  filename = filename.substring(filename.lastIndexOf("\\")+1,filename.length);
}
```

Next, we create a new `File` object that points to the file on the server (we send the full path to the file as an argument to the `File` constructor). This is shown in Listing 8.13. We create a variable called `contents` in which we will store the contents of the file, and then we try to open the file. If we can't open the file, we return a `false` value. Listing 8.14 shows what happens inside the `if` control block.

Listing 8.13 *Opening the file*

```
var inFile = new File(fullFilename);
var contents = "";
if (inFile.open("r")) {
  . . .
}
else {
  return false;
}
}
```

In Listing 8.14 we generate the MIME header that specifies information about the attached file. We set the `contentType` variable previously (either `"text/plain"` or `"text/html"` depending on whether the filename ended with .htm or .html), and it tells the mail client what kind of file we've attached. We also specify the character set (`us-ascii`), the name of the file (minus the extra path information, which we previously removed), and the type of encoding (7-bit for text files or base64 for MIME-encoded files).

Next, we add an extra blank line to separate the attachment header from the actual file. We read the file all at one time and append it to the header information in the variable `contents`. Then we assign the entire string in the variable `contents` to a new element in our array. So now our array `attachments` contains an element that is named the same as the filename and contains a long string consisting of a MIME header followed by a blank line and the entire contents of a text file.

Last, we close the file. If we were able to open the file successfully, the code returns `true`. Otherwise, it returns `false`.

Listing 8.14 *Creating the file attachment*

```
contents = "Content-Type:" + contentType + "; charset=us-ascii name=\"" +
           filename + "\"\n" + "Content-Transfer-Encoding: 7bit\n" +
           "Content-Disposition: inline; filename=\"" + filename + "\"\n\n";
contents += inFile.read(inFile.getLength());
this.attachments[fullFilename] = contents + "\n";
inFile.close();
return true;
```

Creating MIME Attachments

The function for adding a MIME file is quite similar to that for adding a
text file (see Listing 8.15). The major difference is that this function takes
two arguments: the filename and a MIME type. For example, to add a GIF
image you'd specify "image/gif" as the mimeType.

If we don't specify a value (we send a blank string for the second argument), the function checks to see whether the file contains its own header
(some MIME encoders create a MIME header for the file when they convert it to base64). If the file has its own header, we don't do anything else.
However, if the file has no header we use the generic "application/
octet-stream" MIME type for the attachment.

The Content-Transfer-Encoding is base64, and the Content-
Disposition is "attachment". This is because the file is a binary file that's
been changed to base64 encoding. We can't display the contents of this file
in our e-mail message (except in special cases such as GIF or JPG images),
so we set Content-Disposition to "attachment" rather than "inline".

Listing 8.15 *Attaching a MIME-encoded (base64) file*

```
function SuperMail_attachMIMEFile(fullFilename, mimeType) {
  // CREATE FILE ATTACHMENT ARRAY IF IT DOES NOT EXIST
  if (this.attachments == null) {
    this.attachments = new Array();
  }
  var filename = fullFilename;
  if (filename.indexOf("/")) {
    filename = filename.substring(filename.lastIndexOf("/")+1,file name.length);
  }
  if (fullFilename.indexOf("\\")) {
    filename = filename.substring(filename.lastIndexOf("\\")+1,file name.length);
  }
  var inFile = new File(fullFilename);
  if (inFile.open("r")) {
    this.attachments[fullFilename] = inFile.read(inFile.getLength());
    inFile.close();
    var header = this.attachments[fullFilename];
```

Listing 8.15 *Attaching a MIME-encoded (base64) file (Continued)*

```
    if (header.indexOf("Content-Type:") == -1) {
      if (mimeType == "") {
        mimeType = "application/octet-stream";
      }
      this.attachments[fullFilename] =
        "Content-Type: " + mimeType + "; name=\"" + filename + "\"\n" +
        "Content-Transfer-Encoding: base64\n" +
        "Content-Disposition: attachment; filename=\"" + filename + "\"\n\n" +
        this.attachments[fullFilename];
    }
    return true;
  }
  else {
    return false;
  }
}
```

Adding All Attachments to the Outgoing Message

Now we can create attachments from text and binary (base64-encoded), but
we haven't yet added them to the outgoing message. We create a function
called addAttachments() that adds all our file attachments to the body of
the e-mail message. Each file is separated by a unique boundary so that the
mail client knows how to separate them correctly.

Again, we show all the code in Listing 8.16 and then break it into pieces
to show what we're doing. We add all our attachments to the body of the
e-mail message and separate each attachment with a common boundary.
This allows us to add text to the Body property of the message (and set the
content-type of the message) before or after adding any attachments. We
can construct the message in any order, and it will be assembled properly.

Listing 8.16 *Adding all file attachments to a message*

```
function SuperMail_addAttachments() {
  this.Boundary = this.generateBoundary();
  if (this["Content-Type"]) {
    mainMessageType = this["Content-Type"];
  }
  else {
    mainMessageType = "text/plain";
  }
  this["Content-Type"] = "multipart/mixed; boundary=\"" + this.Boundary + "\"";
  this["MIME-Version"] = "1.0";
  var msgBody =
    "\nThis is a multi-part message in MIME format.\n" +
    "--" + this.Boundary + "\n" +
    "Content-Type: " + mainMessageType + "; charset=us-ascii\n" +
    "Content-Transfer-Encoding: 7bit\n\n" + this.Body + "\n\n";
```

Listing 8.16   *Adding all file attachments to a message*

```
for (i in this.attachments) {
   msgBody += "--" + this.Boundary + "\n";
   msgBody += this.attachments[i];
}
msgBody += "--" + this.Boundary + "--" + "\n\n";
this.Body = msgBody;
}
```

First, we create a boundary to separate the various attachments we'll add to the body of the message (see Listing 8.17). The `generateBoundary()` function (not shown) concatenates a bunch of random numbers to generate a boundary unique to this e-mail message. After the boundary is created, we check to see whether the `Content-Type` has been set. If it has, we store the value in the variable `mainMessageType`. Because we're adding attachments, the main body of the e-mail message itself must be an attachment. So we grab whatever `Content-Type` was set for the message, or we set the `Content-Type` to `"text/plain"` if no `Content-Type` was specified.

Next, we set the `Content-Type` for the whole e-mail message to `"multipart/mixed"` because it will contain a plain-text or HTML message and some text or base64 file attachments. By setting the `Content-Type` to `"multipart/mixed"`, we indicate that the message will contain multiple parts—each separated by the specified boundary—and each part may be a different `Content-Type`, such as an image, an HTML document, a spread-sheet, and so on.

We also define the boundary we will use (the one we got by calling the `generateBoundary()` function). This tells the e-mail client where to separate the parts of the message. The mail client receives one big long text string, so it must know how to separate the parts into messages that it displays and attachments that the user can save or view. The mail client uses the boundary to determine where to separate the parts of the message.

Last, we set the `MIME-Version`, which tells the e-mail client which version of the MIME specification this message conforms to. In that way the mail client knows how to handle the message properly.

Listing 8.17   *Specifying the* `Content-Type` *and boundary of the message*

```
this.Boundary = this.generateBoundary();
   if (this["Content-Type"]) {
     mainMessageType = this["Content-Type"];
   }
   else {
     mainMessageType = "text/plain";
   }
   this["Content-Type"] = "multipart/mixed; boundary=\"" + this.Boundary + "\"";
   this["MIME-Version"] = "1.0";
```

In Listing 8.18, we start creating the message body. We add a line that says, "This is a multipart message in MIME format" so that anyone reading the source of the mail message will know it's a MIME-compliant message. We then add the first boundary. Remember that we must append two hyphens (--) to the boundary before we use it. Next, we add the original message and the original `Content-Type` as the first attachment.

Listing 8.18 *Creating the MIME header for the entire message*

```
var msgBody =
    "\nThis is a multi-part message in MIME format.\n" +
    "--" + this.Boundary + "\n" +
    "Content-Type: " + mainMessageType + "; charset=us-ascii\n" +
    "Content-Transfer-Encoding: 7bit\n\n" + this.Body + "\n\n";
```

In Listing 8.19 we add the file attachments. We loop through each element of the `attachments` array, which contains the MIME headers and contents for each file attachment created using the `attachTextFile()` and `attachHTML()` functions. Each file attachment is preceded by a boundary to ensure that the attachments are separated from one another.

Listing 8.19 *Adding all file attachments to the message*

```
for (i in this.attachments) {
  msgBody += "--" + this.Boundary + "\n";
  msgBody += this.attachments[I];
}
```

Now we have a nearly complete e-mail message that contains the original message and all file attachments (and their corresponding MIME headers). The last step is to add a closing boundary as shown in Listing 8.20. This tells the mail client where the last file attachment ends and that the message is complete. Notice that we again append two hyphens (--) to the front of the boundary and also add two trailing hyphens (--) to tell the mail client that the end of the message has been reached.

Listing 8.20 *Completing the message with a final boundary*

```
msgBody += "--" + this.Boundary + "--" + "\n\n";
this.Body = msgBody;
```

Mail

Sending the E-mail Message

Now we have a complete mail message; the original message has been changed to an attachment, and all the file attachments have been added. We are now ready to send the message.

The new Send() method is shown in Listing 8.21. (Note the capitalization. We must differentiate it from the default Send() method in the Send-Mail object.) Send() checks to see whether the attachments array exists (to see whether any files were attached to the outgoing message). If it exists, then Send() calls the addAttachments() method to add all file attachments. Otherwise, it sends only the e-mail message.

This example demonstrates how you can create your own versions of existing methods to better control the object. In this case, we add all requested file attachments to the message and then call the Send() method of the existing SendMail class to send the e-mail message.

Listing 8.21 *The new* Send() *method*

```
function SuperMail_send() {
    // IF ATTACHMENTS EXIST, ATTACH THEM TO THE OUTGOING MESSAGE
    if (this.attachments != null) {
        this.addAttachments();
        this.attachments = null;
    }
    if (this.send()) {
        return true;
    }
    else {
        return false;
    }
}
```

Remember that in Listing 8.8 we added all our functions to SendMail as new methods. We need call the SuperMail function only once from one application on the server. Thereafter, any instances of the SendMail object will contain all the methods and properties we've added. So you should probably add a call to SuperMail in the initial page of one of your applications.

Summary

You can use the SendMail object to send plain-text, HTML, or mime-compliant e-mails (with or without attachments). You can also extend the SendMail object to add custom methods so that you can more easily send e-mail messages with attachments. Now you know all about the SendMail object and sending multipart MIME-compliant e-mail messages.

Figure 8.4 *Sending application login forms via e-mail*

Now it's up to you. Use the `SuperMail` function to extend the `Send-Mail` object and start sending rich-text e-mail messages. Experiment with sending HTML documents and forms. If you want your users to log in to an application every day, send them the login screen via e-mail so that they won't forget (as shown in Figure 8.4). You can use e-mail forms to help route information and requests throughout the company. You can query databases for open employee requests, build HTML pages that let your managers approve or deny those requests with a click of the mouse, and then send the HTML pages to the employee via e-mail. The possibilities are endless.

Mail

9

Extending SSJS Using LiveConnect

Have you ever come up with a cool idea for extending the functionality of an application but you couldn't figure out how to do it with SSJS? In this chapter you'll learn how to harness the power of Java in your applications using a technology in JavaScript called LiveConnect. LiveConnect, introduced in Netscape Enterprise Server 3.0, enables you to communicate directly with Java from inside your JavaScript applications. You can create Java objects in SSJS and then call methods or manipulate properties of those objects as if they were native SSJS objects.

If you're interested in learning Java, the best place to start is by using Java inside your JavaScript applications. You'll find that the JavaScript syntax is remarkably close to that of Java, but remember that Java is not a scripting language. In Java you must explicitly declare your variables and variable types, and you must use classes and instances of classes and all that other hardcore programming stuff. However, Java is a much more powerful language that will help you do things you can't do natively in SSJS. Java programming is the natural evolutionary step for JavaScript programmers.

In this chapter we show you how to access the Java `Math` object directly from JavaScript. Then we show you how to access other Java objects from JavaScript: how to get server properties, how to get a remote Web page as a JavaScript string, and how to get directory listings on the server. By the time you finish this chapter you should have a basic understanding of how the LiveConnect technology allows you to access Java without even knowing that you're using LiveConnect.

The information presented in this chapter extends to Chapter 10, using LDAP. To connect with a directory server from SSJS, you must use Live-Connect. Try the examples presented in this chapter and play around a bit until you feel comfortable with LiveConnect. It's important that you understand the basics of this technology before reading subsequent chapters that build on these concepts.

Setting Up Java on the Server

For LiveConnect to work, it must be implemented in the Java Virtual Machine (VM) that ships with your JavaScript-enabled server. Netscape Web servers ship with the Netscape VM and are thus LiveConnect-ready, and Netscape has taken great pains to ensure that LiveConnect can be implemented in the VMs of other vendors. However, to enable Java and LiveConnect, you must modify the properties of your Netscape Web server (using the server administration application that ships with the server products). Use the following instructions to enable Java (and LiveConnect) on your server. (Figure 9.1 shows the screen where you make the modifications.)

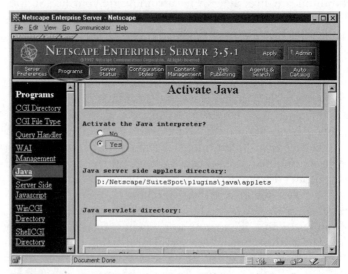

Figure 9.1 *Activating Java on the server (options to select are circled)*

1. Log in to your administration server.
2. Click on the server you wish to administer.
3. Click on the **Programs** button on the top frame.
4. Click on the **Java** link on the left frame.
5. Click on the **Yes** radio button on the right frame to activate the Java interpreter.
6. Click on the **OK** button.
7. Click on the **Save and Apply** button.

Now Java is enabled on your Web server, and you can begin to interact with the Java Virtual Machine (JVM) via LiveConnect. When Netscape Enterprise Server is started, the JVM is also started. The first time you execute a Java class on the server, it may be slow. Subsequent accesses, however, will generally be much faster because the Java class will already be loaded into memory and available to the JVM.

Java Classes

When you install your Netscape Web server, the standard Java classes needed for creating LiveConnect applications are installed in a package in the following location:

```
<server root>/plugins/java/classes/serv3_0.zip
```

Here, `<server root>` is the directory on your server machine into which you installed the Netscape Web server (typically, `/netscape/suitespot`). The Java runtime engine looks for Java class files in the following directories:

```
<server root>/plugins/java/classes/serv3_0.zip
<server root>/plugins/java/local-classes/
<server root>/plugins/java/applets/
```

You can manually add paths to the server's classpath by editing the `<server-root>/https-myserver/config/obj.conf`File. Read the server documentation for information on how to edit configuration files.

The Java runtime engine also searches directories specified in the `CLASSPATH` environment variable. If you wish to add your own Java classes for use with LiveConnect, place them in the `<server root>/plugins/java/local-classes/` directory (or an appropriate subdirectory if you've included all your classes in a package). For example, if you have a Java class called "foo.class" and it's in package "netscape.myclasses", the Java class should be located in the following directory on the server:

```
<server root>/plugins/java/local-classes/netscape/myclasses/foo.class
```

The file serv3_0.zip contains the Java class libraries included with Enterprise Server and FastTrack Server 3.0/3.01 for deploying HttpApplet and LiveConnect applications. (Note that Enterprise Server does not support all of JDK 1.1.) A listing of these packages and classes can be found at the following URLs.

■ Netscape Enterprise Server/FastTrack Server 3.0/3.01 Notes for Java Programmers:

```
http://developer.netscape.com/docs/manuals/enterprise/javanote/es30jpg.html
```

■ Netscape Enterprise Server 3.5.1 Notes for Java Programmers:

```
http://developer.netscape.com/docs/manuals/enterprise/javanote/es351jpg.html
```

To create a simple Java program, simply create a file called HelloWorld.java and add the following code.

```
class HelloWorld {

    // THIS METHOD DISPLAYS "Hello World!"
    static public void main(String[] args)
    {
        System.out.println( "Hello World!" );
    }
}
```

Now compile the code using the Java compiler as follows. (We assume here that you have downloaded and installed the Java Developer Kit (JDK), which contains a Java compiler (javac). You must install the JDK version 1.1 or later if you wish to try examples 3 and 4 in this chapter.)

```
javac HelloWorld.java
```

This code creates a file called `HelloWorld.class` that contains your program in Java byte code format, which any Java VM can execute. Now you can execute your simple Java program:

```
java HelloWorld
```

This code causes the JVM to execute your program, which in turn displays the following:

```
Hello World!
```

We don't go into any more detail on Java basics here—there are a number of excellent books on that topic. This brief tutorial is meant to help those who are new to Java understand the basic steps involved in creating, compiling, and running Java programs.

Accessing Java from JavaScript

You can access Java methods and properties from JavaScript by calling methods or directly manipulating properties (you specify the full classname and package when appropriate). Although the syntax of JavaScript is similar to that of Java, the trickiest part of using LiveConnect is to keep track of the data types returned from your Java calls. We always run into this problem—keeping track of what Java has returned and treating it properly.

You can also pass JavaScript values to Java. However, even though LiveConnect performs some of the data conversions for you, you must manually convert some of them. For example, to pass an integer value to a Java method, use the `parseInt()` function to convert the JavaScript variable to an integer. To pass a Java object from JavaScript to Java (as an argument), you must create the Java object, assign it to a JavaScript variable, and then pass the JavaScript variable (technically now a Java object). You would assign the Java object to a JavaScript variable:

```
var myVar = Packages.java.javaFirstClass(arguments);
```

You could then pass that Java object to another Java method:

```
Packages.java.javaSecondClass(myVar);
```

LiveConnect

JavaScript includes three predefined top-level objects that enable access to Java packages from within JavaScript: `sun`, `netscape`, and `java`. When you reference a class that belongs to these packages, the `Packages` prefix is optional. Therefore, you can refer to the preceding class in either of the following ways:

```
var myVar = Packages.java.javaClassName(arguments);
var myVar = java.javaClassName(arguments);
```

To reference a property or method of a Java class, you would write something like this:

```
var myVar = java.javaClassName.staticMethod(arguments);
var myVar = java.javaClassName.staticProperty;
```

To access a property of a class in the `sun` package, you would use a similar syntax, replacing the `java` package indicator with the `sun` package indicator:

```
var myVar = sun.javaClassName.staticProperty;
```

Accessing JavaScript from Java

A Java method can access an SSJS object only if the Java method was called from SSJS. (On the client, however, Java can initiate a call to CSJS.) To use JavaScript objects in Java, import the `netscape.javascript` package into your Java file. The `netscape.javascript` package defines the `JSObject` and `JSException` classes, which enable Java to access a JavaScript object's methods and properties and to handle errors returned by JavaScript. The `JSObject` and `JSException` classes are described in the JavaScript Guide on the Netscape Web site (see Resources).

When calling a Java method, you can pass a JavaScript object as one of the arguments. Remember, however, that you are passing an object of type `JSObject`. Whenever you reference a JavaScript object from Java, use a `JSException` wrapper so that your Java code can handle JavaScript errors.

Note   If you recompile a Java class that you are using in an SSJS application, the new class definition may not take effect immediately because the server generally continues to use the old Java class definition while it's running. Therefore, you should always restart your Web server after making changes to a Java class on the server.

Data Type Conversion

When you call Java from JavaScript or JavaScript from Java, the JavaScript runtime engine converts argument values into the appropriate data types for the other language. (The JavaScript runtime engine performs the same conversions on the server as it does on the client.) Figure 9.2 illustrates the data type conversions.

Note the following additional details.

- When you convert a Java object to JavaScript, the runtime engine creates a JavaScript wrapper object. Calling a method or accessing a property on the JavaScript wrapper results in a call to the Java object.
- When you convert a JavaScript wrapper to a string, the runtime engine calls the `toString` method on the original Java object.
- When you convert a JavaScript wrapper to a number, the runtime engine calls the `floatValue` method on the original Java object when possible and fails otherwise.
- When you convert a Java Boolean to a JavaScript Boolean, the runtime engine calls the Java `booleanValue` method.
- When you convert a Java array to JavaScript, the runtime engine creates a pseudo-`Array` object that behaves just like a JavaScript `Array` object. You can access array elements using `arrayName[index]`

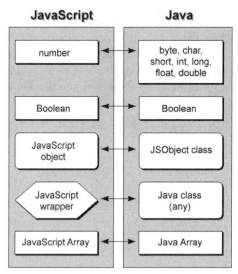

Figure 9.2 *Data type conversion between Java-Script and Java*

LiveConnect

(where `index` is an integer) and determine its length using `arrayName.length`.

■ When you convert a JavaScript wrapper to Java (generally as an argument to a Java method or the value of a Java property), the runtime engine unwraps it to the original Java object.

■ When you convert Java `String` objects to JavaScript strings, use the following syntax:

```
var JavaString = JavaObject.methodThatReturnsJavaString();
var JavaScriptString = JavaString + "";
```

■ When you convert JavaScript strings to Java `String` objects, the runtime engine does the conversion for you, converting JavaScript strings to Java `String` objects and Java `String` objects back to JavaScript strings.

■ When you convert JavaScript objects to Java objects, the runtime engine creates a Java wrapper of type `JSObject` (`netscape.java-script.JSObject`); when a `JSObject` is sent from Java to JavaScript, the runtime engine unwraps it to its original JavaScript object type. The `JSObject` class provides an interface for invoking JavaScript.

Pay close attention to the type of data Java is returning so that you don't make any errors in your code, something that happens to us more often than we care to admit.

OK, that's enough Java class mumbo-jumbo. Let's get to the fun part—extending the capabilities of SSJS applications using LiveConnect. We start with a basic example and then proceed to more exciting examples. The examples are designed to be easy to follow and use. The main idea is to get you up and running with LiveConnect as quickly and easily as possible.

Example 1: Generating Random Numbers

We start with a simple example: getting a random number from Java. After Java is enabled on Netscape Enterprise Server, you can access all the class libraries that come with the server (and any classes you write and install in an appropriate directory). In this example, we get a random number from JavaScript and then get a random number from Java using LiveConnect. To see random numbers generated by JavaScript and by Java, add the code in Listing 9.1 to an HTML page in your application.

Listing 9.1 *Displaying random numbers using JavaScript and Java*

```
<SERVER>
write("<H2>JavaScript Random Number: " + Math.random() + "</H2>");
write("<H2>Java Random Number: " + java.lang.Math.random() + "</H2>");
write("<H2>PI: " + java.lang.Math.PI + "</H2>");
write("<H2>E: " + java.lang.Math.E + "</H2>");
</SERVER>
```

See how easy that was? Notice that in lines 2 and 3 the syntax for getting a random number in Java is very similar to the syntax used in JavaScript. The biggest difference is that to get the Java random number we must specify "`java.lang`", which tells the server to use Java's `Math` object rather than JavaScript's `Math` object. You can access any of the properties of the Java `Math` object by using this syntax; you specify the class you wish to use (`java.lang.Math`) and the methods or properties of that class (`random()`, `PI`, `E`, and so on). `Random` is a method of the Java `Math` object, whereas `PI` and `E` are properties. To access `PI` and `E` you use the same syntax used to access the `random()` method, but omit the parentheses, as shown in lines 4 and 5 of Listing 9.1.

You can reference Java properties, create Java objects, and call any Java methods using this syntax. Example 2 demonstrates how to call a Java method and handle a returned Java object. It also introduces you to the concept of wrappers, which are used in later examples.

Figure 9.3 displays properties of the Java and JavaScript math objects.

Figure 9.3 *Example 1: generating random numbers*

Example 2: Displaying System Properties

Next, we use the Java `System` object in the `"java.lang"` library to get a listing of server properties, including operating system information, Java classpath, and so on. We access the `getProperties()` method of the `System` object, which returns all the property values as a Java `Properties` object (see Listing 9.2).

Listing 9.2 *Displaying system properties—unformatted*

```
<SERVER>
    // GET PROPERTIES
    var properties = java.lang.System.getProperties();

    // PRINT PROPERTIES STRING
    write("<P><H3>Properties:</H3>\n<HR>" + properties + "\n\n<P></HR>");
</SERVER>
```

Instead of simply writing the properties returned by Java, we assign the Java properties to a JavaScript variable and then print that variable. Remember that the variable does not contain a JavaScript string but rather contains a Java `Properties` object. If we want to manipulate the property values using JavaScript we must first convert it to a JavaScript string. This example simply demonstrates how to assign a Java object (a `Properties` object) to a JavaScript variable.

Note The toughest part of using LiveConnect is that you're accessing Java objects and variables that do not directly correlate to JavaScript objects and variables. Because Java is a strongly typed language, you should always keep track of what's being passed to and from it.

Now we format the properties using regular expressions and then display the properties (see Listing 9.3). We first convert a Java `Properties` object to a JavaScript string by adding an empty string (you can add the empty string to the beginning or end of a Java `String` object to convert it to a JavaScript string). To make the conversion, JavaScript calls the Java object's `toString()` method.

After converting the Java object to a JavaScript string, we use a regular expression to replace linefeeds with HTML line-break tags (<BR>) to properly format the output. Then we remove the brackets and display the resulting values. The main point of this exercise is to show that JavaScript can convert Java objects to values (such as JavaScript strings) that JavaScript can use natively. In addition, it shows how regular expressions can be used in Netscape Enterprise Server 3.0 and later. Anything you can do in core Java-Script 1.2 you can do in SSJS on NES 3.0.

Listing 9.3 *Displaying system properties—formatted*

```
<SERVER>
    var properties = java.lang.System.getProperties();
    var  propString = "" + properties;

    // REPLACE COMMAS WITH <BR> CHARACTERS
    var pattern = /, /g;
    var props   = propString.replace(pattern,"\n<BR>");

    // REMOVE {} FROM PROPERTIES STRING
    props = props.substring(1,props.length-1);

    // PRINT PROPERTIES STRING
    write("<P><H3>Properties:</H3>\n<HR>" + props + "\n\n<P></HR>");
</SERVER>
```

Figure 9.4 shows an example of this application in action.

Now let's throw a wrench into the works. JavaScript can easily call Java, but JavaScript 1.2 and earlier versions cannot catch Java exceptions. (Exceptions are a mechanism by which Java signals that an unexpected error condition has occurred. If a Java program "catches" the exception, it can handle it so that the application doesn't crash.) If Java throws an exception and you don't catch it, your application, and perhaps your server, will crash. (Remember, SSJS runs inline with the server, and that's why the applications are so much faster than CGI. However, it also means that if the inline application fails, it can potentially bring the server down with it.) As you've probably surmised, crashing your server is a bad thing. It almost goes without saying that catching Java exceptions is important.

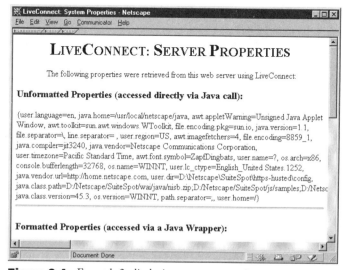

Figure 9.4 *Example 2: displaying system properties*

Java Wrappers

To catch the exceptions in Java before they propagate to SSJS, we'll create a Java *wrapper*. Java wrappers are Java classes that you create to catch Java exceptions. (In JavaScript 1.3 and later, this step is unnecessary because you can catch Java exceptions and can even throw and catch JavaScript exceptions.) To implement a wrapper, you create a Java class that creates your Java objects, calls Java methods, and so on and then passes the appropriate objects, values, or messages back to your calling JavaScript program. The wrapper catches any thrown exceptions and handles them as needed.

We make little effort here to show correct Java coding styles, teach how to create Java applications, or cover the Java language. Addison Wesley produces a comprehensive series of books on the Java language. If you plan to use LiveConnect in your applications, we recommend that you purchase some of these books to assist you in your Java coding efforts. (Note the shameless plug for our publisher.)

In the preceding example, the `getProperties()` method does not throw any exceptions, so we can't demonstrate the try/catch functionality until example 3. Here, we illustrate how a Java wrapper works. Simply create your Java file as shown in Listing 9.4. (Remember that the name of the Java file must be the same as that of the class you create.)

Listing 9.4 *Using a Java wrapper*

```
package netscape.ssjs;

import java.lang.*;

public class propertiesWrapper {

    public static java.util.Properties getProperties() {
        return System.getProperties();
    }
}
```

Listing 9.4 creates a small Java file that calls the `getProperties()` method and returns the resulting Java `Properties` object. Notice that we place it in a package, a technique that helps us organize our Java classes. We compile the Java file into a class using the following syntax (this assumes that you've already properly installed a Java compiler on your system):

```
javac -verbose propertiesWrapper.java
```

Next, we copy the `propertiesWrapper.class` file to the appropriate directory on the server, placing the file in the proper directory hierarchy so that the Java VM on the server can find it. Because it's in a package called `"netscape.ssjs"`, the VM will look for a `"netscape/ssjs/ propertiesWrapper.class"` file. We therefore place our Java class file in the following location:

```
<server root>/plugins/java/local-classes/netscape/ssjs/propertiesWrapper.class
```

Then, we call the wrapper in SSJS as shown in Listing 9.5.

Listing 9.5 *Calling a Java wrapper*

```
<SERVER>
    write("<P><H3>Properties Wrapper:</H3>\n<HR>" +
    Packages.netscape.ssjs.propertiesWrapper.getProperties() + "\n\n<P></ HR>");
</SERVER>
```

The `"Packages"` portion of the call is optional. The example shows how to create a simple Java wrapper that calls a Java method and returns an object or value. In example 3 we expand on this concept so that we can catch Java errors and keep them from making our lives difficult.

Example 3: Accessing Remote Content

Here's a problem we run into frequently: we want to access information in a document. If the document is located on the local server, the solution is easy—simply use the SSJS `File` object to read the file and then manipulate the contents using regular expressions.

But what do you do if the document or file is located on a remote server? The answer is easier than you might think: you simply use Live-Connect to access a Java method that facilitates HTTP requests. You can thus grab any file on any accessible server and manipulate the contents in your application.

To do this, we first create a Java class—the part of the application that issues the HTTP request, collects the file contents, converts the contents into string format, and returns the string to the SSJS application (see Listing 9.6). Notice that we use a Java wrapper to catch any Java exceptions that might get thrown. (For example, if you enter an incorrect URL, a `"MalformedURLException"` is thrown.) We catch Java exceptions in our Java class so that they don't propagate back to the SSJS application.

Listing 9.6 *Using a Java wrapper to catch Java exceptions*

```java
package netscape.ssjs;
import java.io.*;
import java.lang.*;
import java.net.*;
import java.util.*;

public class getFileWrapper {
    public static String getFile(String url) {
        // 2^15 CHARACTERS (ASSUMED LENGTH OF FILE - // ANYTHING LARGER WILL LOAD SLOWER)
        int len =  32768;
        int input;
        StringBuffer htmlDoc = new StringBuffer(len);
        // CATCH ANY EXCEPTIONS (CAUSED BY MALFORMED URLS OR IO PROBLEMS)
        try {
            // CREATE NEW URL OBJECT (IN java.net.URL CLASS)
            URL dest = new URL(url);
            // OPEN URL AS AN INPUT STREAM -
            // THIS REQUESTS THE HTML DOC FROM A REMOTE SERVER
            DataInputStream dis = new DataInputStream(dest.openStream());

            // LOOP THROUGH THE HTML DOC - PUTTING IT IN A STRING BUFFER
            while ((input = dis.read()) != -1) {
                htmlDoc.append((char) input);
            }
            // CLOSE THE INPUT STREAM
            dis.close();
        // HANDLE ERRORS
        } catch (MalformedURLException me) {
            return ("Error - MalformedURLException: " + me);
        } catch (IOException ioe) {
            return ("Error - IOException: " + ioe);
        }
        // RETURN HTML PAGE AS A STRING
        return htmlDoc.toString();
    }
}
```

Notice in Listing 9.6 that when we create the URL object and interact with the `DataInputStream`, we place all the statements within the `try{}` block. If a Java exception occurs, the `catch{}` statements will be processed; if we've caught the exceptions, we can handle them in our Java class (in this case we return an error string). If we did not catch the exceptions, they would propagate back to JavaScript and crash the application.

The Java class `getFileWrapper` contains a single method, `getFile()`, which takes a string argument and returns a Java `String` object. In the `getFile()` method, we create a URL object called `"dest"` and give it a valid URL as an argument (the Java `String` `"url"` is passed into the `getFile()` method as an argument):

```
URL dest = new URL(url);
```

We use the variable `dest` to create the `DataInputStream` object, which causes Java to issue the HTTP request and put the results (an HTML page or file) into a buffer:

```
DataInputStream dis = new DataInputStream(dest.openStream());
```

Next, we read from the input buffer, or stream, and put the contents into a `StringBuffer` object:

```
while ((input = dis.read()) != -1) {
    htmlDoc.append((char) input);
}
```

After the stream has been read, we convert the `StringBuffer` object HTML document to a Java `String` object and return the Java `String` object to SSJS. That's all there is to it. We're simply issuing an HTTP request for a file on the Web, converting it to a Java `String` object, and passing it back to our SSJS application. What could be simpler?

The next step is to compile the Java code into a class file using the following command:

```
javac -verbose getFileWrapper.java
```

Then we copy the `getFileWrapper.class` file to the following directory:

```
<server root>/plugins/java/local-classes/netscape/ssjs/
```

Now we can call the `getFileWrapper.getFile()` method from within our SSJS application:

```
var javaFile = netscape.ssjs.getFileWrapper.getFile(request.url);
```

If we request an HTML document and simply write the Java string we get back from the `getFile()` method, the tags will be interpreted as HTML and we won't be able to see the actual code. Therefore, in the sample application we convert the brackets that surround HTML tags into character equivalents. To do this, we first convert the Java `String` object we receive using `getFile()` into a JavaScript string that we can manipulate using JavaScript 1.2 regular expressions. By appending a blank string, we make the conversion from a Java `String` object to a JavaScript variable:

```
var htmlDoc = "" + javaFile;
```

That is easy. Now we can use JavaScript regular expressions to replace all the angle brackets that surround HTML tags with their HTML character equivalents:

```
// REPLACE OPEN AND CLOSE TAG CHARACTERS WITH CHARACTER EQUIVALENTS
    var openTag = /</g;
    var closeTag = />/g;
    htmlDoc    = htmlDoc.replace(openTag,"&lt;");
    htmlDoc    = htmlDoc.replace(closeTag,"&gt;");
```

Then we write the results, as shown in Listing 9.7. The listing contains both the SSJS code we use and the actual HTML so that you can also see the form we create. The form appears at the top of every page in the example, allowing the user to easily enter another URL. It is a good practice to include such search forms at the top of any documents that display search results so that users can quickly and easily enter alternative search requests.

Listing 9.7 *Calling the Java wrapper methods*

```
<HTML>
<HEAD>
    <TITLE>LiveConnect: Get Web File</TITLE>
</HEAD>
<BODY onLoad="document.myForm.url.focus()">
<CENTER>
<H2>
<FONT SIZE=+3>L</FONT>IVE<FONT SIZE=+3>C</FONT>ONNECT:
<FONT SIZE=+3>G</FONT>ET
<FONT SIZE=+3>W</FONT>EB
<FONT SIZE=+3>F</FONT>ILE
</H2>
</CENTER>
<CENTER>
<H3>Please enter the URL for a document you wish to retrieve from the Web:</H3>
</CENTER>
```

Listing 9.7 *Calling the Java wrapper methods (Continued)*

```
<CENTER>
<FORM NAME="myForm" METHOD="GET" ACTION="getfile.html">
<TABLE BGCOLOR=lightgrey CELLSPACING=0 CELLPADDING=0 BORDER=0>
<TR>
<TD ALIGN=right>
<B>URL:</B>
<TD><INPUT TYPE=text NAME="url" VALUE="http://" SIZE=40 MAXLENGTH=256>
<TD><FONT SIZE=-1 COLOR="#888888"></FONT></TD>
</TR>
<TR>
<TD COLSPAN=2><CENTER>
<INPUT TYPE="RESET" NAME="Clear" Value="Clear">
<INPUT TYPE="SUBMIT" NAME="getfile" VALUE="Get File">
</CENTER></TD>
</TR>
</TABLE>
</FORM>
</CENTER>

<SERVER>
if (request.url) {
    var len     = 16384;
    var javaFile = netscape.ssjs.getFileWrapper.getFile(request.url);
    var htmlDoc = "" + javaFile;

    // REPLACE OPEN AND CLOSE TAG CHARACTERS WITH CHARACTER EQUIVALENTS
    var openTag = /</g;
    var closeTag = />/g;
    htmlDoc    = htmlDoc.replace(openTag,"&lt;");
    htmlDoc    = htmlDoc.replace(closeTag,"&gt;");

    write("<CENTER><FONT SIZE=+2 COLOR=blue>" + request.url  +
        "</FONT></CENTER>\n<HR>\n");
    write("<PRE>\n");
    write(htmlDoc);
    write("</PRE>\n");
    write("<HR>\n");
}
</SERVER>
</BODY>
</HTML>
```

Figure 9.5 shows an example of this application in action.

We close with one last LiveConnect example. This one uses the `File` class, and does not generate any Java errors, so we don't use try/catch. It shows an example of something you can do with LiveConnect that you cannot do with SSJS: get a directory listing from the server.

LiveConnect

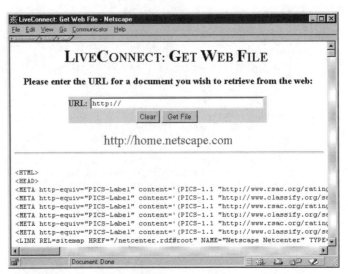

Figure 9.5 *Example 3: accessing remote content*

Example 4: Local File System Access

The JavaScript File object is fairly robust for manipulating individual files on the operating system. However, what happens if you need to get a list of files in a given directory on the server? Maybe you need to process all text or HTML files in a directory. Because you can't do it with JavaScript, the answer again is to use LiveConnect and Java.

Example 4 shows you how to get a directory listing on the server for any valid directory path you enter and pass that information back to SSJS. Please resist the urge to install this sample application on your public Web servers; it's meant as a demonstration of how to use LiveConnect to find files on the server's file system. It's doubtful you would ever *display* file system information in an application, although it is likely that you would *use* such information in an SSJS app.

The fileSystem Java class is shown in Listing 9.8 with an explanation to follow. Note that we simply create a Java File object if that file object points to a directory, we can call the list() method to get a listing of all the files in that directory. We loop through the list of files, gathering information about each of them and we then compile that information into a list and return it to SSJS. We ignore any files that don't contain the optional filter (*.html, *.txt, and so on). Note that the filter in this example is case-sensitive. Although very basic, this example gives you a little more exposure to the concepts we've previously discussed before we delve into LDAP in Chapter 10.

Listing 9.8 *Using Java to get a directory listing*

```
package netscape.ssjs;

import java.io.*;
import java.lang.*;
import java.util.*;

public class fileSystem {

    public static String fileSeparator = System.getProperty("file.separator");
    public static String getDirList(String dir) {
        int len        = 4096;              // 2^10 BYTES
        String dirName;
        String filter;

        // CHECK FOR EXISTENCE OF A FILENAME FILTER (*.html, etc.)
        if (dir.indexOf("*") != -1) {
            dirName = dir.substring(0,dir.indexOf("*"));
            filter  = dir.substring(dir.indexOf("*")+1,dir.length());
        }
        else {
            dirName = dir;
            filter  = null;
        }
        File currentDir  = new File(dirName);

        if (currentDir.exists() && currentDir.isDirectory()) {
            String dirList[] = currentDir.list();
            StringBuffer dirListing = new StringBuffer(len);

            for (int i=0; i < dirList.length; i++) {
                if (filter == null || dirList[i].indexOf(filter) != -1) {
                    File currentFile = new File(dirName +
                        fileSeparator + dirList[i]);
                    Date fileDate    = new Date(currentFile.lastModified());

                    // FILE TYPE
                    if (currentFile.isDirectory()) {
                        dirListing.append("DIR");
                    }
                    else if (currentFile.isFile()) {
                        dirListing.append("FILE");
                    }
                    else {
                        dirListing.append("UNKNOWN");
                    }
                    dirListing.append(",");

                    // FILE NAME
                    dirListing.append(dirList[i]);
                    dirListing.append(",");

                    // FILE SIZE
                    dirListing.append(currentFile.length());
                    dirListing.append(",");
```

Listing 9.8 *Using Java to get a directory listing (Continued)*

```
                    // DATE LAST MODIFIED
                    dirListing.append(fileDate.toLocaleString());
                    dirListing.append("\n");
            }
        }
        if (dirListing.length() > 0) {
            return dirListing.toString();
        }
        else {
            return "No files found that match " + dir;
        }
    }
    return "Invalid Directory: " + dirName;
  }
}
```

The only argument passed into the `fileSystem` class is a string argument that presumably contains a valid directory name. (Note that we test to see whether the directory name is valid. If it's not, we return an error message.)

The user can also include an optional filename filter so that only files with a specific extension (such as `.html`, `.txt`, `.sys`, and so on) are listed. We check for the existence of a filter by looking for an asterisk (*) character. If it's found, we assign everything following the asterisk to `filter` and everything preceding the asterisk to the `dirName` variable. Otherwise, we assign a `null` value to `filter` and assign the entire directory name to `dirName`.

```
if (dir.indexOf("*") != -1) {

    dirName = dir.substring(0,dir.indexOf("*"));
    filter  = dir.substring(dir.indexOf("*")+1,dir.length());
} else {
    dirName = dir;
    filter  = null;
}
```

We create a `File` object using the string argument we passed into the class.

```
File currentDir  = new File(dirName);
```

We then check to ensure that the `File` object we've created actually exists and is a valid directory.

```
if (currentDir.exists() && currentDir.isDirectory()) {
```

If `currentDir` is a valid directory, we call the `list()` method to return an array of string objects: the names of all the files in the directory. We create a string array called `dirList` to hold them. Unfortunately, after a Java `String` object is assigned a value, it becomes relatively static and you can't add anything to it. A Java `StringBuffer`, however, can be a contiguous, dynamically sized string value. For efficiency, you can specify the initial value when creating the `StringBuffer`, but it's not required.

```
String dirList[] = currentDir.list();
StringBuffer dirListing = new StringBuffer(len);
```

Next, we loop through the list of filenames.

```
for (int i=0; i < dirList.length; i++) {
```

If a filter was included, we check to ensure that each filename contains whatever was in the filter (`.html` and so on) before continuing. (Remember that the filter is case-sensitive.)

```
if (filter == null || dirList[i].indexOf(filter) != -1) {
```

If the filter is `null`, or if the filter value is found in the filename, we create a new Java `File` object. This is necessary so that we can use the `File` object's `lastModified()` method to determine when the file was last modified (so that we can display this information to the user).

```
File currentFile = new File(dirName + fileSeparator + dirList[i]);
Date fileDate = new Date(currentFile.lastModified());
```

Each line of the string we create will contain "DIR" or "FILE" to indicate the file type, the filename, the size of the file (in bytes), and the date the file was last modified. We append the information to the `dirListing` `StringBuffer` object using the `append()` method.

```
if (currentFile.isDirectory()) {
    dirListing.append("DIR");
}
```

LiveConnect

Then we convert the `StringBuffer` object to a `String` object before returning it to SSJS.

```
if (dirListing.length() > 0) {
    return dirListing.toString();
}
```

Listing 9.9 shows the SSJS application that uses LiveConnect to call the `fileSystem` class we've created.

Listing 9.9 *Formatting and displaying the directory listing*

```
<SERVER>
if (request.dir) {
    var javaFile = netscape.ssjs.fileSystem.getDirList(request.dir);
    var htmlDoc = "" + javaFile;

    // REPLACE COMMAS WITH TABLE CELLS AND NEWLINES WITH TABLE ROWS
    var comma = /,/g;
    var returnChar = /\n/g;
    htmlDoc = htmlDoc.replace(comma,"</TD><TD>");
    htmlDoc = htmlDoc.replace(returnChar,"</TD></TR><TR><TD>");

    // REPLACE FILE AND DIR LABELS WITH GRAPHICS
    var file = /FILE/g;
    var dir = /DIR/g;
    htmlDoc = htmlDoc.replace(file,"<IMG SRC='images/file.gif' BORDER=0>");
    htmlDoc = htmlDoc.replace(dir,"<IMG SRC='images/dir.gif' BORDER=0>");
    htmlDoc = "<CENTER>\n<TABLE CELLSPACING=2 CELLPADDING=2 ><TR><TD>" +
            htmlDoc;
    htmlDoc += "</TD></TR></TABLE>\n</CENTER>\n";

    // WRITE OUT DIRECTORY LISTING
    write("<CENTER><FONT COLOR=blue SIZE=+2><B>" + request.dir  +
        "</B></FONT></CENTER>\n<HR>\n");
    write("<PRE>\n");
    write(htmlDoc);
    write("</PRE>\n");
    write("<HR>\n");
}
</SERVER>
```

With a single LiveConnect command, we retrieve a file listing from Java, we pass our JavaScript string, which contains the name of a directory and an optional filename filter.

```
var javaFile = netscape.ssjs.fileSystem.getDirList(request.dir);
```

We then use JavaScript 1.2 regular expressions to replace the commas with HTML table markup tags. In this way, our directory listing appears in neat columns and rows.

```
// REPLACE COMMAS WITH TABLE CELLS AND RETURNS WITH TABLE ROWS
var comma = /,/g;
var returnChar = /\n/g;
htmlDoc = htmlDoc.replace(comma,"</TD><TD>");
htmlDoc = htmlDoc.replace(returnChar,"</TD></TR><TR><TD>");
```

We then replace the "DIR" and "FILE" labels with graphics and print the output, and we're finished.

```
// REPLACE FILE AND DIR LABELS WITH GRAPHICS
var file = /FILE/g;
var dir = /DIR/g;
htmlDoc = htmlDoc.replace(file,"<IMG SRC='images/file.gif' BORDER=0>");
htmlDoc = htmlDoc.replace(dir,"<IMG SRC='images/dir.gif' BORDER=0>");
```

Figure 9.6 shows this example in action.

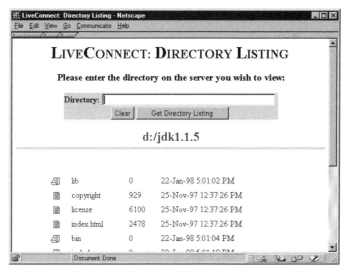

Figure 9.6 *Example 4: local file system access*

Summary

Calling Java from JavaScript is relatively easy. The straightforward syntax for accessing Java properties and methods from JavaScript using Live-Connect looks very much like JavaScript syntax. The trickiest part of using LiveConnect is to keep track of the type of values you receive from Java and to ensure that you convert them properly before using them.

Example 1 shows how to access properties of a Java class. Example 2 shows how to access a method of a Java class and how to use Java wrappers to catch Java exceptions before they propagate back to JavaScript. Example 3 illustrates how to use Java to get the contents of an HTML document from anywhere on the Web by passing a valid URL to the Java class you create. Example 4 shows how to access the file system on the server to get a listing of files in a given directory, something SSJS cannot do natively.

Now you know the basics of LiveConnect and have taken your first steps toward extending your SSJS applications with Java. Refer to this chapter if you get stuck with LiveConnect. We present the basics here so that you have a foundation to build on. Chapter 10 delves into LDAP, which relies heavily on the use of Java and LiveConnect.

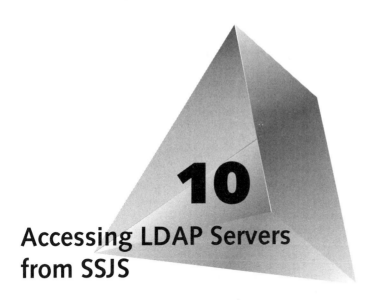

10

Accessing LDAP Servers from SSJS

In this chapter we do more than show you how to connect and conduct LDAP searches—any book can do that. We show you how to connect, search, sort, and authenticate and how to add, delete, and modify attributes and entries. This chapter covers nearly everything you'll want to do with LDAP. Why would you want to use an LDAP directory server in the first place? Many applications that you create probably include some sort of username or password functionality to restrict access to the application. Often, you must create this portion of the application yourself. Eventually you have several applications, each with its own store of user information (see Figure 10.1). A directory server enables you to store user information in a central location so that all applications can authenticate against a central repository. (This is called "single sign on" and it is a valuable capability for an intranet.) In addition, coding time for the application is reduced because you don't need to create a portion of the application to manage user information, and maintenance is simplified because you can manage all users and groups from a central location. That's only one use of a directory server, but it's an important one.

LDAP and Directory Servers

In Chapter 9 we explain how to use LiveConnect and Java to extend the functionality of SSJS. We show you how to use Java wrappers to trap Java exceptions and how to call those Java wrappers from

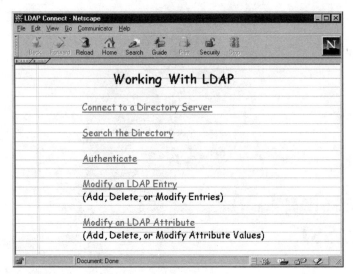

Figure 10.1 *Sample application main screen*

JavaScript. Now we build on those LiveConnect concepts and teach you how to access a directory server using Java. However, before we begin, it's important to know a little about LDAP and directory servers.

Lightweight Directory Access Protocol (LDAP) was developed at the University of Michigan and is a lightweight version of the ISO X.500 Directory Access Protocol (DAP) standard. Although LDAP was designed to work with the older X.500 protocol, it was also designed to be easier to use and implement. It all boils down to the idea that people want a simple way to store relatively static data so that it is optimized for searching.

In an LDAP directory the data is stored in a b-tree format that is optimized for fast searches. All the related data is stored in one place so that you can get to it quickly and get all the information at once. Remember that relational databases store information so that you can quickly insert, update, and delete records or search and manipulate the data to generate reports. Directories weren't built for this. They're mainly intended for the fast searching of static data (such as employee information, computer hardware, and so forth). So directories are faster than relational databases for searching but are slower for data modifications, and they are not suited for generating robust reports. Table 10.1 compares the two approaches.

Table 10.1 *Comparison of directdories and relational databases*

Directory	RDBMS
Optimized for basic retrieval	Optimized for transactions (read/write operations) and relational searches
Uses a simple hierarchical data model	Uses a complex relational data model
Uses a standard, cross-application database schema	Uses a custom, application-specific database schema
Uses a standard access protocol (LDAP)	Uses proprietary access protocols (SQL-net, and others)
Retrieves directory entries only	Can perform count, sum, and so forth

Directory servers are ideal if you want the following:

- Centralized administration of user and group data
- Single password and single sign-on capabilities
- Location independence (for roaming users)
- Secure data publishing over an extranet
- High-speed data lookups
- Access to common information from multiple distributed applications
- A common network registry

You should not use a directory server when your application

- Has a high volume of writes (more than 30–50 per second)
- Requires complex data analysis and reporting

Web servers generally listen on port 80 (HTTP) or port 443 (HTTPS), whereas directory servers listen on port 389 (LDAP) or port 636 (LDAP over SSL). Both types of servers respond to client requests; a Web server returns files, whereas a directory server returns *entry* information (explained in a moment). You can even enter an LDAP query in your Web browser. To get the entry for Airius (the organization listed in the `airius.ldif` file that ships with the Netscape directory server), you would enter the following:

```
ldap://machine.domain.com/o=airius.com
```

LDAP

To get the entry for Sam Carter of Airius you would enter this:

```
ldap://machine.domain.com/uid=scarter,ou=people,o=airius.com
```

Reading from right to left, the directory server first locates the organization (o), which is Airius.com. Then it locates the organizational unit (ou) people and traverses the tree until it finds the user ID (uid) scarter. After it locates this information, the directory server returns the entry.

The entry is the basic unit of information in a directory server. It is a collection of attributes, each of which has a type (case-insensitive string, case-exact string, binary, distinguished name, telephone, and so forth) and one or more values. The attribute type specifies the kind of values that can be stored in the attribute.

As you can see in Figure 10.2, each LDAP entry has one or more attributes, and each attribute can have one or more values. One or more of these attributes are used to form the relative distinguished name (RDN) of the entry. Entries are generally arranged in a hierarchical, tree-like structure, although this is not required. The distinguished name (DN) of an entry consists of its RDN and the RDN of its ancestors. See Figure 10.3 for an example of how a directory server is generally arranged.

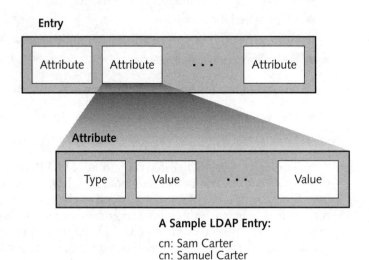

A Sample LDAP Entry:

cn: Sam Carter
cn: Samuel Carter
sn: Carter
mail: scarter@micromanage.com
jpegphoto: /9j/4AAQSkZJRgABAA. . .
objectclass: top
objectclass: person

Figure 10.2 *LDAP entry for Sam Carter*

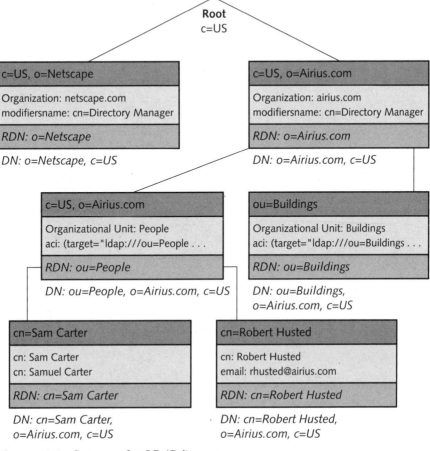

Figure 10.3 *Structure of an LDAP directory*

For us, the hardest part about using LDAP was the need to shift to a new way of thinking about how data is organized. We were used to SQL and expected LDAP to behave in the same way, but it doesn't. LDAP directories are organized differently, and the syntax used to search for data is different. Therefore, we thought it might be useful to talk about LDAP initially in terms of SQL so that you can see the similarities and the differences between the two.

LDAP versus SQL

No doubt you're familiar with Structured Query Language (SQL), which enables you to extract information from a relational database. Although

SQL is hard to grasp at first, it becomes almost second nature over time. LDAP is very much the same except that it was created to facilitate the searching of directory databases.

Data in a relational database is stored in a series of related tables. Records in the table are linked using keys; ideally, the only duplicate data in the database is the keys. In a directory, all the data is stored together in a b-tree format and is referenced by a distinguished name. The DN stores the minimum amount of information needed to quickly locate an LDAP entry and its associated values, or attributes. The only duplicate data that generally exists in a directory is the DN, which functions as a sort of database key. Given the DN, a directory server can almost instantly find the values associated with that DN by traversing the tree. (Like a primary key in a database, a DN is always supposed to be unique.)

Fortunately, Netscape has provided the Java SDK, which you can use to access LDAP. The SDK contains everything you need to manipulate the directory server, although you'll find that you use only a small subset of the available classes to do what you want. The remainder of this chapter focuses on the Netscape Java SDK, which you can download from the following location:

```
http://developer.netscape.com/docs/manuals/dirsdk/dirsdk.htm
```

Install the Java SDK in the following directory:

```
<server-root>/plugins/java/local-classes
```

When Enterprise Server starts up, this is one of the directories where it will look for Java class files, so it's easiest to uncompress the Java classes into that directory. If you decide to uncompress the Java classes into another directory, please remember to add that directory to your classpath.

Connecting to a Directory Server

In Chapter 9 we encourage you to use Java wrappers when calling Java from JavaScript so that you can trap Java exceptions and prevent them from affecting your application. We continue to do this in the code examples. Note that listings in this chapter generally include the Java code as well as the JavaScript code.

The first thing we do is to create an `LDAPConnection` object and then connect to a directory server. Listing 10.1 shows the Java code required to do this. If we try to connect with an invalid server name or port, an LDAPException is thrown. We catch any exceptions that occur in Java and simply return a null value if no connection was established; otherwise, we return the LDAPConnection object. (When you call the getLdapConnection() method from JavaScript, remember to convert the port number to an integer using the parseInt() function.)

Listing 10.1 *Java: connecting to an LDAP server in Java*

```
// THIS METHOD CONNECTS TO THE SPECIFIED DIRECTORY SERVER
public static LDAPConnection getLdapConnection(String server, int port);
{
    LDAPConnection conn = new LDAPConnection();
    try {
        conn.connect( server, port );
    }
    // CATCH ANY EXCEPTIONS SO THAT THEY DON'T CRASH YOUR SSJS APP
    catch (LDAPException e) {
        return null;
    }
    return conn;
}
```

You call the preceding Java method from JavaScript as shown in Listing 10.2. This code assigns the Java LDAPConnection object to the project object property ldapConnection.

Listing 10.2 *JavaScript: calling a Java method to create an LDAP connection*

```
var project.ldapConnection = null;
project.ldapConnection = Packages.netscape.ssjs.ldapJS.getLdapConnection(server,
parseInt(port));
```

After you have attempted to connect to the directory server, you may want to test the connection as shown in Listing 10.3. Use the isConnected() method of the Java LDAPConnection object to test the connection. The method returns a true value if you are connected to the server and returns false if you're not connected. It's generally best to test the connection before executing any searches or trying to modify the directory.

Listing 10.3 *Java: verifying a connection to a directory server*

```
// ENSURE THAT A CONNECTION TO THE LDAP SERVER EXISTS
if (project.ldapConnection.isConnected()) {
    // CONNECTED TO A DIRECTORY SERVER
}
else {
    // NOT CONNECTED TO A DIRECTORY SERVER
}
```

LDAP

LDAP Searches

Now that we've connected to a directory server, let's do a search
(Figure 10.4). Searching in a directory is a little different from searching a
database. Rather than receive rows and columns (which are then available
via the `cursor` object), you receive a bunch of Java `LDAPEntry` objects. If
you convert them to a string value, they look like the values in Listing 10.4.

Listing 10.4 *A typical LDAP entry*

```
LDAPEntry: uid=husted, ou=People, o=airius.com; LDAPAttributeSet: LDAPAttribute
{type='objectclass', values='top,person,organizationalPerson,inetOrgPerson'}LDAPAttribute
{type='ou', values='Product Development,People'}LDAPAttribute {type='l',
values='Sunnyvale'}LDAPAttribute {type='facsimiletelephonenumber', values='+1 408 555
9751'}LDAPAttribute {type='roomnumber', values='4321'}LDAPAttribute {type='manager',
values='uid=husted, ou=People, o=airius.com'}LDAPAttribute {type='cn', values='Robert
Husted'}LDAPAttribute {type='sn', values='Husted'}LDAPAttribute {type='givenname',
values='Robert'}LDAPAttribute {type='uid', values='husted'}LDAPAttribute {type='mail',
values='husted@airius.com'}LDAPAttribute {type='telephonenumber', values='+1 650 937 1213'}
```

Although the LDAP entries themselves aren't very readable, the LDAP
Entry object has a number of methods we can use to get the exact attribute
values we want, a functionality we discuss in a moment. First, let's start with
a basic directory search as shown in Listing 10.5.

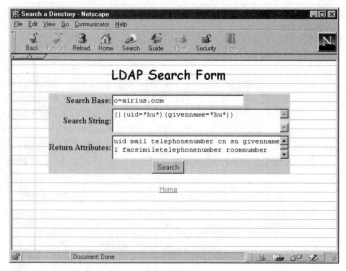

Figure 10.4 *Searching an LDAP Directory*

Listing 10.5 *A typical LDAP search command*

```
// A Typical LDAP SEARCH
return myLDAPConn.search(
    base,        // where to start searching on the LDAP tree
    scope,       //
    filter,      // check attributes (use AND "&" OR "|" and NOT "!")
    attrArray,   // attributes to return (null=all)
    false);      // true = names only, false = names and values
```

The arguments required for an LDAP search are similar to those you'd use in SQL. Table 10.2 shows how the LDAP arguments roughly equate to SQL arguments. Hopefully, this will help you better understand the LDAP syntax.

When we try to do a search, the LDAP search method throws an LDAPException if an error occurs. Therefore, it's important to catch this exception using a Java wrapper (most of the examples in this chapter use a wrapper called "ldapJS.class" to catch the exceptions).

Table 10.2 *LDAP versus SQL arguments*

LDAP	SQL Equivalent	Description
base	from	Where to start searching in the directory tree. If the base is "ou=People,o=Netscape Communications, c=US", your search will start with the "People" portion of the tree rather than perhaps the "Location" portion of the tree.
scope	No equivalent	The base indicates the starting point for the search and the scope indicates how far down to go. Whether to search only at the same level as the base, search one level below the base, or search all levels below the base.
filter	where	Describes which entries to bring back. If the filter contains "cn=au", only those entries that have a common name (cn) starting with the letters "au" will be returned.
attrArray	select	Specifies which attributes to return. A null value tells the directory to return all the attributes for all entries that match your filter parameters. This parameter must be an array of attribute names. Your array might consist of values such as "cn, givenname, mail".
boolean	No exact equivalent	"True" most nearly equals desc <tableName>, where the names of all columns in a table are returned. A true value for the boolean returns only attributes; no values are returned. A "false" value specifies that you want both the names and the values returned for each entry.

In the sample LDAP search (Listing 10.6), we pass the `LDAPConnection` object and several search parameters. Note that we do not pass a Boolean value or the integer for the scope. The Boolean value indicates what the LDAP search should return; `true` returns only attribute names, and `false` indicates that you want both the attribute names and all associated values. Assume here that we always want names and values and simply hard-code a Boolean `"false"` in the `ldapSearch()` method of the wrapper. We also assume that the scope of our search is always the current branch of the tree and all subbranches. Therefore, we hard-code these assumptions in our Java wrapper to make the method easier to use.

Listing 10.6 *Java: searching the directory*

```
// SEARCH THE DIRECTORY, IF ANYTHING GOES WRONG RETURNED A NULL VALUE
    public static LDAPSearchResults ldapSearch(
        LDAPConnection conn,
        String        base,
        String        filter,
        String        attrs)
    {
        try
        {
            // CONVERT JS STRING OF ATTRIBUTES INTO A JAVA STRING ARRAY
            String[] attrArray = stringToArray( attrs );
            // PERFORM THE SEARCH
            return conn.search(
                base,          // WHERE IN THE TREE TO BEGIN THE SEARCH
                netscape.ldap.LDAPv2.SCOPE_SUB,
                filter,        // CRITERIA FOR THE SEARCH (cn='au', etc.)
                attrArray,     // ATTRIBUTES TO RETURN (null=all)
                false);        // false = RETURN NAMES AND VALUES
        }
        catch (LDAPException e)
        {
            return null;
        }
    }
```

In Listing 10.6 we make a call to the `stringToArray()` method, which takes a space-delimited string and converts it to a Java array. We do this so that we don't have to pass a Java array into the `ldapSearch()` method. Instead, we pass a JavaScript string, which contains a space-separated list of attributes. We then convert the JavaScript string into a Java string array of attribute names that we want to return for each entry in the search. The `stringToArray()` method is shown in Listing 10.7.

The Java `Vector` class is an expandable array, so you can add and remove objects from a vector and it will automatically grow or shrink accordingly. The `StringTokenizer` class separates a Java `String` object into separate elements. We then get the size of the `Vector` class (the number of elements it contains) and create our array of Java `String` objects accordingly.

Listing 10.7 *Java: convert a comma-separated list into a Java array*

```
// THIS METHOD CONVERTS A SPACE-DELIMITED STRING TO A JAVA STRING ARRAY
static private String[] stringToArray( String str )
{
    Vector tmp = new Vector();
    {
        StringTokenizer toks = new StringTokenizer( str, " " );
        while ( toks.hasMoreElements() )
        {
            tmp.addElement( (String) toks.nextElement() );
        }
    }
    String[] array = new String[tmp.size()];
    for ( int i = 0;  i < tmp.size();  i++ )
    {
        array[i] = (String) tmp.elementAt( i );
    }
    return array;
}
```

We use the JavaScript code shown in Listing 10.8 to call the `ldapSearch()` method from SSJS. In our example, the base, filter, and requested attributes are all submitted via a form so we use the `request` object to reference them.

Listing 10.8 *JavaScript: searching the directory*

```
// ENSURE THAT AN LDAP CONNECTION EXISTS
if (project.ldapConnection.isConnected()) {
    // PERFORM LDAP SEARCH IF ALL FORM VALUES WERE ENTERED
    if (request.searchBase &&
        request.searchString &&
        request.returnAttributes) {
        // DO LDAP SEARCH
        var searchResults = Packages.netscape.ssjs.ldapJS.ldapSearch(
            project.ldapConnection,
            request.searchBase,
            request.searchString,
            request.returnAttributes);
    }
}
```

When we call the `ldapSearch` method, we pass a comma-delimited list of attributes. (JavaScript arrays are not equivalent to Java arrays, so we can't just pass a JavaScript `array` object.) However, an LDAP search requires that the attributes we want returned appear in an array. So we must convert the

LDAP

comma-delimited list of attribute names into a Java array of attribute names. The `stringToArray` method, which we described earlier, takes a comma-delimited string and converts it to a Java array (as shown previously in Listing 10.7).

Sorting LDAP Result Sets

After performing our search, we get back a Java `LDAPSearchResults` object. We show you how to manipulate this object in a moment. However, before we start parsing through the entries returned from the search, we may want to sort them (rather like using "ORDER BY" in SQL). LDAP includes a sort method for the `LDAPSearchResults` object, so we call that method.

When calling the `LDAPSearchResults.sort()` method, we must pass the name of the attribute we want to search on and pass a Boolean value indicating the direction of the sort, either ascending (`true`) or descending (`false`). If we want to sort on more than one attribute, we must send a Java `String` array *and* a Java `Boolean` array. To keep things simple in the example, we demonstrate how to sort search results based on a single attribute. Listing 10.9 shows how to do the sort: simply pass a Java `String` object and a Java `Boolean` object to the `LDAPSearchResults.sort()` method.

Listing 10.9 *JAVA: sorting the LDAP result set*

```
public static LDAPSearchResults ldapSort(
    LDAPSearchResults searchResults,
    String attribute,
    boolean direction)
{
    searchResults.sort(
        new netscape.ldap.LDAPCompareAttrNames(
        attribute,
        direction ) );
    return searchResults;
}
```

Listing 10.10 shows how to call the `ldapJS.ldapSort()` method. Because `sort()` is a method of the `LDAPSearchResults` object, you could call it directly from JavaScript. However, remember that you must create and pass a Java `String` object. Given this fact, it's easier to simply create a wrapper and pass a JavaScript string, which is converted automatically to a Java `String` object.

Listing 10.10 *JavaScript: sorting the LDAP result set*

```
// SORT THE RESULTS BASED ON THE FIRST ATTRIBUTE (true = ascending)
Packages.netscape.ssjs.ldapJS.ldapSort(searchResults, attribute, true)
```

Authentication

Another use of a directory server is for user authentication—ensuring that a user's name and password exist in the directory (see Figure 10.5). In this example we authenticate using the connection we've assigned to the `project` object. Authentication is necessary if you want to modify attributes or entries (which we discuss later in this chapter).

Most directories are set up so that each user can modify some or most of the attributes in his or her entry. Additional control is given to administrators so that they can add, delete, and modify all attributes and entries. (This is generally the `"cn=Directory Manager"` user, and the password for this user is generally specified when you install your directory server.).

In Listing 10.11 notice how easy it is to authenticate: pass the `dn` (distinguished name) and password to the `authenticate` method of your `connection` object. If the authentication is successful, the `LDAPConnection` object is authenticated and you can start manipulating your directory attributes and entries. It really is that simple.

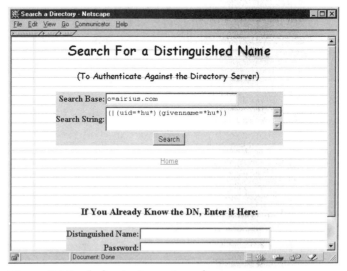

Figure 10.5 *Authenticating against a directory server*

Listing 10.11 *Java: authenticating against a directory server*

```
// AUTHENTICATE WITH THE SPECIFIED LDAP CONNECTION
public static void ldapAuthenticate( LDAPConnection ldapConnection,
                                     String dn,
                                     String pwd )
{
    try {
        ldapConnection.authenticate( dn, pwd );
    }
    catch ( LDAPException e ) {
        // EXCEPTION HANDLING CODE GOES HERE
        return false;
    }
    return true;
}
```

Listing 10.12 shows the required JavaScript code for calling the
ldapAuthenticate() method of ldapJS.class.

Listing 10.12 *JavaScript: authenticating against a directory server*

```
// AUTHENTICATE THE CONNECTION WITH A DN AND PASSWORD
Packages.netscape.ssjs.ldapJS.ldapAuthenticate(
    project.ldapConnection,
    request.dn,
    request.password);
```

After we've attempted to authenticate, we check the LDAPConnection
object to see whether the attempt was successful by calling the isAuthen-
ticated() method of LDAPConnection. The isAuthenticated()
method returns a Boolean value to indicate whether the connection is
authenticated. No exceptions are thrown, so we can make the same call from
Java or from JavaScript, as shown in Listings 10.13 and 10.14, respectively.

Note   In these code examples and in the sample LDAP application included on the CD-
ROM (ldap.web), we use the **project** object to maintain the connection. After the
connection is authenticated, anyone accessing the application can use that
authenticated connection because the **project** object is shared by all users. When
you create your own applications, you may want to protect your application itself
with the directory server to ensure that only authorized persons have access.

Listing 10.13 *Java: checking whether authentication was successful*

```
// CHECK TO SEE IF AUTHENTICATION WAS SUCCESSFUL
if (ldapConnection.isAuthenticated()) {
    . . .
}
```

Listing 10.14 *JavaScript: checking whether authentication was successful*

```
// CHECK TO SEE IF AUTHENTICATION WAS SUCCESSFUL
if (project.ldapConnection.isAuthenticated()) {
   . . .
}
```

Modifying Attributes

After authenticating the connection, we may want to add, delete, or replace directory entries. If we don't authenticate the connection, any attempt to modify entries in the directory will result in an LDAPException, so it's important to authenticate before trying to change attributes. The attributes shown in Figure 10.6 are examples of the kinds of attributes you might have in your directory.

Although entries in a directory don't change frequently, they do change, so you need a way to modify the attributes of an entry. The first step is to get the entry. Whenever you try to change an attribute, you must use the DN of the entry to identify it. (Remember that the DN, like the primary key in a relational database table, should always be unique.)

To modify an attribute, we start by creating a Java LDAPAttribute object to contain the name of the attribute and the new value. Listing 10.15 shows how to create a Java LDAPAttribute object.

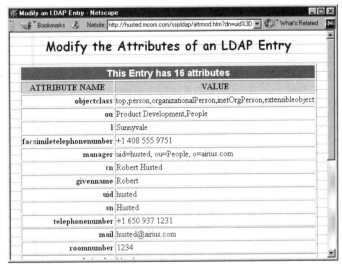

Figure 10.6 *Modifying LDAP attributes*

Listing 10.15 *JavaScript: creating a Java* LDAPAttribute *object*

```
attribute = new Packages.netscape.ldap.LDAPAttribute(
    request.attributeName,
    request.attributeValue);
```

After creating the attribute, we create a Java LDAPModification object in which we specify the type of modification we want to make (ADD, DELETE, or REPLACE) and the LDAP attribute we want to change (the Java LDAPAttribute object we previously created). Listing 10.16 shows how to create a Java LDAPModification object.

Listing 10.16 *JavaScript: creating a Java* LDAPModification *object*

```
modification = new Packages.netscape.ldap.LDAPModification(
    Packages.netscape.ldap.LDAPModification.REPLACE,
    attribute);
```

Now we're ready to submit the change request to the directory server. Listing 10.17 shows the Java code required to make the change. The modify() method of the LDAPConnection object throws an LDAPException if an error occurs (usually because the user is not authenticated or because the attribute doesn't exist or can't be added). The modify() method does not return a value. If no exception occurs, the modification was successful.

Note that the same Java method is used for modifying, deleting, and adding attributes. All you have to change is the parameter that specifies the type of change you are making (ADD, DELETE, or REPLACE).

Listing 10.17 *Java: modifying an attribute*

```
// ADD, DELETE, OR REPLACE AN ATTRIBUTE FOR A SPECIFIED DN
static public String modifyAttribute(
    LDAPConnection conn,
    String dn,
    netscape.ldap.LDAPModification modification)
{
    try
    {
        conn.modify(dn, modification);
    }
    catch (LDAPException e)
    {
        // HANDLE EXCEPTION
    }
}
```

In Listing 10.16 we created the modification variable that holds a Java `LDAPModification` object. We now use this modification object when calling the `modifyAttribute()` method of `ldapJS.class` (see Listing 10.18). Remember that the `LDAPModification` object contains a single Java `LDAPAttribute` object, which specifies the name and value of the attribute we wish to change.

Listing 10.18 *JavaScript: modifying an attribute*

```
result = Packages.netscape.ssjs.ldapJS.modifyAttribute(
    project.ldapConnection,
    request.dn,
    modification);
```

The only significant difference between adding, deleting, and replacing an attribute is the type of modification you specify when you create the `LDAPModification` object (see Table 10.3). There is one additional catch to adding an attribute, which we discuss next.

If you try to replace an attribute that doesn't exist, it will be added. Remember that `REPLACE` overwrites all existing attribute values, whereas `ADD` simply adds another value to the attribute. If you try to delete an attribute that doesn't exist, an `LDAPException` occurs. You also get an `LDAPException` if you try to add or replace an attribute that does not appear in the schema.

Usually, the directory manager defines the directory schema. Typically, each entry contains certain values in its `objectclass` attribute that identify the attributes that are allowed for that entry. If the `objectclass` allows or defines specific attributes, they can be added to an entry. If you wish to add a new attribute that is not allowed or has not been defined, there are three ways to do it.

Table 10.3 *Ways to modify an LDAP attribute*

Parameter	Attribute Affected	Value
ADD	New or existing attribute	New value (adds the specified value)
DELETE	Existing attribute	Current value (deletes only the specified value; all other existing values remain)
REPLACE	Existing attribute	New value (replaces all existing values)

1. You can ask the directory manager to add the attribute. This is generally the best option because the directory manager will likely want to
   maintain some control over the directory schema to ensure that
   entries are as consistent as possible.

2. You can add `"extensibleobject"` as a value to the `objectclass`
   attribute in any LDAP version 3-compliant directory. Adding `exten-
   sibleobject` allows you to add any attribute to an entry in the direc-
   tory. It largely depends on how much control your directory manager
   wants to maintain over the directory schema.

3. You can programmatically retrieve and alter the schema, changing an
   `objectclass` to accommodate additional attributes. This option is
   beyond the scope of this book. In addition, it creates the same directory consistency problems as option 2. Generally speaking, option 1 is
   best.

To see this feature in action, in the sample application you can add
`"extensibleobject"` to the `"objectclass"` attribute and then add any
attributes you want.

Modifying Entries

When you add, delete, or modify an attribute, you are simply working with
a single attribute. However, when adding or modifying an entry you typically work with several attributes at once. You just learned how to modify a
single attribute, so we start here by showing you how to modify multiple
attributes, a similar process. Remember that to add, delete, or modify an
entry you must be authenticated (generally as the directory manager or
equivalent).

The biggest difference is that instead of creating an `LDAPModification`
object that holds a single `LDAPAttribute` object, we create an `LDAPModi-
ficationSet` object that will hold multiple `LDAPAttribute` objects (see
Listing 10.19). In the form that displays the LDAP entry (Figure 10.7) and
allows the user to modify the attributes, each field has a corresponding hidden field starting with `"mod_"`. If the original field is modified, the client-
side `onChange` event triggers and sets the corresponding `"mod_"` field. In
this way, we change only the values for attributes that have changed. (It also
simplifies the example because we don't have to worry about checking for
multiple preexisting values, parsing those values, replacing the first value,
and adding each additional value as a separate attribute.) If the value of the
`"mod_"` pair is a blank string, we assume that it wasn't changed.

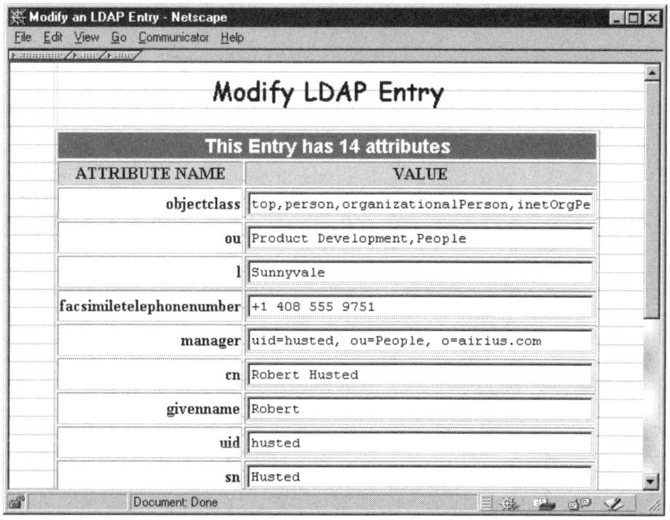

Figure 10.7 *Modifying an LDAP entry*

Listing 10.19 *JavaScript: creating an* LDAPModificationSet

```
// CREATE NEW MODIFICATION SET TO CHANGE ATTRIBUTE VALUES
modificationSet = new Packages.netscape.ldap.LDAPModificationSet;
// LOOP THROUGH ALL INCOMING FORM NAME-VALUE PAIRS
for (name in request) {
    if ((name.indexOf("mod_") != -1) && request[name] != "") {
        nameString = name.substring(4,name.length);
        attribute = new Packages.netscape.ldap.LDAPAttribute(
            nameString,
            request[name]);
        modificationSet.add(
            Packages.netscape.ldap.LDAPModification.REPLACE,
            attribute);
        modifications++;
    }
}
```

After we'e created the LDAPModificationSet we again call the
LDAPConnection.modify() method, this time passing it an LDAPModifi-
cationSet rather than an LDAPModification. The Java code is shown in
Listing 10.20, and the JavaScript code in Listing 10.21.

Listing 10.20 *Java: modifying an LDAP entry*

```
// THIS METHOD MODIFIES THE ENTRY FOR A SPECIFIED DN
static public String modifyEntry(
    LDAPConnection conn,
    String dn,
    netscape.ldap.LDAPModificationSet modifications)
```

LDAP

Listing 10.20 *Java: modifying an LDAP entry (Continued)*

```
{
    try
    {
        conn.modify(dn, modifications);
    }
    catch (LDAPException e)
    {
        // ERROR HANDLING CODE GOES HERE
    }
    return "Success";
}
```

Listing 10.21 *JavaScript: modifying an LDAP entry*

```
// MODIFY LDAP ENTRY
result = Packages.netscape.ssjs.ldapJS.modifyEntry(
    project.ldapConnection,
    request.dn,
    modificationSet );
```

Now let's look at deleting an entire entry and then at adding an
entire entry. Deleting an entry is almost too easy—you simply specify the
DN of the entry you wish to delete. See Listing 10.22 for the Java code,
and Listing 10.23 for the JavaScript code. We use the **LDAPConnec-
tion.delete()** method to delete the entry. This method takes only one
parameter—DN—and on error throws an exception.

Listing 10.22 *Java: deleting an LDAP entry*

```
// THIS METHOD DELETES AN LDAP ENTRY
static public String deleteEntry( LDAPConnection conn, String dn)
{
    try
    {
        conn.delete(dn);
    }
    catch (LDAPException e)
    {
        // ERROR HANDLING ROUTINE GOES HERE
    }
        return "Success";
}
```

Listing 10.23 *JavaScript: deleting an LDAP entry*

```
result = Packages.netscape.ssjs.ldapJS.deleteEntry(
    project.ldapConnection,
    request.dn );
```

Now we show you how to add a new entry to the directory server. To add an entry you must ensure that all the attributes that are specified as required are filled in. Check with your directory manager to get a list of these attributes. In the sample application we simply duplicate an existing entry and change the dn, uid, cn, and a few other values to ensure uniqueness and then submit the entry.

To add a new LDAP entry we create an LDAPAttributeSet and add several LDAPAttribute objects to it. It's similar to the way in which we modified attributes except that here we use an LDAPAttributeSet rather than an LDAPModificationSet because we are adding all the attributes rather than modifying existing ones.

In Listing 10.24 we first create an LDAPAttributeSet object and then parse through all the values sent from the form, stripping out all the irrelevant properties of the request object. We then create a new LDAPAttribute object for each valid attribute we wish to add. Next, we add each LDAPAttribute object to the LDAPAttributeSet. After we add all the attributes to the LDAPAttributeSet, we're ready to create and add a new entry.

Listing 10.24 *JavaScript: creating an* LDAPAttributeSet

```
// ADD NEW LDAP ENTRY
var attributeSet = new Packages.netscape.ldap.LDAPAttributeSet();
// LOOP THROUGH ALL INCOMING FORM VALUES
for (name in request) {
    // REMOVE SSJS VARIABLES FROM REQUEST OBJECT
    if (name == "add" ||
        name == "ip" ||
        name == "protocol" ||
        name == "method" ||
        name == "agent" ||
        name == "uri" ||
        name == "dn" ||
        (name.indexOf("mod_") != -1))
    {
        // LEAVE OUT HIDDEN mod_ FIELDS
    }
    // ADD ALL VALID ATTRIBUTES TO THE LDAP modificationSet
    else {
        // SPLIT ENTRY INTO INDIVIDUAL ATTRIBUTES
        var attrArray = request[name].split(",");
        // LOOP THROUGH ATTRIBUTE ARRAY
        for (var i=0; i < attrArray.length; i++) {
            attribute = new Packages.netscape.ldap.LDAPAttribute(
                name,
                attrArray[i]);
            attributeSet.add( attribute );
        }
    }
}
```

LDAP

Listing 10.24 creates an `LDAPAttributeSet` and adds all the `LDAP-Attribute` objects for each attribute we wish to add for the new entry. Now we create an `LDAPEntry` object that contains our newly created `Attribute-Set` and the DN for the new Entry (a Java `String` object). Ask your directory manager how DNs are set up in your directory so that you'll know how to create one, or just look at some existing ones; most DNs are similar (although unique). Listing 10.25 shows how to create a new LDAP entry.

Listing 10.25 *JavaScript: creating a new* `LDAPEntry` *object*

```
// CREATE LDAP ENTRY
var newEntry = new Packages.netscape.ldap.LDAPEntry(
    request.dn,
    attributeSet );
```

Then, we call the `LDAPConnection.add()` method to create the new entry in the directory. Listing 10.26 shows the Java code, and Listing 10.27 shows the JavaScript code.

Listing 10.26 *Java: adding a new LDAP entry*

```
// THIS METHOD ADDS A NEW LDAP ENTRY
static public String addEntry(
    LDAPConnection conn,
    netscape.ldap.LDAPEntry entry)
{
    try
    {
        conn.add(entry);
    }
    catch (LDAPException e)
    {
        // ERROR HANDLING CODE GOES HERE
    }
    return "Success";
}
```

Listing 10.27 *JavaScript: adding a new LDAP entry*

```
result = Packages.netscape.ssjs.ldapJS.addEntry(
    project.ldapConnection,
    newEntry );
```

In addition to the preceding sample application (which lets you connect with a directory server and search, authenticate, and modify attributes and entries), a second application is provided. The org chart application (shown in Figure 10.8) dynamically builds the organizational structure for an indi-

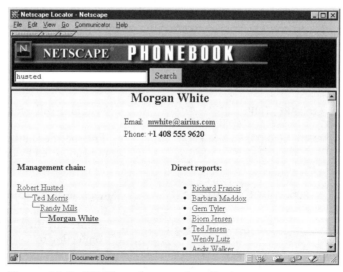

Figure 10.8 *LDAP org chart sample application*

vidual, showing all his or her managers and reports. This simple application demonstrates the usefulness of directories.

LDAPException Error Codes

Table 10.4 lists LDAPException error codes that will come in handy as you begin to debug your LDAP applications.

Table 10.4 LDAPException *error codes*

Error Number	Name	Description
0	SUCCESS	The operation completed successfully.
1	OPERATION_ERROR	An internal error occurred in the LDAP server.
2	PROTOCOL_ERROR	Your request does not strictly comply with the LDAP protocol.
3	TIME_LIMIT_EXCEEDED	The search operation could not be completed within the maximum time limit.
4	SIZE_LIMIT_EXCEEDED	The search found more than the maximum number of results.

LDAP

Table 10.4 LDAPException *error codes (Continued)*

Error Number	Name	Description
5	COMPARE_FALSE	No matching value found.
6	COMPARE_TRUE	Matching value found.
7	AUTH_METHOD_NOT_SUPPORTED	The specified authentication method is not supported by the LDAP server that you are connecting to.
8	STRONG_AUTH_REQUIRED	A stronger authentication method (more than the default LDAP_AUTH_SIMPLE) is required by the LDAP server that you are connecting to.
9	LDAP_PARTIAL_RESULTS	The LDAP server is referring your client to another LDAP server.
10	REFERRAL	Version 3: The server does not hold the requested entry.
11	ADMIN_LIMIT_EXCEEDED	Version 3: The adminstrative limit on the maximum number of entries to return was exceeded.
12	UNAVAILABLE_CRITICAL_EXTENSION	Version 3: The server received an LDAP v3 control that is marked critical and either (1) is not recognized or supported by the server or (2) is inappropriate for the operation requested.
13	CONFIDENTIALITY_REQUIRED	Version 3: A secure connection is required for this operation.
14	SASL_BIND_IN_PROGRESS	Version 3: The server requires the client to send a new SASL bind request to continue authentication.
16	NO_SUCH_ATTRIBUTE	The specified attribute could not be found.
17	UNDEFINED_ATTRIBUTE_TYPE	The specified attribute is not defined.
18	INAPPROPRIATE_MATCHING	An inappropriate type of matching was used.

Table 10.4 LDAPException *error codes (Continued)*

Error Number	Name	Description
19	CONSTRAINT_VIOLATION	An internal error occurred in the LDAP server.
20	ATTRIBUTE_OR_VALUE_EXISTS	The value that you are adding to an attribute already exists in the attribute.
21	INVALID_ATTRIBUTE_SYNTAX	The request contains invalid syntax.
32	NO_SUCH_OBJECT	The entry specified in the request does not exist.
33	ALIAS_PROBLEM	A problem occurred with an alias.
34	INVALID_DN_SYNTAX	The specified DN uses invalid syntax.
35	IS_LEAF	The specified entry is a leaf entry (it has no entries beneath it in the directory tree).
36	ALIAS_DEREFERENCING_PROBLEM	An error occurred when dereferencing an alias.
48	INAPPROPRIATE_AUTHENTICATION	The authentication presented to the server is inappropriate (for example, the userpassword attribute is missing).
49	INVALID_CREDENTIALS	The authentication credentials are not valid (for example, the password is invalid).
50	INSUFFICIENT_ACCESS_RIGHTS	The authenticated user does not have the access privileges to perform this operation.
51	BUSY	The LDAP server is busy.
52	UNAVAILABLE	The LDAP server is unavailable.
53	UNWILLING_TO_PERFORM	The LDAP server is unable to perform the specified operation.
54	LOOP_DETECT	A loop has been detected.
60	SORT_CONTROL_MISSING	The server-side sorting control was not included with the virtual list view control in the search request.
61	INDEX_RANGE_ERROR	An index range error occurred.

LDAP

Table 10.4 LDAPException *error codes (Continued)*

Error Number	Name	Description
64	NAMING_VIOLATION	A naming violation has occurred.
65	OBJECT_CLASS_VIOLATION	The requested change does not comply with the schema.
66	NOT_ALLOWED_ON_NONLEAF	The requested operation can be performed only on a leaf entry.
67	NOT_ALLOWED_ON_RDN	The specified operation cannot be performed on a relative distinguished name (RDN).
68	ENTRY_ALREADY_EXISTS	The specified entry already exists (for example, you're adding an entry that already exists or you are creating a duplicate entry).
69	OBJECT_CLASS_MODS_PROHIBITED	You cannot modify the specified object class.
71	AFFECTS_MULTIPLE_DSAS	Version3: The client attempted to move an entry from one LDAP server to another by requesting a "modify DN" operation.
80	OTHER	General result code for other types of errors that may occur.
81	SERVER_DOWN	The LDAP server cannot be contacted.
89	PARAM_ERROR	Parameters incorrectly specified for constructor or method.
91	CONNECT_ERROR	Client failed to connect to the LDAP server.
92	LDAP_NOT_SUPPORTED	LDAP version doesn't support the request.
93	CONTROL_NOT_FOUND	The requested control is not found.
94	NO_RESULTS_RETURNED	No results have been returned from the server.
95	MORE_RESULTS_TO_RETURN	More results are being returned from the server.

Table 10.4 `LDAPException` *error codes (Continued)*

Error Number	Name	Description
96	`CLIENT_LOOP`	Your LDAP client detected a loop in the referral.
97	`REFERRAL_LIMIT_EXCEEDED`	The maximum number of sequential referrals has been exceeded.

Summary

This chapter shows you everything you need to know about LDAP for most applications. Generally, you use LDAP for searching and authenticating, but we include the additional information in case you want to develop location-independent applications in which preferences and data are stored in the directory server.

LDAP

Netscape Application Server

As all Web developers know, the Internet is a fast-changing world. The phrase Internet time was coined to describe the breakneck speed with which languages, platforms, tools, and applications are being built to meet the growing demand for bigger and better Internet and intranet applications. The latest demand is for platforms to support the building of scalable and highly reliable Web-based enterprise applications. It is here that Netscape Application Server comes in.

Platforms such as Netscape server-side JavaScript and Microsoft Active Server Pages are terrific for building small to mid-sized applications. But let's face it—scripted applications written on Web servers have their limits. If you want to develop something such as a real-time e-commerce site serving thousands of users, Netscape Application Server (NAS) can give you the power and scalability you need between your intranet Web server and your corporate databases. NAS is the right choice for larger applications that will benefit from a multitier architecture and for applications that have heavy performance demands that SSJS isn't designed to handle.

In this chapter we explain the basics of application servers and introduce you to NAS. We go on to describe how NAS can help you build scalable, flexible Web applications and how it can integrate with SSJS. Finally, we run through an initial evaluation of NAS and summarize its strengths and weaknesses.

If your organization is committed to the Netscape platform or if you anticipate developing a range of applications from small workgroup applications to large, enterprise-wide applications, you need the information presented in this chapter. SSJS and NAS are two Web application platforms that offer different levels of application services for different needs. If you understand what NAS provides and where it differs from SSJS, you can make better decisions in the future about which platform is most appropriate for your needs. If you understand what NAS provides and where it differs from SSJS, you can make better decisions in the future about which platform is most appropriate for your needs. Additionally, in the future Netscape may provide a direct migration path from SSJS applications to NAS applications. In that case, you can economically build applications on SSJS initially and then esaily scale up to the heavy-duty NAS platform as your application and user requirements demand.

Application Servers and NAS

What exactly is an application server? Simply put, it's an engine that handles the serving of requests for application logic, just as Web servers serve requests for documents. An application server provides distributed, multiuser access to objects that contain application logic.

Note   **An Application Server Glossary**

This glossary helps explain some of the newer terms used to describe application server functionality so that you can better understand the concepts presented in this chapter.

application logic Any kind of application code that performs operations specific to the application or necessary for the application to function. Examples include security or user authentication and memory management.

business logic A specific kind of application logic that deals primarily with functions that relate to a real-world operation. Examples include processing online credit card payments and calculating loan payments.

business object Any object that contains logic that relates to a real-world entity or operation, such as a customer or a product. For example, an application for a mortgage company might contain business objects such as **property**, **owner**, and **mortgage**. The mortgage object might contain methods that calculate the monthly payment based on the interest rate.

business rule A rule that defines the boundaries and restrictions of the real-world business processes being modeled by the application. Examples include "All employees must have a unique employee identification number" and "An order can exist in the system only if it is associated with one and only one customer. "

multitier (or n-tier) application A Web or client/server application that divides application responsibilities among multiple logical services, called tiers. For example, a traditional SSJS application can be considered a three-tier application, with presentation logic on the browser in client-side JavaScript, business logic in SSJS code on the Web server, and data validation rules in stored procedures on the database server.

presentation logic Code that generates HTML or other user interface elements. Such code generally doesn't perform any business functions but instead calls on business objects to retrieve data and then takes care of formatting the data for output.

As an SSJS developer, you've already used an application server; the SSJS engine that's built into Netscape Enterprise Server can be considered an embedded application server. The Microsoft Active Server Pages engine can also be considered an embedded application server. Both engines execute application logic based on a user request. In addition, these application servers take care of handling simultaneous requests from multiple users without forcing you to consider the multiuser environment except in a few cases, when you must consider locking certain objects. You can write your application as if it were destined for a single user, and you don't have to worry about the complexities that trouble traditional multiuser client server applications.

To be useful, an application server should have some or all of the following capabilities:

- Allow developers to write objects as if for a single user
- Handle simultaneous connections for multiple users automatically, including threading and memory management
- Provide state maintenance mechanisms
- Provide an API or component framework for developing objects that run on the server
- Contain an administrative interface for managing the server as well as for packaging objects into "applications" and deploying those objects

Netscape Application Server has all these features and more. It hosts and processes application logic written in Java or C/C++, and it's designed to handle much heavier loads than SSJS was intended to handle.

Aftere you set up your business objects in NAS, any application can access them. Unlike SSJS, NAS doesn't require clients to be Web clients, and NAS doesn't require that only one client application access a given object. You can have an SSJS application access objects on NAS at the same time that a stand-alone Java application accesses the objects. By contrast, if you wrapped your business logic in your SSJS application, you'd have to rewrite it for the Java application and any other applications that needed to do the same thing.

NAS was originally created by an independent company, Kiva Software, that had no particular ties to Netscape. Kiva created the server to be platform-agnostic within reason. Thus, NAS runs on both NT and UNIX and should work consistently with most popular Web servers, browsers, and databases.

Using NAS in Web Applications

To give you a better idea of how NAS might be used in a typical Web application, let's look at a real-world project that one of the authors designed last year before sophisticated application servers existed. The example is a three-tier SSJS e-commerce application that serves documents over the Internet to customers who purchase them online using credit cards. The payments are then processed online using the CyberCash CashRegister payment server so that customers receive immediate feedback on their purchases. The first tier consists of HTML and some client-side JavaScript. The middle tier consists of an SSJS application that generates HTML through presentation logic and implements application logic, such as processing online payments, through SSJS function libraries. An Informix database server—filled with integrity constraints, basic data retrieval code in stored procedures, and business rules implemented through triggers and stored procedures—makes up the final tier. A separate administrative application runs internally, allowing customer service representatives to modify available products and make changes to customer accounts. This application performs some of the same operations as the customer application.

All in all, the basic three-tier architecture works well, but there are problems. In many instances, the application logic is tied tightly to the presentation logic, because that approach required less development time up front. Making changes, however, often requires more development time than it would if the responsibilities had been better separated. Also, even though the Informix server handles heavy loads quite well, SSJS tends to become a bottleneck when subjected to extremely heavy, simultaneous user sessions because the SSJS application is responsible for much processing. Finally, with both the administrative and the customer applications written in SSJS, sharing application code becomes a bit of a problem, especially if the applications run on two different Web servers.

Adding a NAS tier between the Web server and the database server, as shown in Figure 11.1, would solve or at least reduce these problems. We could move most or all of the application logic, such as payment processing, into reusable Java objects running on NAS. Then if we needed to change the look-and-feel of the application by way of the presentation logic, we

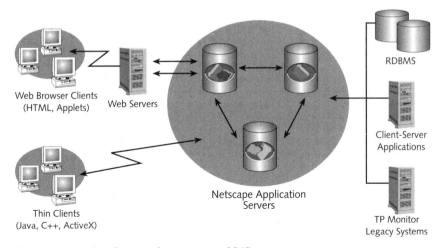

Figure 11.1 *A multitier architecture using NAS*

wouldn't have to worry about tangling with important application logic. Because the objects running on NAS (called AppLogics) would be reusable by any application, the administrative application could directly reuse them. We wouldn't have to recompile both the customer and the administrative applications each time someone changed shared SSJS code, nor would we have to track the different versions running on different servers. Finally, NAS would no doubt help improve the performance of the application, because we would have pushed some of the heaviest processing from the SSJS tier to the NAS tier.

Although we believe strongly that scripting will always have a place in the world of Web development, the advent of application servers means that scripting may be used somewhat differently in the future for large applications. As you can see, when you throw an application server into the mix of a large application, there's little value in putting anything other than presentation logic into script code except that it might be faster to create some code in script. The last thing you want to do is to create a bottleneck at the Web server with a bunch of fat SSJS logic that could be run more efficiently across more users inside objects running under NAS. Thus, for large systems with an application server, scripting should be used as the glue that ties the client to the back-end tiers, such as the application and database servers. Scripting still plays an important role and is responsible for generating HTML views on the data, but application logic is moved to an application server.

This approach allows you to take advantage of NAS while still using SSJS and your Web server for the tasks they're designed for: generating and serving HTML documents. Although there is no direct integration between

SSJS and NAS at the time of this writing, it is possible to call NAS AppLogics from SSJS through the NAS Open Client Library (OCL) interface. The OCL interface allows almost any type of application—from SSJS to Visual Basic—to call AppLogics. In the case of SSJS, you use LiveConnect to call out to Java classes that in turn talk to the NAS AppLogics through OCL. In this manner, you can pass data between SSJS and NAS AppLogics and can call AppLogic methods as long as you make arrangements for this in your go-between Java class.

It's important to realize that we aren't saying SSJS will no longer be used to handle business logic. On the contrary, there are plenty of work-group-sized applications to be built that do not require an expensive platform such as NAS. For such applications, SSJS does an excellent job of serving both HTML and application logic, especially if you focus on a good design up front.

Advantages of a Multitier Approach

When it comes to building large applications that will serve tens of thousands or perhaps hundreds of thousands of users, a multitier approach that integrates an application server becomes increasingly important. Consider a typical scenario: developing an information system from scratch. One multitier approach might implement business rules in database servers through stored procedures, implement system and business application logic in objects running on an application server, and implement presentation logic through a combination of client-side and server-side JavaScript.

Another approach might implement business logic and business rules in objects running on an application server and use the database server simply as a data store. Such an approach would be beneficial if your objects might need to talk to different types of databases or if your database might change; that's because you wouldn't have to rewrite a mass of stored procedure code for each new or different database server. The approach you choose depends in part on the needs of your application and in part on the design philosophies of your application architects.

Whichever approach you choose, using an application server and multiple tiers promotes maintainability, code reuse, and performance, as illustrated by our earlier example of the e-commerce application; it can also enhance reliability. Let's examine each of these advantages in turn. For more information on multitier Web development using NAS, see the white paper "Deploying and Managing Web-Based Enterprise Applications" on Netscape's Web site.

Maintainability

Maintainability is all about responding to change. It's the ease with which changes can be made to the code in responding to changing requirements, fixing bugs, adding new functionality, and so on. Good programming practices, such as commenting code and using modular design, increase the maintainability of an application, but the application architecture also affects maintenance.

For example, if you bundle business rules, application logic, and presentation code in one place rather than isolate each element in its own tier, you're asking for trouble. Suppose that your customer wanted a change in the look-and-feel of an application. With the critical application logic, such as calculation of employee compensation, closely tied to the presentation logic, you will have to be much more careful about changing the code if you wanted to avoid accidentally introducing a bug in the application logic. If you used a multitier architecture instead, you would be able to isolate the presentation code, which is running on a Web server, from the business objects running on an application server. With this architecture, changing the look-and-feel of the application on the Web Server shouldn't even require that you look at the highly critical business logic on the application server.

Code Reuse

The ability to reuse code is a critical success factor in designing medium-sized to large applications. The greater the reuse of code in a project, the less time and money you spend developing it. A multitier structure promotes code reuse for the same reason it promotes maintainability: it helps you isolate pieces of the application in logical layers of functionality.

Ask yourself how much you've focused on separating application logic from presentation logic when creating SSJS applications. The answer is probably not much, even though you should be. It's tempting to lump the two together, resulting in an application that's harder to maintain and doesn't promote reuse. NAS provides an environment in which not only is it less tempting to bundle application logic and presentation logic, but also it makes less sense to do so. That said, however, you can apply the same good design techniques to your SSJS applications—better logical separation between application and presentation logic—even if both layers are controlled by the same SSJS engine.

Performance

It's no secret that a three-tier architecture can improve the performance of Web applications. For example, putting some logic in the browser in the form of client-side JavaScript reduces the need to communicate with the server to perform calculations or other tasks. Using stored procedures and triggers to hold data validation and business rules and to perform other SQL tasks has long been known to provide a performance advantage because stored procedures are compiled and execute faster than pass-through SQL statements from Web servers.

NAS provides several performance-enhancing features that you won't find in SSJS or many other Web server application environments.

- Dynamic load balancing: NAS applications can implement load balancing, which causes requests to be routed to the least loaded server. This feature allows you to control performance by adding more servers when the number of requests exceeds your tolerated load levels.

- Results caching: In a highly transactional application, caching dynamic results can improve performance significantly. Imagine that you've used NAS to help create a popular Internet store that sells Beanie Babies and you've just gotten in a coveted Jerry Garcia bear. Suddenly your site is swamped with hundreds of thousands of hits from people requesting pricing information for the bear. The first request for a price goes from the browser across the Internet, through the Web server, and through NAS to a database server, and the price is returned. That's a lot of overhead for retrieving the price of a bear. However, if you configure NAS so that it caches the result in memory, subsequent requests retrieve the price from the cache without having to access the database server each time.

  NAS gives you a good deal of programmatic control over the caching so that you're not forced to simply turn caching on or off. You can enable or disable caching depending on your own criteria, you can dirty the cache manually, and you can even set a timeout for cached results. In addition, the cache is prioritized so that cached results that receive greater numbers of accesses remain in the cache longer than results that are rarely accessed.

- Results streaming: Streaming is a technique for managing how data is returned to the user. When results are streamed, data is returned to the user as soon as it's available rather than when the entire result set can be returned. For example, suppose 10,000 people placed a bid for the Jerry Garcia bear on your Internet store and you wanted to view all the bids. It might take several seconds to return and show 10,000 records, but you could use streaming to return results as soon as they were returned by your query.

Reliability

Mission-critical applications are those that the business depends on for daily or critical operations, such as calculating how much vacation time you have left. These applications demand high system reliability and data integrity. You can improve system reliability by distributing responsibility for system functions across different servers or services. NAS has powerful built-in deployment and fault tolerance features that enable you to distribute all or part of an application across multiple servers. If one server goes down, the other servers can continue to handle requests. NAS can even maintain client state in the face of server crashes as long as more than one NAS server is running in a cluster with the server that crashed.

Data integrity is usually even more important than system reliability. If your system isn't reliable, that situation can last only in the short term and must be fixed quickly. If your system allows dirty, corrupt data to be stored in the database, it can affect the long-term reliability of your system and is much harder to detect after the fact. A system with garbage for data isn't worth much even if its mean time between failures (MTBF) is 300 days. Generally, the database should be the entity responsible for ensuring storage and integrity of data, so you must add preventive measures at your database server to protect the integrity of the data. Part of this protection is to enforce business and data validation rules.

For example, if your order entry system has a business rule that hot dogs can be ordered only in packs of eight and that hot dog buns can be ordered only in packs of ten, you must make sure that no one is allowed to order only eight hot dog buns. You could enforce this business rule in your SSJS code on the Web server or in objects on the application server, but your SSJS application might not be the only application that accesses the same database. What if there's also a Java application used internally that allows people to order hot dogs and hot dog buns, but that application hasn't enforced the bun count business rule? Your data will be corrupted, and the hot dog bun industry will surely have some unkind words for you. There is, after all, a reason that vendors sell ten buns to a pack even though hot dogs come eight to a pack. Of course, no one knows what that reason is, but we're sure it's a good one! And even if it's not, it's a business rule that must be supported. It is better to take advantage of a multitier architecture and put your business and data validation rules in the database server.

NAS Evaluation

You should have a good idea by now of how NAS can be used to build scalable and flexible multitier Web applications and of the advantages this mode of development offers. But how easy and convenient is it to use? Next, we give you our impressions of the administrative, project management, and development tools, as well as the costs of using NAS.

 These evaluations are based on NAS 2.0.

We should note that we're also familiar with Microsoft Transaction Server (MTS). Some people might argue that MTS isn't a true application server, but we tend to think of it as one and it can certainly be used like one in combination with COM objects. We don't discuss MTS here except to say that it's also a valid choice as an application server, especially if the rest of your components are running under Windows NT and you're a fan of COM. Of course, if you're running on UNIX, you can forget about MTS. NAS runs on both UNIX and Windows NT. Finally, MTS 2.0 doesn't include features, such as load balancing and fault tolerance that NAS ships with today.

Administration

One aspect of NAS that struck me early in our evaluation was how easy it is to use the administrative tools. It is easy to manage the services, configure applications for load balancing, add projects, and so on using the intuitive administrative interfaces. Their primary disadvantage is that they're written in Java and are fairly slow. We hope that this will improve as Java speed issues are addressed in the near future. Another disappointment is the lack of directory server integration at the administrative level. If you want to create users and groups for administrative access, you must deal with the internal NAS user database for now.

Project Deployment

NAS provides several options for deploying application code. The most basic option is to group several server objects (AppLogics) that are related to an application into a project and deploy these grouped objects to one or more application servers. You can also deploy some objects related to an application to one server and other objects related to the same application to another server. You might do this for security, performance, or other reasons.

For example, suppose that you've written an e-commerce application that lets users search for items and then purchase them online with a credit card. As you might guess, far more users will search for items than actually make purchases. So to improve performance, you might want to deploy the heavily used objects related to your search-and-select engine on one server and deploy the less frequently used objects on another server. You could also deploy the objects redundantly on multiple servers and take advantage of the load balancing features. The NAS project management tools make such deployments straightforward.

You can also use the tools to deploy applications with load balancing by simply checking a box. NAS takes care of the details, and, best of all, you don't have to code differently to use load balancing. It's a great feature and remarkably easy to use.

Component Development

If you're going to develop AppLogics for use with NAS, for now you should have your own development tool, such as Symantec Visual Café (for Java applications) or Microsoft Visual C++. The Netscape Application Builder (NAB) tools, such as AppLogic Designer, still lack the maturity of tools such as Visual Café and Visual Basic. By the time this book is published, however, Netscape should have released updated development tools that address some of these usability issues. NAB offers some convenient wizards, such as a visual SQL query builder, that are easy to use and definitely save time. When you settle on a set of development tools you're comfortable with, you'll find developing for NAS to be like working with any other server product of its kind. There are new classes and methods to learn, new state management features to deal with, and a new database API to work with, as with most other application servers. Netscape has announced that future versions of NAS will support Enterprise JavaBeans, and that is exciting news for Java developers.

Costs

When you consider its cost, you'll see that NAS isn't appropriate for all Web applications. For one thing, it's quite expensive compared with a copy of Enterprise Server, which comes with SSJS. NAS requires formal or informal training to operate efficiently, so you must have to devote time, money, or both to getting one of your administrators up to speed. It also requires the use of Java or C++, so your JavaScript developers will have to acquire skills in one of those languages if you don't already have any in-house Java or C++ programmers. Also, although object-oriented programming and multitier architectures have definite advantages, they can be costly to plan and build. Despite the eventual cost savings of such an approach, sometimes the budget of the moment rules all and an NAS solution may prove too costly up front. Finally, it's one more service to monitor, administer, and maintain.

Evaluation Summary

Table 11.1 summarizes the strengths and weaknesses we identified in our test drive of NAS.

NAS

Table 11.1 *NAS strengths and weaknesses*

Strengths	Weaknesses
Has good fault-tolerance features	Uses slow Java-based administration tools
Has good scalability features	Uses proprietary AppLogic API instead of an industry standard, such as Enterprise JavaBeans
Includes intuitive administration tools	Uses poor development tools
Supports flexible object/application deployment	Has no direct integration between NAS and SSJS and forces you to go through OCL
Lets you use either Java or C++ to build objects	
Lets you call objects from any client and not just Web clients	
Works with several Web servers and not just Netscape Enterprise Server	

Don't be fooled by the simplistic look of the tools. We're convinced that you'll find great value in this server for larger Web projects that would benefit from a multitier approach. We also wouldn't limit the scope of its usefulness to only Web applications. It has just as much utility serving objects for C++, Java, Visual Basic, Delphi, and other kinds of clients. In fact, that's one of its primary advantages because many administrative applications are written in an operating-system-specific language such as Visual Basic even though the corresponding customer-side application might be a cross-platform Web application.

Summary

For small to moderate-sized applications, you probably don't need a hefty application server such as NAS. Scripting works just fine for such applications when they are designed properly. But if you're designing a mission-critical system or an enterprise-wide information system for thousands of users, you'll be sorely disappointed with a solution that doesn't include a heavy-duty, scalable application server. NAS is a good choice, with many current strengths and planned improvements on the way.

Index

Java™ Technology from Addison-Wesley

ISBN 0-201-37949-X

ISBN 0-201-37963-5

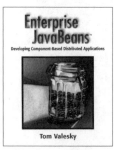

ISBN 0-201-60446-9

ISBN 0-201-43329-X

ISBN 0-201-48543-5

ISBN 0-201-61563-0

ISBN 0-201-30972-6

ISBN 0-201-18393-5

ISBN 0-201-32573-X

ISBN 0-201-32582-9

http://www.awl.com/cseng
⋀⋁ Addison-Wesley

Addison-Wesley Computer and Engineering Publishing Group

How to Interact with Us

1. Visit our Web site

http://www.awl.com/cseng

When you think you've read enough, there's always more content for you at Addison-Wesley's web site. Our web site contains a directory of complete product information including:

- Chapters
- Exclusive author interviews
- Links to authors' pages
- Tables of contents
- Source code

You can also discover what tradeshows and conferences Addison-Wesley will be attending, read what others are saying about our titles, and find out where and when you can meet our authors and have them sign your book.

2. Subscribe to Our Email Mailing Lists

Subscribe to our electronic mailing lists and be the first to know when new books are publishing. Here's how it works: Sign up for our electronic mailing at **http://www.awl.com/cseng/mailinglists.html**. Just select the subject areas that interest you and you will receive notification via email when we publish a book in that area.

3. Contact Us via Email

cepubprof@awl.com
Ask general questions about our books.
Sign up for our electronic mailing lists.
Submit corrections for our web site.

bexpress@awl.com
Request an Addison-Wesley catalog.
Get answers to questions regarding your order or our products.

innovations@awl.com
Request a current Innovations Newsletter.

webmaster@awl.com
Send comments about our web site.

mary.obrien@awl.com
Submit a book proposal.
Send errata for an Addison-Wesley book.

cepubpublicity@awl.com
Request a review copy for a member of the media interested in reviewing new Addison-Wesley titles.

We encourage you to patronize the many fine retailers who stock Addison-Wesley titles. Visit our online directory to find stores near you or visit our online store: **http://store.awl.com/** or call **800-824-7799**.

Addison Wesley Longman
Computer and Engineering Publishing Group
One Jacob Way, Reading, Massachusetts 01867 USA
TEL 781-944-3700 • FAX 781-942-3076

Warranty

Addison Wesley Longman warrants the enclosed disc to be free of defects in materials and faulty workmanship under normal use for a period of ninety days after purchase. If a defect is discovered in the disc during this warranty period, a replacement disc can be obtained at no charge by sending the defective disc, postage prepaid, with proof of purchase to:

Addison Wesley Longman, Inc.
Computer and Engineering Publishing Group
One Jacob Way
Reading, MA 01867

After the 90-day period, a replacement will be sent upon receipt of the defective disc and a check or money order for $10.00, payable to Addison Wesley Longman, Inc.

Addison Wesley Longman makes no warranty or representation, either express or implied, with respect to this software, its quality, performance, merchantability, or fitness for a particular purpose. In no event will Addison Wesley Longman, its distributors, or dealers be liable for direct, indirect, special, incidental, or consequential damages arising out of the use or inability to use the software. The exclusion of implied warranties is not permitted in some states. Therefore, the above exclusion may not apply to you. This warranty provides you with specific legal rights. There may be other rights that you may have that vary from state to state.

CD-ROM Contents

NetObjects ScriptBuilder 3.0 for Windows
NetObjects ScriptBuilder is the only script development environment for the Web, offering the most effective way to create client and server scripts for Web sites. ScriptBuilder integrates a powerful script editor and innovative scripting methodologies with point-and-click development for fast clean code. ScriptBuilder is the perfect complementary tool to any Web developer's toolkit. To purchase ScriptBuilder, visit the online store at www.netobjects.com.

Other programs/features included on the CD-ROM are:
• Code examples from the book
• JavaScript reference (CORE, CLIENT, and SERVER)
• JavaScript guide (CORE, CLIENT, and SERVER)
• Writing SSJS Apps tutorial
• LDAP SDK (Java)
• Messaging SDK (Java)

System Requirements
The software available on the CD-ROM will run on the following platforms:
• Windows 95/98/NT
• UNIX